להאיר עולם חשוך

TO ILLUMINATE A DARKENED SOCIETY
2ND EDITION

ESSAYS ON JEWISH THOUGHT AND CONTEMPORARY LIFE

BY RABBI RONALD H. GROSS

FOREWORD BY CHAPLAIN COL. STERLING WETHERALL

Copyright 2025 by Rabbi Ronald H. Gross

❧ *Dedication* ☙

This Sefer is dedicated to the blessed memory of my beloved parents:

ר' משה פסח ניסן בן ר' צבי הירש הכהן ע"ה
Moses Gross a"h
and
מרת חיה לאה בת ר' אלטר משה ע"ה
Lilyan Gross a"h

Their faith in me has always been unshakeable, and their love and concern have been my illuminating light.

❧☙

And to the blessed memory of my revered uncle and mentor:
הרב חיים בן ר' אלטר משה ז"ל
Rabbi Hyman Tuchman z"l

His cherished teachings and personal example continue to serve as the most important influence on my life.

תנצב"ה

✺ Dedication ✺

This Sefer is also dedicated to the blessed memory of

ר' מרדכי בן ר' צבי הירש ז"ל

Rabbi Mutel Pinter z"l

He was the beloved father of my dear sister-in-law, Lea Fink.

Reb Mutel was a giant in his מצות בין אדם למקום as well as in his interpersonal relationships. He was an outstanding Talmid Chacham, a very wise, thoughtful, and considerate individual, as well as an advisor and confidant to many people.

In the over 40 years that I had the pleasure of knowing him, his חכמה, his decency, and his overall mentschlichkeit which he extended to me and to my family knew no bounds. He was always there whenever we needed him.

We will truly miss him. However, our lives are so much more enriched because of the wonderful example he set for all who knew him and loved him.

May his memory be for a blessing.

תנצב"ה

<u>Foreword</u>

This compilation of essays on Jewish thoughts represents the work of Chaplain (Captain) Rabbi Ronald H. Gross as he has ministered to the Jewish community of Fort Benning for the last two years. Nearly all of these essays in this work have appeared in earlier publications by the Rabbi as parts of his weekly and monthly newsletter to his people. They express the religious concerns of the Rabbi for his people and their faith as it is practiced in the daily life. I believe their value in compilation as a collection of the Rabbi's thoughts will make a fitting memento to the Jewish people as they finish their military experience at Fort Benning or are reassigned to other posts and duties throughout the world. Rabbi Gross has spent countless hours writing, editing, and producing these contemporary essays so that his people might not sit in darkness, but might let the light of their faith be an expression for the total society of which they are a part. To this end I sincerely hope that all our Jewish people will read and consider these writings.

Col. Sterling A. Wetherell,
Chief Chaplain
Fort Benning, Georgia
April 12, 1973

Table of Contents

- INTRODUCTION TO THE FIRST EDITION 9
- INTRODUCTION TO THE SECOND EDITION 13

The Parshiyos and Pirkei Avos

1. PARSHAS BEREISHIS - ACCEPTING RESPONSIBILITY 20
2. PARSHAS NOACH - NOACH'S INFLUENCE ON TWO GENERATIONS 30
3. PARSHAS LECH LECHA - TO WALK WITH HASHEM 41
4. PARSHAS CHAYEI SARAH - THE PRICE 46
5. PARSHAS VAYEITZEI - YAAKOV'S TRANSFORMATIVE DREAMS 54
6. PARSHAS VAYIGASH - SHALOM, PEACE THAT REIGNS SUPREME 66
7. PARSHAS VAYIGASH - SEPARATE BUT VERY EQUAL 78
8. PARSHAS SHEMOS - TO BE A MAN 87
9. PARSHAS BESHALACH - A TIME TO ACT 100
10. PARSHAS YISRO - A FRIEND AT ALL TIMES 111
11. PARSHAS MISHPATIM-PARSHAS SHEKALIM - DONATING FUNDS; PREPARING FOR FREEDOM 123
12. PARSHAS TERUMAH - THE MISHKAN IN OUR HEART 132
13. PARSHAS KI SISA-PARSHAS PARAH - PURIFYING THE IMPURE 136
14. PARSHAS KI SISA - WHAT WILL ISRAEL SAY? 147
15. PARSHAS PIKUDEI - BUILDING OUR OWN MISHKAN 162
16. PARSHAS BAMIDBAR - TRANSFORMING A DESERT INTO A PARADISE 172
17. PARSHAS KORACH - CONTROVERSIES 176

Table of Contents

18. PARSHAS CHUKAS - SHALOM: AHARON HAKOHEN'S LEGACY 183

19. PARSHAS KI SEITZEI - BATTLING TWO DIFFERENT ENEMIES 192

20. PIRKEI AVOS - OUR THREE PILLARS 198

21. PIRKEI AVOS - WHO WILL BE FOR ME? WILL I ONLY BE FOR MYSELF? 204

The Yom Tovim

22. ROSH HASHANAH - TO REACH THE PRESENT DAY 212

23. YOM KIPPUR - REMEMBERING THE PAST; PRESERVING THE FUTURE 220

24. THE HOLINESS AND THE SPECIAL SIGNIFICANCE OF CHAG HASUKKOS 230

25. CHANUKAH - TO ILLUMINATE A DARKENED SOCIETY .. 239

26. PARSHAS ZACHOR - AFTER AMALEK, WHY PRETEND? .. 248

27. PURIM - FASTING AND FEASTING 255

28. PESACH - MATZAH: THE EVERLASTING MEMORIAL 260

29. HAGGADAH SHEL PESACH - דם ואש ותימרות עשן 265

30. YOM HASHOAH - DEATH NEED NOT BE FINAL 269

31. LAG BAOMER - REBBE AKIVA'S MESORAH 279

32. CELEBRATING A NEW BEGINNING: LAG BAOMER - A NEW PERSPECTIVE 287

33. YOM YERUSHALAYIM - G-D'S GIFTS AND ISRAEL'S RESPONSIBILITY 293

34. SHAVUOS - WHO IS A JEW? 304

35. TISHA B'AV - A DAY TO MOURN, A TIME TO HOPE 312

Table of Contents

Special Occasions

36. BAR MITZVAH OF YEHUDA GROSS - SINGULARLY IMPORTANT (PARSHAS EKEV) 324

37. BRIS OF DANIEL KOHN - GRATITUDE AND LAUGHTER (PARSHAS VAYEIRA) 336

38. HESPED OF MR. MOSES GROSS A"H - A MAN OF KINDNESS, COURAGE, AND PRINCIPLE 346

39. HESPED OF MRS. LILYAN GROSS A"H - FINALLY AT PEACE 354

40. TRIBUTE TO RABBI STEVEN DWORKEN (PARSHAS LECH LECHA) 360

41. HESPED FOR MRS. YETTA GROSS - A WOMAN FOR ALL SEASONS 368

42. MY SUGGESTIONS FOR THE ENHANCEMENT OF OUR LIVES IN AMERICA 378

43. THE SIMCHAS TORAH MASSACRE 384

44. THE LAST PESACH 402

45. AWAITING OUR GREATEST VICTORY - THE BIRTH AND BRIS OF OUR FIRST GREAT-GRANDSON 407

46. OUR VERY BLESSED AND CHERISHED TIME - CELEBRATING OUR GOLDEN FIFTIETH ANNIVERSARY 416

INDEX 424

OTHER WORKS BY THIS AUTHOR 429

Introduction to the First Edition

Charles Dickens, in *A Tale of Two Cities*, wrote: "It was the best of times, it was the worst of times." The words of this late 19th century English author are most applicable even today. While we are blessed with living in a most propitious time – the most prosperous era in world history, we are also cursed with the sight of hundreds of millions of individuals who border on the very brink of starvation. While we are spared either nuclear holocaust or global confrontation by the superpowers, we sadly observe small local wars, terrorism, air piracy, and total disregard for another man's rights and property.

Judaism is also faced with apparent contradictions. Today, thanks in large part to our brothers and sisters in the State of Israel, the Jewish people are at its zenith in world prestige. Due to the courage of our brethren in the Soviet Union, our own determination to fight against tyranny and oppression has been strengthened. And because of the wide and diversified contributions which Jews have made in all aspects of society, Judaism is held in high esteem by most thinking persons.

However, while these may be the best of times, they are also perhaps the worst of times. For, as the secular and non-traditional Jew becomes more socially acceptable to his neighbors, and as his bank account grows increasingly larger, his commitment to Judaism and to the Jewish way of life becomes steadily weaker. Observance of Jewish laws and customs in the non-Orthodox camp is presently at an all-time low, while assimilation and intermarriage are at increasingly high numbers. These two factors – more than anything else – threaten to completely engulf and cause a great deal of harm to Judaism.

Thousands of years ago, Hashem chose *Am Yisrael* to be an example to other people. Through our actions, the name of G-d was to be sanctified and hallowed. We were to be an אור לגוים, a light unto the nations. We were to show the world the path toward righteousness and piety, spirituality and peace. For centuries, when the world was filled with darkness, gloom, and immorality, we were that illuminating light, the brightness, the shining beacon on the hill. Today, we are needed ever so desperately. We are faced with great and difficult challenges. If we rise to the occasion, if we fulfill our goal, if we do our part, we will certainly help to "Illuminate our darkened society."

Introduction to the First Edition

The chapters of this book represent a selection of the sermons, lectures, and discussions, which I have delivered during my two years as the Jewish chaplain at Fort Benning, Georgia. Most of the essays have appeared at one time or another in either the "Jewish Center's Monthly Bulletin" or in the "Thought of the Week" series. Some chapters, however, are being presented to the reading public for the first time.

The topics discussed range from interpretations of the Yom Tovim, the weekly parshah, and various and diversified *minhagim*, to discourses on the State of Israel, Soviet Jewry, civil rights, and Vietnam. Each topic is presented from a traditional Jewish point of view with a modern and contemporary outlook.

There are many people who are responsible for this publication and to whom I owe a debt of gratitude: Dr. Murray Kohn, whose original idea led to the development of the "Thought of The Week" series; Rabbi Sheldon Goldsmith and Rabbi Theodore Lauer, who both urged me to consolidate my articles and publish them in book form; Chaplain Richard Nybro, whose comments and suggestions on a number of chapters were most helpful; Chaplain (Col) Sterling A. Wetherell, the United States Army Infantry Center Chaplain, whose encouragement and support during this project were most instrumental in transforming it from an idea into a reality; and Mrs. Teresa Leibson

Introduction to the First Edition

and Thomas Kujawa who helped with the layout as well as with the art work.

I am also very deeply grateful to Mrs. Jane Linnane who meticulously typed the entire manuscript and without whose help this project could never have been brought to fruition. Most notably, I offer a heartfelt appreciation to my dear friend, Dr. Howard Shaw, who painstakingly read and edited each chapter and offered extremely constructive and practical criticism and advice. His friendship will forever be treasured, and his help and assistance will never be forgotten. Lastly, I wish to thank the members of my congregation for their inspiration and friendship during my two years as their Rabbi.

Ronald H. Gross
Fort Benning, Georgia
April, 1973

Introduction to the Second Edition

I recently discovered that this past year, 2023, was the "Yovel," the Jubilee year, which commemorated fifty years since this book's original publication. A great deal has transpired during this past half-century. My life has truly been fulfilled. I have, Baruch Hashem, been married to my wonderful and amazing wife, Rivkie, for over forty-nine glorious and phenomenal years. We have been blessed with three fantastic and marvelous children, three amazing in-law children, eighteen adorable and incredible grandchildren, two of whom are married, and – to date – we have three beautiful great-grandchildren. These fifty years have also seen the passing of my dear parents, Mr. and Mrs. Moe and Lil Gross *a"h*, my dear in-laws, Rabbi and Mrs. Samuel Fink *z"l*, my uncles and aunts, as well as my only sibling, Eamie Fruchter *a"h,* and a number of dear cousins and some very close friends.

During this period, I served as the Rabbi of Congregation Sinai Torath Chaim in Hillside, New Jersey, for five glorious years, from 1973-1978. I spent the next 38 years in the business world, working for and subsequently serving at the helm of a family concern. In addition, for many of these years, I was

Introduction to the Second Edition

also very involved in helping the Jewish community in Elizabeth, New Jersey. I was fortunate enough to assist both the Jewish Educational Center and The Elmora Hills Minyan (now Congregation Bais Hillel) to grow, develop, and flourish.

With my retirement from the business world in 2016, Rivkie and I became "snow birds" and we currently spend our winters in Boca Raton, Florida. We also relocated from Elizabeth to Lakewood, New Jersey, where we spend our springs and summers.

Five years ago, I embarked on a new career and pastime, the writing of English *seforim* on various Jewish topics. The series was entitled *From Sinai Came Torah*. These included themes on the Yom Tovim, the Jewish Life Cycle, and a two-volume commentary on the Torah. I also recently completed writing my autobiography: *A Blessed Life: From the Halls of Toras Emes to the Kollel of BRS*. It was recently published in the winter of 2023. I then chose to rewrite and republish this, my first book, which was originally written, published, and distributed when I was a young United States Army Chaplain in 1973.

While the title of this book will remain the same as in the first edition, it has been amended, expanded upon, and totally updated. Many of the sources have also been modified. I have added the Hebrew text of the *pesukim* quoted in this work. In addition, many of

Introduction to the Second Edition

the *meforshim*, the commentaries which appeared in the first edition only in English, will now include their original Hebrew text as well. I have also added a number of new chapters which were not included in the first edition. These, I feel, will enhance and give additional depth and perspective to the new edition.

My intended audience for the first edition was my Ft. Benning congregation, most of whom were quite removed from authentic and traditional Judaism, as well as for the non-Jewish chaplains who were stationed together with me in Ft. Benning. I have chosen in the second edition to focus on my dear children, my grandchildren, my extended family, and some very dear and close friends, all of whom are *frum* and completely committed to a genuine and observant Torah lifestyle. Thus, I have updated this book to make it more reader friendly for my new intended audience.

In addition, I have modified the structure of the sub-titles as well as the chapters. There will be three sections:

I. The Parshiyos and Pirkei Avos
II. The Yom Tovim
III. Special Occasions

I hope that this edition will be well received by both laymen as well as scholars. It is my fervent wish that my message resonates with many different segments of our community. As with all my other

Introduction to the Second Edition

books, this volume has been, from its very inception, a true labor of love. I took great pride in writing and publishing it in 1973 as a young 27-year-old. Now, 50 years later, as a 77-year-old senior citizen, I continue to take enormous satisfaction in rewriting and preparing it for its new publication and its new audience.

There are a number of people whom I wish to acknowledge for their help and assistance in developing and preparing this *sefer*. I first would like to thank each of my wonderful children: Frumie and Hillel Drebin, Goldie and Aryeh Gross, and Dena and Yaakov Kibel for their constant encouragement and assistance in many areas of this Sefer.

I also wish to express my heartfelt appreciation to my dear son-in-law, Rabbi Yaakov Kibel, for his ongoing technical assistance, for his many ideas, suggestions, and emendations throughout the entire project. In addition, I want to truly express my *hakaras haTov* to him for the countless hours he spent, both day and night, in reading, reviewing, and editing each and every chapter. Without his assistance, this venture would not have come to fruition.

Lastly, אחרון אחרון חביב, to my wonderful wife of almost a half-century, Rivkie, for reading each chapter and offering very fine and constructive comments and suggestions. If this book reads well and flows very smoothly, it is no small measure due to her help, her assistance, and especially to her love. For that and for so much more, I can never thank her enough.

I would like to wish each of you, my amazing family and my very special friends, a wonderful and very pleasant life. It should be one with אריכת ימים, long life, *gezunt*, good health, and continued *nachas* from each of your families. Thank you for your continuous and ongoing love and friendship.

Ronald H. Gross
November, 2024 – Cheshvan 5785

THE PARSHIYOS AND PIRKEI AVOS

1. Accepting Responsibility
Parshas Bereishis

This week we once again begin the annual Torah reading cycle. The Torah is divided into fifty-four portions; usually one *parshah* is read on each Shabbos throughout the year. On certain *Shabbosim* two *parshiyos* are read. The goal of *Chazal* who instituted this policy was to fulfill the Torah's command (Devarim 6:6-7):

וְהָיוּ הַדְּבָרִים הָאֵלֶּה אֲשֶׁר אָנֹכִי מְצַוְּךָ הַיּוֹם עַל לְבָבֶךָ׃ וְשִׁנַּנְתָּם לְבָנֶיךָ וְדִבַּרְתָּ בָּם בְּשִׁבְתְּךָ בְּבֵיתֶךָ וּבְלֶכְתְּךָ בַדֶּרֶךְ וּבְשָׁכְבְּךָ וּבְקוּמֶךָ׃

And these words which I command you today shall be on your heart. You shall teach them diligently to your children, and you shall speak of them when you are sitting at home and when you go on a journey, when you lie down and when you rise up.

In essence, our *rabbanim* felt that the most effective method of teaching the Torah was to incorporate it into our *Tefilos*, our prayers. Thus, three times weekly, on Monday and Thursday mornings and on Shabbos afternoon, a small section of the weekly *parshah* is read. On Shabbos morning, when people are free from the cares and difficulties of their busy work week and have more time to devote to *davening* and learning, the entire *sedra* is read.

The *sedra* for this week is Parshas Bereishis, the first chapters of *Sefer Bereishis*. It is the very basis and foundation of our religion and serves as a prologue to the historical drama that unfolds in the following pages of the Torah. Parshas Bereishis proclaims loudly and unmistakably the absolute subordination of all creation to the *Ribono shel Olam*, our Creator, our G-d, Who Himself created the forces of nature and has made use of them to fulfill His mighty deeds. Bereishis informs us that Hashem, the Creator of the Heavens and Earth and all of the world, is one incorporeal, eternal, omnipotent, omniscient and omnipresent G-d. He is the One who not only created the world but continually serves as its guiding light throughout its development and growth.

Hashem, in His infinite wisdom, formed and created all the vegetative life and the entire animal kingdom. And G-d, in His mercy and compassion, formed and breathed life into the crown-jewel of His creation, man. Man is a G-d-like entity uniquely blessed with dignity, honor, and infinite worth. In his hands, Hashem entrusted mastery over all the rest of His creation.

The story of man, his very beginning, his promising future, his first challenges and tests, and his

Parshas Bereishis

earliest failures, occupy a major section of this week's *parshah*. Two incidents – more than any other in Parshas Bereishis – perplex and disturb our *chachamim*. They are:

1. Man's first transgression against G-d.
2. His first sin toward his fellow man.

The former was the eating from the *Eitz HaDa'as,* the Tree of Knowledge, by Adam and Chava after G-d had specifically forbidden them from eating its fruit. The latter was the first incident of fratricide, Kayin's murder of his brother Hevel.

The *meforshim* are perplexed by a number of problems. Firstly, why did Adam, who was created by G-d Himself and who lived in *Gan Eden,* a perfect environment with everything he could possibly want, fail the only test which was given to him?

Secondly, when contrasting the stories of Adam and Kayin, one notices a significant distinction. When Adam was given his Mitzvah, it came along with a warning from *HaKadosh Baruch Hu* (Bereishis 2:17):

בְּיוֹם אֲכָלְךָ מִמֶּנּוּ מוֹת תָּמוּת

"On the day that you eat from the tree, you shall surely die."

Indeed, this threat was materialized through the consequence that Adam lost his immortality. Upon his exile from the Garden of Eden, Hashem set up angelic guards, the *Keruvim,* to prevent Adam from partaking of the *Eitz HaChaim,* the Tree of Life, which would have restored his immortality.

Kayin, on the other hand, seems to have been held to a different standard. After murdering his brother Hevel, he was forced to become a fugitive and wander throughout the world. He was never allowed to settle in any one area. Kayin's punishment is difficult to understand. *Chazal* teach us the fundamental principle that for a person to be liable for punishment for performing an illegal act, he must be forewarned, and his punishment must be specified. Unlike his father Adam, Kayin was given no warning against murder. Prior to his murderous act, G-d rebuked Kayin for his jealousy, but there is no hint of a consequence (Bereishis 4:7):

הֲלוֹא אִם תֵּיטִיב שְׂאֵת וְאִם לֹא תֵיטִיב לַפֶּתַח חַטָּאת רֹבֵץ וְאֵלֶיךָ תְּשׁוּקָתוֹ וְאַתָּה תִּמְשָׁל בּוֹ:

Is this not so - if you improve, there is forgiveness. But if you do not improve, sin crouches at the door and unto you its desire, but you have the capacity to rule over it.

Why then was Kayin subjected to such a severe punishment without warning when his father was only punished after being forewarned?

We may answer the first question concerning Adam's failing his one test by understanding the very nature of the *Eitz HaDa'as.* The tree, explains Rav Samson Raphael Hirsch of blessed memory, was similar to every other tree in the garden. It had no external differences or outstanding physical characteristics. It differed from the other trees only in that it revealed to Adam the basic concept that good and evil is solely defined by G-d's will. Adam was taught that strict adherence and observance of the *mitzvos* – not human reasoning or understanding – must be the final judge in determining moral values.

In man's first rebellion against the *ratzon Hashem*, we see the core of all physical evil and the origin of death. Adam attempted to affirm his independence from Hashem by setting up his own standards for good and evil. He attempted to fix the limits of moral judgement according to his own rationale, his own set of judgement. By so doing, he defied and transgressed the will of G-d, his creator.

In regards to Kayin, although he did not receive any prior warning nor any description of his punishment, none was actually needed. The Torah states (Bereishis 1:27): בְּצֶלֶם אֱלֹקִים בָּרָא אֹתוֹ – *"In the image of G-d he was created."* Man's main purpose in life, his modus operandi, is to perfect himself. He must intuitively realize that the spilling of human blood is an inherently forbidden act, as it is diametrically opposed to his goal of becoming G-d-like. It, instead, lowers him to the basest form of animal life. For the act of killing, no rational man needs a warning. He who

Parshas Bereishis

murders his fellow man deserves the most severe punishment possible. It was only due to the compassion and pity, the *rachamim* of Hashem, that Kayin did not receive the punishment that was due him, instant and immediate death.

Once the first questions are answered, our *chachamim* are still faced with yet a third difficulty: the responses of both Adam and Kayin following their acts of defiance. When confronted by Hashem, both Adam and Kayin did not respond with a sense of contriteness and sorrow. Neither of them accepted full responsibility for their acts. Instead, they behaved in a very immature and childlike manner by either casting the blame elsewhere, as in Adam's case, or by denying the commission of the crime altogether, as in Kayin's case. What, ask our rabbis, is the moral lesson to be learned from these two distinct but ultimately similar responses?

When Hashem asked Adam and Chava whether they ate from the *Eitz HaDa'as,* Adam replied (Bereishis 3:12):

הָאִשָּׁה אֲשֶׁר נָתַתָּה עִמָּדִי הִוא נָתְנָה לִי מִן הָעֵץ וָאֹכֵל:

The woman whom You gave to me, she gave me of the tree, and I did eat.

Adam appears first to blame Hashem for giving him a wife. It is as if he said, "If You, Hashem, hadn't been so good to me and acted as a matchmaker and instead allowed me to be alone, I never would have committed this transgression." He went on to explain that Chava enticed, cajoled, and convinced him to join her in eating the forbidden fruit. "It really was not my fault," he said, "too many external forces compelled me to act this way."

After Hevel's death, Hashem said to Kayin (Bereishis 4:9):

אֵי הֶבֶל אָחִיךָ

"Where is Hevel your brother?"

Kayin replied:

וַיֹּאמֶר לֹא יָדַעְתִּי הֲשֹׁמֵר אָחִי אָנֹכִי:

"I do not know; am I my brother's keeper?"

Our *Chachamim* comment that it seems that this exchange was purposeless. G-d certainly knew that Hevel was dead, and Kayin understood that every human action is recorded and known to the *Ribono Shel Olam*. However, they say, this dialogue serves to pinpoint the responsibility for Hevel's death. Hashem said to Kayin: "You, alone are responsible for Hevel. You had the power to choose between right and wrong. You chose wrong, and, therefore, you must bear the consequences of your actions which resulted in your brother's death."

Kayin, however, believed that since he succeeded in killing Hevel, his death must have been decreed and approved by Hashem. He, Kayin, was

Parshas Bereishis

merely G-d's instrument in fulfilling this Divine plan. He therefore asked, "Am I my brother's keeper?" You, Hashem, are the keeper of all the world. Nothing occurs on earth without being ordained from above. It was thus Your plan that I kill my brother; I certainly deserve no punishment.

Our rabbis explain that both Adam and Kayin were in grievous error. Whether man does good or evil is not predestined. It rather depends on his own choice. He certainly has בחירה חפשית, complete free will. G-d never forces man's hand, and man, therefore, is strictly accountable and responsible for all of his actions.

This moral lesson can be applied to our own times. All too often, people commit illegal acts – whether it be thievery, vandalism, sabotage, or murder – and then try to cast the blame elsewhere. The Nazis, ימח שמם וזכרם, from the elite of the S.S. to the average soldier, to even many thousands of average Germans, tortured and murdered six-million Jews. However, when they were confronted with their inhuman acts, they said that they could not help themselves. They received orders from their superiors and could not disobey. "We are not responsible for our actions," they claimed.

An even more irresponsible response is when a purportedly impartial third party condones the barbarous acts of murderers and instead blames society. One such incident occurred in 1972 at the summer Olympic games held in Munich, Germany. There, Palestinian terrorists mercilessly and sadistically murdered eleven members of the Israeli Olympic team, השם יקום דמם, may Hashem avenge their deaths. Following that tragic event, the world community was horrified. The Olympic games were halted for one day, and terrorism and murder were condemned by every responsible world leader.

However, after just a few days, attempts were made to understand the "anger and bitterness of the Palestinian terrorists." "After all," many claimed, "these poor people were forced to flee their country and live in refugee camps for twenty-five years. It is quite understandable that hatred and revenge have been implanted in their hearts. Naturally, kidnapping and murder should be avoided, but these people are not really responsible for their actions. They are driven blindly to such actions."

In fact, in a most ironic twist of logic, the world community subsequently blamed the State of Israel for the events leading up to the massacre. They claimed that Israel's policy of inflexibility and aggressive actions *vis-à-vis* the Palestinians as well as their "usurping Palestinian land" has led to the radicalization of the Palestinians. This was merely the PLO venting their "understandable anger."

Unfortunately, over the past five decades since that tragic day, things have not really changed at all. The State of Israel has continuously been condemned and castigated by the world community for each of its actions. This has occurred in spite of Israel's numerous attempts to always act in a virtuous, moral, and high-minded manner, even in times of war.

Let us hope and pray that the day will soon come when all mankind will learn from the mistakes of Adam and Kayin. We will realize that whatever man does is of his own free choice, and if he acts in a favorable manner, he will be rewarded. However, if he does evil, he alone must pay the price. At that time, we will be able to truly understand and internalize the words at the beginning of the Torah (Bereishis 1:27):

וַיִּבְרָא אֱלֹקִים אֶת הָאָדָם בְּצַלְמוֹ בְּצֶלֶם אֱלֹקִים בָּרָא אֹתוֹ:

And G-d created man in His own image, in the image of G-d He created him.

And then Hashem will once again declare over His handiwork (Bereishis 1:31):

וַיַּרְא אֱלֹקִים אֶת כָּל אֲשֶׁר עָשָׂה וְהִנֵּה טוֹב מְאֹד:

And G-d saw everything that He created and behold, it was very good.

We pray for that day to arrive soon. *Amen.*

2. Noach's Influence on Two Generations

Parshas Noach

This week we are introduced to two ancient generations, the *Dor HaMabul,* the era of the Great Flood, and the *Dor Haflagah,* the age of the Tower of Babel. We also meet for the first time a man whom the Torah describes as an איש צדיק ותמים, "one who was righteous and wholesome." He alone in his generation walked with G-d, as it says (Bereishis 6:10):

אֶת הָאֱלֹקִים הִתְהַלֶּךְ נֹחַ.

This righteous individual was Noach.

Both of these *doros* achieved notoriety for being exceptionally wicked and depraved. Both generations sinned against G-d, and both were punished by the *Yad Hashem,* the Hand of *HaKadosh Baruch Hu.* *Chazal* go to great lengths to compare and contrast these two infamous peer groups.

Ten generations after He created the world, the *Ribono shel Olam* decided to destroy mankind with a cataclysmic deluge and said (Bereishis 6:13):

קֵץ כָּל בָּשָׂר בָּא לְפָנַי כִּי מָלְאָה הָאָרֶץ חָמָס מִפְּנֵיהֶם וְהִנְנִי מַשְׁחִיתָם אֶת הָאָרֶץ:

Parshas Noach

The end of all flesh has come before Me, for the earth is filled with violence; and behold, I will destroy them with the earth.

Rashi says: לא נחתם גזר דינם אלא על הגזל – "The fate of the generation of the flood was sealed on account of the robbery they committed."

Rashi (Bereishis 6:11), commenting earlier on the word "וַתִּשָּׁחֵת", says that they sinned through "*Ervah and Avodah Zarah.*" Their transgressions were based on indecency, immorality, and idolatry. Many of our *chachamim* question this interpretation. They ask that if the people of that generation were guilty of such wicked and heinous crimes as idolatry, immorality, and indecency, why were they punished for the transgression of robbery which is apparently a lesser crime?

Chazal explain that when one commits a capital offense for which he deserves to be killed, Hashem does not immediately impose the death penalty on him. He first punishes the sinner by depriving him of his wealth and his worldly possessions. Only when that does not produce any positive change, *Teshuvah Sheleimah,* complete repentance, does Hashem take the sinner's life.

Our *meforshim* explain that a person's material wealth can be taken as a substitute for his death only if he acquired it in an honest, legitimate, and legal manner. Once he loses his wealth, it is an indication that he has paid for his sin by having his possessions taken from him. It serves as a *kaparah,* an atonement, a substitute. However, if this individual acquired his wealth through illegal and unjust means such as thievery and misappropriation, it does not actually belong to him. Thus, its loss is not considered as a penance for his sins. Therefore, he will be given the death penalty which he surely deserves.

If the *Dor HaMabul,* the generation of the flood, had been guilty strictly of indecency and immorality, Hashem would have first taken away their material possessions before inflicting them with physical suffering and death. However, since their wealth was accumulated in an unlawful and illegitimate manner, it did not really belong to them; thus, its loss could not serve as an atonement for their other sins. Therefore, their fate was sealed on account of the thievery and embezzlement that they committed.

The lesson of the *Migdal Bavel,* the Tower of Babel, is very different. The Torah relates about the Tower-builders (Bereishis 11:4):

וַיֹּאמְרוּ הָבָה נִבְנֶה לָּנוּ עִיר וּמִגְדָּל וְרֹאשׁוֹ בַשָּׁמַיִם וְנַעֲשֶׂה לָּנוּ שֵׁם פֶּן נָפוּץ עַל פְּנֵי כָל הָאָרֶץ:

And they said: "Come let us build ourselves a city and a tower with its top in heaven, and let us make a name, lest we be scattered abroad upon the face of the earth."

The Torah then appraises their motives:

וַיֹּאמֶר ה' הֵן עַם אֶחָד וְשָׂפָה אַחַת לְכֻלָּם וְזֶה הַחִלָּם לַעֲשׂוֹת וְעַתָּה לֹא יִבָּצֵר מֵהֶם כֹּל אֲשֶׁר יָזְמוּ לַעֲשׂוֹת:

And G-d said, "Behold they are one people, and they have all one language, and this is what they begin to do, and now nothing will be withholden from them which they purpose to do."

The *Pirkei D'Rebbe Eliezer* (Ch. 24) explains that they began their grandiose project with brotherly love and with a desire for the unification of all mankind. However, they eventually became completely unconcerned with human life and substituted instead a high esteem for material achievements.

ואם נפל אדם ומת לא שמים את לבם עליו, ואם נפלה לבנה אחת היו יושבין ובוכין ואומרין אוי לנו אימתי תעלה אחרת.

If a man fell down during the building of the tower and he died, no one would give him a second thought. On the other hand, if a brick fell down, they would mourn the brick and cry out "Woe is to us, when shall we be able to make another brick in its stead."

Thus, the Torah relates the words of Hashem to the ministering angels (Bereishis 11:7):

הָבָה נֵרְדָה וְנָבְלָה שָׁם שְׂפָתָם אֲשֶׁר לֹא יִשְׁמְעוּ אִישׁ שְׂפַת רֵעֵהוּ:

"Let us go down and confuse their language, that they may not understand one another's language."

The crime of the builders of the Tower, says Rav Ovadia Seforno, the great medieval Italian commentator, was that they tried to force through totalitarian means a uniformity of thought upon the rest of their generation. They wanted to coerce the entire human race to accept the worship of idolatry which they made manifest through their tower. If that would have occurred, says Seforno:

אם כן אין מונע להם מהשלים כונתם ותהיה אותה עבודה זרה אשר יבחרו כללית לכל מין האדם ולא יפנה אחד מהם לדעת את הבורא יתברך ולהבין כי יוצר הכל הוא. והפוך זה יקרה כשתהיה מחלוקת בענין האלהות כי כל אחד יחשוב שיש אלהי האלהים שכל האלוהות מסכימים לדעתו ובו ישלם סדרם וסדר המציאות כאמרו כי ממזרח שמש ועד מבואו גדול שמי בגוים.

It would have been almost impossible for anyone to ever have the opportunity of eventually recognizing Hashem as the true creator of the universe. However, if diversity of opinion or disagreement concerning even the form of idol worship developed, there would still be hope for humanity. There would, hopefully, come a day when mankind would realize the existence of the one and true G-d.

Seforno says that *Hashem's* punishment of the *Dor Haflagah* was of a preventive measure. Its purpose was to frustrate the tower builders at an early stage of their evil course before more great damage could be done.

The moral of the *Migdal Bavel* therefore, was the ultimate inadequacy of even the most grandiose of human endeavors before Hashem's infinite superiority. Great heights are meaningless, and even that skyscraping tower became a senseless creation. What is important are not the outstanding achievements of society but rather the human heart which alone can forge a link with *HaKadosh Baruch Hu*. Man can and must recognize and accept Him as our Creator and the Shaper of all human destiny.

Even a superficial reading of this week's *sedra* would show the strong relationship between Noach and the *Dor HaMabul,* the generation of the Deluge. However, does any relationship exist between Noach and the *Dor Haflagah,* the era of the Dispersion?

To answer this question, it is necessary to read the Torah's account of Noach, the man. The Torah states (Bereishis 6:9):

אֵלֶּה תּוֹלְדֹת נֹחַ נֹחַ אִישׁ צַדִּיק תָּמִים הָיָה בְּדֹרֹתָיו:

These are the generations of Noach. Noach was in his generation a righteous and whole-hearted man.

The Torah further explains that the earth had become totally corrupt. Immorality and violence were the order of the day. Therefore, G-d decided to destroy all mankind except Noach and his family. *Chazal*, as quoted by Rashi, are undecided on the specific merits

Parshas Noach

of Noach. They are disturbed by the addition of the word "בְּדֹרֹתָיו" – *"in his generation."* Rashi says:

יֵשׁ מֵרַבּוֹתֵינוּ דּוֹרְשִׁים אוֹתוֹ לְשֶׁבַח, כָּל שֶׁכֵּן אִלּוּ הָיָה בְדוֹר צַדִּיקִים הָיָה צַדִּיק יוֹתֵר. וְיֵשׁ שֶׁדּוֹרְשִׁים אוֹתוֹ לִגְנַאי, לְפִי דוֹרוֹ הָיָה צַדִּיק וְאִלּוּ הָיָה בְדוֹרוֹ שֶׁל אַבְרָהָם לֹא הָיָה נֶחֱשָׁב לִכְלוּם.

Some interpret it to his credit, while others interpret it to his discredit. Those who feel that it has negative connotations say that he was righteous in his generation but not necessarily in any other generation. (They contend that Noach appeared righteous only when compared to the other members of his depraved and corrupt generation. When compared to immoral and unethical individuals, even a man such as Noach stands out.) *However, had Noach lived in a generation of righteous and worthy persons such as Avraham Avinu, he would have appeared as an average man with no extraordinary qualities or attributes.*

Another *Midrash* quotes a debate between two *Tana'im* of the Mishnah, Rav Yehuda and Rav Yosi. They also debate the righteousness of Noach. They both conclude, however, that when the sinners of the *Dor HaMabul* were to be destroyed, Hashem anxiously wanted to save them. However, there was no one with sufficient virtue and righteousness capable of rescuing them from their future cataclysmic ending. Noach's righteousness was of a degree to enable the rescue of himself and his family alone. His merit was not great enough to save the rest of mankind. To redeem the world, ten individuals of integrity and uprightness were needed, and there were only eight such people: Noach, his wife, his three sons and their wives.

It has always puzzled me as to why *Chazal* were so concerned with determining whether Noach was a truly righteous man or a comparatively righteous man. The fact remains that Noach was the first man in the Torah to defy public opinion and acknowledge and accept Hashem as the *Borei Olam;* in so doing exposed himself to much abuse and derision. In a generation which had forsaken morality and ethics, the very foundations of G-dliness, Noach alone upheld these principles.

Chazal, however, feel that for a man to be considered truly righteous, his character and his actions must be exemplary, at all times, throughout his lifetime. If one acts virtuously and piously during one stage of his life but later acts in an unseemly manner, he certainly cannot be considered completely wholesome and pure. For one hundred twenty years, following Hashem's command to build the ark which would rescue him, Noach's conduct was superb and exemplary. He was a true man of *Emunah* and *Bitachon*. He did everything that Hashem asked of him.

However, once the flood ended and mankind was totally annihilated, Noach desired to return to his former carefree and *laissez-fair* way of life. The tragedy of mankind's destruction did not leave an indelible and everlasting mark on him. It should have made him a completely different person, one filled with grandiose ideas for building a new and better world which would never again sink to the spiritual abyss of its predecessor. Noach, however, unfortunately began where he left off one hundred twenty years earlier.

His former heavenly thoughts became earthbound. He no longer was the *Tzadik*, the איש תמים, the completely righteous and wholesome man who walked with Hashem. Instead, he became the איש האדמה, the man who planted a vineyard and became intoxicated. He remained unproductive and ineffective for the remainder of his life. He had an opportunity and an obligation to set a positive example for his descendants. However, instead of leaving them a proud, beautiful, and meaningful heritage of spiritual ideals and values, Noach left his children an inheritance of love for the mundane, the earthly, and for material achievements.

Thus, it was no wonder that only a few generations following Noach, the *Tzadik* and *Tamim*, the righteous, whole-hearted, and G-dly man, that the descendants of this earthbound, materialistic, and inebriated Noach built the potentially disastrous and deleterious *Migdal Bavel*, the Tower of Babel. That was his heritage; that was his legacy.

My dear friends, our own times are very similar to those of Noach's *Dor*. An inordinate amount of our great moral and spiritual heritage was lost in the devastating and most destructive *Mabul* of the 20th century, the Shoah. Many of our outstanding *Talmidei Chachamim, Roshei Yeshivos,* and distinguished and prestigious Rabbanim in Europe were tortured and killed. Great centers of Torah learning and piety were destroyed. Most of European Jewry was annihilated and uprooted from the face of the earth.

We, as the survivors of that tragic and disastrous catastrophe, have an obligation, an important and genuine *chiyuv,* to set an example for future generations. We have the choice to walk with *HaKadosh Baruch Hu* and be wholesome and pure at all times and in all situations. By so doing, we will be considered truly righteous and complete. On the other hand, we could decide to be like Noach and be righteous on a part time basis. We could be moral and ethical and uphold the Torah's principles only when circumstances require it. We could become emergency Jews and assist our brethren only when difficult situations arise.

However, we must always remember that the decision we make will not only affects us and our present time. The generations that follow us will either reach for spiritual heights or will stoop low for the material and the mundane, primarily because of our decision. Let us not make the same mistake as Noach. Let it be said of our era that we were at all times a righteous and a wholesome generation, את האלקים התהלך דורינו – we were a generation who at all times walked together with Hashem.

3. To Walk with Hashem
Parshas Lech Lecha

This week's *sedra*, Parshas Lech Lecha, deals for the first time exclusively with the one individual who was called an אוהב השם, a friend of G-d, the founder of Judaism, our first patriarch, Avraham. Who was this man? What special qualities did he possess so as to be chosen to found *Am Yisrael*? We cannot say that he was chosen solely because of his belief in monotheism, for we know that ten generations before Avraham, Noach had already accepted the *Ribono shel Olam* as the one G-d and Creator, who is Omnipotent and Omniscient. Subsequently, Noach and his family were the only survivors of the great *Mabul,* the catastrophic and ruinous deluge, which destroyed and devastated the rest of humanity. Noach, we are told, was a *Tzadik* and a *Tamim*, a righteous and wholehearted man who walked with G-d. However, Avraham was chosen to be the patriarch, the founder, and the first of the *Avos* of *Am Yisrael.*

The choice of Avraham was made because he was an אדם השלם, a complete and total man. He was not one who was satisfied in doing what was right merely for himself. Rather, he also tried to help, influence, and encourage others to follow on the דרך הישר, the right and correct path.

To illustrate this point further, we must compare the life of Noach with that of Avraham.

The Torah says about Noach (Bereishis 6:9):

נֹחַ אִישׁ צַדִּיק תָּמִים הָיָה בְּדֹרֹתָיו אֶת הָאֱלֹקִים הִתְהַלֶּךְ נֹחַ:

Noach was a righteous man, flawless in his generation, Noach walked with G-d.

Chazal, as quoted by Rashi, are divided on the inclusion of the words "בְּדֹרֹתָיו" – *in his generation*. Rashi says:

יש מרבותינו דורשים אותו לשבח, כל שכן שאלו היה בדור צדיקים היה צדיק יותר.

The *Midrash Rabbah* says that some of our *Chachamim* believe that even though he lived in a generation of such wicked and depraved people, nevertheless, he remained unspotted and untainted by their corruption.

ויש שדורשים אותו לגנאי: לפי דורו היה צדיק, ואלו היה בדורו של אברהם לא היה נחשב לכלום.

Others interpret this to mean that judged by the standards of the moral depravity and the unequalled decadence of his time, Noach was indeed a righteous man. However, had he lived in another era, another generation, perhaps in Avraham's *dor*, he would not have been conspicuous at all by his goodness and would not even have been worthy of special praise, let alone of being rescued.

According to a number of our *meforshim*, the latter is the generally accepted approach; that *Noah's* righteousness was merely that of a comparative nature. Contrasted to the rest of his immoral and extremely wicked generation, he was a very good and decent man, and that was why Hashem chose to rescue him and his family. However, he was not, in essence, an exceptionally righteous and exemplary personality.

When Hashem informed him that he intended to destroy the world with a flood, Noach spent the next one hundred twenty years constructing and preparing an ark to save himself and his family. He did very little in utilizing these precious years to try to convince his neighbors to do *Teshuvah,* to ameliorate their behavior and thus be saved from annihilation. He didn't make much effort to try to save or even have any impact on the other citizens of his society. What a contrast to Avraham!

In Parshas Vayeira (Bereishis 18:20), Hashem informed Avraham that the cities of Sedom and Amorah were to be destroyed due to their cruelty and debased behavior. Instead of rejoicing at the downfall of the wicked, he made an impassioned plea to G-d to spare the lives of these cities' inhabitants if there be

Parshas Lech Lecha

found even ten righteous men among them. Unfortunately, none were to be found.

When Avraham was informed about the capture of his nephew Lot in the battle with the four Axis powers, he did not merely send his soldiers to help the cause. Avraham himself led the counteroffensive and with the help of Hashem was victorious.

Lastly, when Hashem commanded him to take his beloved son and successor, Yitzchak, and offer him as a sacrifice, Avraham did not say, "How could You, G-d, Who promised that my children will be as numerous as the stars in the sky and the sand in the earth, now ask me to kill my own son?" Instead, Avraham rose early in the morning and hastened toward Har Moriah, the mountain where Yitzchak was to be sacrificed, specifically because it was the will of G-d. Avraham only desired to follow Hashem's dictate and to observe His command at all times.

Therefore, when the Torah discusses Noach, it says (Bereishis 9:1):

אֶת הָאֱלֹקִים הִתְהַלֶּךְ נֹחַ

"Hashem walked together with Noach," since without G-d's help and assistance he would have sunk perhaps as low as his immoral, unethical, and wicked contemporaries. When discussing Avraham, however, the Torah says (Bereishis 17:1):

הִתְהַלֵּךְ לְפָנַי וֶהְיֵה תָמִים

Walk before Me and be wholehearted.

Avraham did not need the *Ribono shel Olam's* assistance to live a truly moral life in his society. He was able to do so through his own deep and personal religious beliefs.

Noach was a good, decent, and very upstanding man. That is why he and his immediate family were saved, while the rest of his generation perished. Avraham, on the other hand, was an אדם השלם, a complete man, and that is why he alone had the *zechus,* the merit, and fortune to be chosen as the first of our *Avos,* the founder of the עם קדוש לה', a nation holy and sanctified unto G-d.

4. The Price
Parshas Chayei Sarah

All too often when confronted by personal tragedy and misfortune, man becomes overwhelmed by his troubles. His spirit is broken, and he no longer has the desire or the fortitude to continue on life's journey. This situation is frequently found when a person loses a spouse or a very close and dear relative. He continually mourns his loved one and refuses to pick up the pieces and live life as completely as he can.

The Torah, however, sets a specific limit on *aveilus,* mourning. Thirty days is the maximum that one can formally grieve for all relatives, save for his parents. For one's mother and father, the Torah sets a year as the bereavement period. It is forbidden to prolong even that *aveilus* after this time.

The Torah understood that when a person loses a loved one, a most important part of his life has ended. Nevertheless, life must continue. Each of us, with the memory of the wonderful years spent with the deceased, must continue living and offering our contributions to society.

Avraham Avinu, the first of our *Avos,* while living hundreds of years before *Matan Torah,* nevertheless fulfilled this precept. This week's *Parsha*, *Chayei Sarah*, discusses the death of Sarah, Avraham's beloved wife and life-long partner. It relates his deep personal loss and his sense of despondency. However, immediately after the Torah discusses Sarah's death, it continues (Bereishis 23:3):

וַיָּקָם אַבְרָהָם מֵעַל פְּנֵי מֵתוֹ

Avraham arose from before his dead.

The Torah goes on to relate about Avraham's purchase of a family burial plot in Chevron and his subsequent burial of Sarah. I would like to share an interpretation that I recently saw in a *sefer* called *Zichron Tzvi*. When the Torah tells us that "Avraham arose from before his dead," it is giving us the message that while still grieving at the loss of his life-long partner, Avraham realized that all human beings share the same fate; we eventually all experience the same destiny. Each of us, rich or poor, strong or weak, good or evil, must ultimately meet our maker. We all will one day pass away and must give a *din v'cheshbon* to the *Ribono shel Olam*.

Avraham understood that his time to depart this world was not too distant; he was already 137 years old. Thus, there was very little time to complete his life's work. As soon as the *aveilus*, the mourning period, for Sarah was concluded, Avraham picked up the pieces and rose to his full stature. His time was now occupied with a question of monumental importance – the choosing of a wife for his son, Yitzchak.

Would the work to which he and Sarah devoted their lives be in vain? Would the concept of an Omnipotent and Omniscient G-d Who alone created the world, an idea which they introduced into their idolatrous society, die with them? Avraham was fully aware that his son Yitzchak would carry on his work with the same faith, devotion to G-d, and vigor that he and Sarah had. Of that he was certain. Yitzchok, however, was 37 years old and not yet married. Should he die, who would follow? The nation which was to be consecrated and dedicated unto G-d would never be formed.

Avraham, therefore, wanted to find a suitable and exceptional wife for Yitzchak, one who would be his true spiritual partner. He was searching for a young lady who could aid and assist Yitzchak in his own life-long endeavor just as Sarah had helped Avraham.

We then read how Avraham sent his trusted servant Eliezer to his homeland in Aram Naharayim to find a proper and righteous wife for Yitzchak. Many of our *meforshim* are puzzled by Avraham's actions. Why did he specifically forbid Eliezer from choosing a wife from amongst his Canaanite neighbors? Why instead did he send him back to the very land from which, years earlier, Hashem said (Bereishis 12:1):

לֶךְ לְךָ מֵאַרְצְךָ וּמִמּוֹלַדְתְּךָ וּמִבֵּית אָבִיךָ אֶל הָאָרֶץ אֲשֶׁר אַרְאֶךָּ:

Go out of your land, and from your family, and from your father's house unto the land that I will show you.

Was the reason perhaps because the Canaanites were idolators? Surely the inhabitants of Aram Naharayim were no better; they too were עובדי עבודה זרה. We could understand why, years later, Yitzchak ordered his son Yaakov not to intermarry with the local women because of his unfortunate experience with his other son Eisav, who had already intermarried. Avraham, however, had no such experience to justify this avoidance of the Canaanites. His relatives in his homeland were just as idolatrous. Why then did he insist that Eliezer travel to a distant land and bring back a wife for Yitzchak?

The answer may lie in understanding the nature of the evils perpetrated by the inhabitants of Canaan and those performed by the citizens of Aram Naharayim. While the ideas and beliefs of the residents of the latter were faulty, they were nevertheless a moral and ethical people. The inhabitants of Canaan, on the other hand, were particularly notorious for their immorality and other acts of abomination. Unethical behavior, thus, is far worse than idolatry.

In addition, had Yitzchak intermarried with the *Bnos Canaan,* they would have endangered the entire Jewish nation through heredity, example, and education. Thus, Avraham sent Eliezer to a distant land to bring back a wife for Yitzchak.

Rabbi Samson Raphael Hirsch suggests another reason. He says that Avraham realized that the influence of a Canaanite girl on Yitzchak would be completely deleterious. Not only the girl herself, but her entire family and acquaintances who lived in close proximity would exert a cumulatively negative and destructive influence on his son. If, however, he married a girl from a distant country, the girl would be bound to assimilate into the environment of Avraham's household. Thus, thousands of years ago, Avraham HaIvri, the founder of our religion, established a policy which has been instrumental in preserving *Yahadus,* the prohibition against marrying out of the Jewish fold, the ban on intermarriage.

Since Avraham's time, we have remained alive as a nation and as a people, for even when we were physically weak, we were nevertheless spiritually strong. In the face of Roman persecutions, Crusader attacks, Spanish expulsions, and Nazi crematoriums, we exclaimed loudly and boldly: אני מאמין באמונה שלימה. "I believe in our past history as well as in the future destiny of the Jewish people, and if I must, I am willing to give my life to sanctify the Holy and Sacred Name of my G-d and my people."

Today, the Jewish people are physically more powerful than at any other time in our history. However, spiritually, we are at a crossroad. While the traditional frum communities are growing, developing, and even thriving, the rate of intermarriage and assimilation in the non-Orthodox world is at its highest rate ever. In some Scandinavian countries, almost 50% of the Jewish population is intermarried. While the Jewish intermarriage rate in the United States is somewhat lower, it too is reaching epidemic proportions.[1]

The past few generations have seen Jewish homes in America become spiritually empty. There is very little respect for Jewish learning, Jewish knowledge, and Jewish wisdom. There is very little relationship to Torah, to traditions, and to Jewish customs.

The non-Orthodox Jewish child sees the same lifestyle and the same foods at the homes of his non-Jewish friends that he does at his own. He, therefore, sees nothing wrong with admiring the background of his non-Jewish playmates; and why wouldn't he?

---

[1] This was written in 1972-1973. Today in 2023-2024, the rates in the United States are significantly higher than they were in the Scandinavian countries during the early years of the 1970's (RHG).

Their social and family lives are identical. The child later becomes embittered against his parents when they oppose his marrying someone who, while not Jewish, is similar to him in every way that counts to him.

Arthur Cohen, writing in an issue of *Commentary Magazine* a few ago, presents a short story entitled 'The Last Jew on Earth.' In it, he tells of a time when the entire world population embraces Christianity. However, one person, a Jew, refuses to renounce his loyalty and devotion to the G-d of Avraham, Yitzchak, and Yaakov. For that he is severely punished.

While the story is fictitious, it is nevertheless horrifying to think that at the rate which Jewish intermarriage and assimilation is progressing, that dreadful day could possibly occur. It can be averted only if we immediately begin to combat the engulfing wave of intermarriage.

In order to stem the tide, we must develop all resources available to us. First and foremost, we must plan and develop more effective yeshivos and day-schools. Their purpose should be to plant in our children a genuine love and respect for their religion and heritage.

Parents also have a great responsibility. They must create better homes and families by providing a rich and meaningful religious experience for their children within the home and through the examples of their personal lives. We must try to increase the Jewish self-consciousness of our young people. They must be made to feel that they are deserting, which they are, if they marry out of the fold. The child who respects and honors both the moral and ethical values, as well as the practice of *mitzvos*, is unlikely to disregard the significance of that heritage when choosing a life-long partner.

We must teach our youth that to be a Jew is to be like a fish and swim against the stream. Judaism exacts a price, but it is well worth that price. This was the way of Avraham HaIvri who stood against the entire world in his belief of G-d and who forbade his son from intermarrying.

And herein lies the strength of our own very survival. If our children can learn to live with the ideal of Jewishness, they will take pleasure in paying the price of being different. They will become very proud and dedicated Jews who will never, under any circumstances, give up their religion or their ties with their people. They will become the proud bearers of the next generation, the next link in our wonderful chain, our *mesorah*. They will help guarantee the growth, development, and the furtherance of *Yiddishkeit*. It is our responsibility. Let us not miss our opportunity.

5. Yaakov's Transformative Dreams
Parshas Vayeitzei

This week's *sedra*, Parshas Vayeitzei, relates the continuing story of the enigmatic and turbulent life of Yaakov Avinu, our third patriarch. After receiving his father Yitzchak's *berachos* and arousing the wrath of his brother Esav, Yaakov left his home and made his way to Aram Naharayim. There he hoped to find a wife from amongst the daughters of his uncle, Lavan. He wanted to eventually build the nation about which Hashem had told his grandfather Avraham (Bereishis 13:16)

וְשַׂמְתִּי אֶת זַרְעֲךָ כַּעֲפַר הָאָרֶץ אֲשֶׁר אִם יוּכַל אִישׁ לִמְנוֹת אֶת עֲפַר הָאָרֶץ גַּם זַרְעֲךָ יִמָּנֶה:

And I will make your descendants as the dust of the earth, so that if a man can count the dust of the earth, then your descendants too will be countable.

After his first weary day of travel, Yaakov spent the night in the same locale where his father, Yitzchok, was prepared to offer his life to Hashem. He rested on the very spot which would eventually become the holiest and most sacred of all Jewish possessions, Har HaMoriah in Jerusalem. That night, Yaakov experienced the first of two dreams, both of which were to have a profound impact on his life.

In the first dream, Yaakov saw a ladder which extended from heaven to earth. *Malachim,* celestial angels, were ascending and descending this ladder. After beholding this transformative sight, Yaakov was filled with great fear and trepidation. However, Hashem put his mind to rest and alleviated his concerns.

Chazal, in the *Midrash Tanchuma,* tried to explain Yaakov's fear. They say that his dream depicted the rise and fall of some of the world's most powerful and dominant nations. Each of the *Malachim* represented the princes of these countries and the influence of their different cultures and heritage on the arena of world history. The ascent of the angels symbolized the rise of these countries to world supremacy.

The *Midrash* begins:

א"ר שמואל בר נחמן אלו שרי אומות העכו"ם דא"ר שמואל בר נחמן מלמד שהראה לו הקב"ה לאבינו יעקב שרה של בבל עולה שבעין עוקים ויורד, ושל מדי חמשים ושנים, ושל יון מאה ויורד, ושל אדום עלה ולא ידע כמה:

Rav Shmuel ben Nachman said that Hashem told Yaakov that these angels represented the most powerful nations of the world. The representative of Bavel ascended seventy rungs on the ladder and then descended. *Persia's angel went up fifty-two rungs and then came down. Greece's Malach ascended to a height of one hundred rungs and then came down. Rome's representative kept on going up and never descended.*

Each of these nations; Babylonia, Persia, Greece, and Rome, would one day grow in power and strength until it became master of its world. Each would occupy and control vast areas of land and millions of inhabitants. However, while the first three of these nations ascended the ladder of material and physical success and reached the zenith of power and dominion, they would also eventually fall from glory and be displaced from its position of power. Their empires will be lost and their contribution to civilization will be no more than a mere footnote in the pages of history texts. Yaakov, however, did not see the angel of Rome ever descending.

Yaakov's fear was two-fold. His first fear was that he saw that the mighty Roman Empire would ascend the ladder of power and world dominion. However, unlike the other superpowers who preceded her, it appeared in his dream that perhaps, their climb was endless. It seemed that Edom would never fall from their position of supremacy and power.

To this, continues the *Midrash,* Hashem responded:

ואתה אל תירא עבדי יעקב ואל תחת ישראל כביכול אפילו
אתה רואהו עולה אצלי משם אני מורידו.

"Do not fear, My servant Yaakov. Even if you see Rome climbing and rising in an apparent unstoppable manner, I myself will cause their fall and destruction."

Yaakov's second concern was that perhaps the same fate that impacted the other nations would also befall his children and grandchildren, the future *Am Yisrael*. One day, they might conceivably climb the same ladder of power and dominion and may also reach its summit. However, just as the other nations before it fell and eventually disappeared from the community of nations, *Klal Yisrael* too might fall to the ground and eventually disappear and would no longer exist. It was this fear that caused Yaakov to awaken with a great deal of concern and trepidation.

Once again, the *Midrash Tanchuma* quotes Hashem's response, and it was quite instructive:

א"ל הקב"ה אם אתה עולה אין לך ירידה.

Hashem said, "Yaakov, my son, do not be afraid. The fate of your children will not be the same as that of other nations. When your descendants will indeed climb this ladder, I will never allow them to fall into oblivion. They will never disappear as a nation. They will forever remain the most exalted of all the nations.

"There may be times when it will seem that the Jewish people are on the verge of collapse. They will appear to be standing on their last leg and in only a matter of time will disappear from the face of the earth. However, they will –phoenix-like – arise as a force with which to be reckoned. The prophecy which I gave to your grandfather Avraham (Bereishis 12:3):

וַאֲבָרֲכָה מְבָרְכֶיךָ וּמְקַלֶּלְךָ אָאֹר וְנִבְרְכוּ בְךָ כֹּל מִשְׁפְּחֹת הָאֲדָמָה:

'Whoever blesses you will be blessed, whoever curses you shall themselves be cursed, through your seed shall all the families of the earth be blessed,' will be fulfilled through you and your children."

    Yaakov was quite relieved and satisfied with the words of comfort and encouragement from Hashem. He was now no longer afraid of the future. His communion with G-d left him a changed man. When he awoke in the morning, he dedicated a pillar of stone to Hashem and vowed his complete and total allegiance to the *Ribono shel Olam*. With renewed spiritual strength and an optimistic view of the future, Yaakov left this *makom kodesh*, this holy place, which he named *Beis El*. He then continued on his journey to Lavan's home.

    Twenty years later, Yaakov dreamed his second dream. He was no longer a lonely, penniless traveler as he was when he arrived at Lavan's home. He was now blessed with four wives, eleven children, and an extremely large estate. This time, however, his dream did not center around spiritual and lofty ideals. His dream did not offer any indication of the future of his progeny. It consisted solely of his material and temporal possessions.

Yaakov now dreamt of many sheep and goats, some streaked, some speckled, and some spotted. This dream marked the nadir, the low point of his immersion in the mundane affairs of Lavan's society. He had spent all twenty years outside of Eretz Yisrael in the home and under the influence of his cunning, wicked, and idol worshipping uncle and father-in-law, Lavan.

Immediately upon his arrival in Aram Naharayim, Yaakov threw himself completely into the business world. With a great deal of concentration and ingenuity, Yaakov became a shepherd par excellence. Although Lavan used every possible means to cheat him of his due earnings, Yaakov defeated him at his own game and amassed a fortune.

After awakening from this dream, Yaakov was once again very fearful. This time his fear was that he himself may have changed. He was separated for so long from his parents and their positive religious influences. He had lived for two decades in the immoral and depraved environment of Lavan and perhaps was influenced by his evil ways. He did not now dream of sacred and spiritual ideals as he did when he had left his father's home. Instead, he now dreamed solely about material wealth and financial gain.

The 18th century great Chassidic Rebbe, Reb Meir of Przemysl, explained that a person's thoughts and aspirations are in essence detailed in the dreams which he experiences. When Yaakov had his first dream soon after leaving Be'er Sheva and his parents' home, it mirrored his greatness. For at that time, all his thoughts, his very essence, were based on spirituality and *kedusha*.

Now, however, two decades later, his daily activities and his very dreams centered around temporal, mundane, and physical ideas. He was now extremely bothered and concerned for both himself and for his family's future.

A *Malach Hashem,* a celestial angel, then appeared to Yaakov towards the end of his dream and said (Bereishis 31:13)

אָנֹכִי הָקֵל בֵּית אֵל אֲשֶׁר מָשַׁחְתָּ שָּׁם מַצֵּבָה אֲשֶׁר נָדַרְתָּ לִּי שָׁם נֶדֶר עַתָּה קוּם צֵא מִן הָאָרֶץ הַזֹּאת וְשׁוּב אֶל אֶרֶץ מוֹלַדְתֶּךָ:

I am the G-d of Beth-El where you anointed a pillar and where you made a vow unto Me. Now arise and leave this land and return unto the land of your birth.

Yaakov obeyed the command of the angel and left Lavan's evil environment before he could be influenced even more adversely. With his family and his possessions, he fled from Lavan and returned to Eretz Yisrael to his father Yitzchak.

Chazal fully understood Yaakov's fear. In the first chapter of *Pirkei Avos* (Mishnah 7), Nitai HaArbeli teaches us, הרחק משכן רע ואל תתחבר לרשע – "*Keep far from an evil neighbor, and consort not with the wicked.*"

Our *Chachamim* recognized the positive as well as the negative influences that an environment and a surrounding milieu can have upon individuals. They maintained that one of the foremost factors involved in determining a person's character is the people with whom he lives.

The *tzaddik*, Reb Shlomo Leib of Lenchna, relays a most poignant lesson from this story. He says that if a man so steeped in religious tradition as Yaakov Avinu could be adversely affected by living in a deleterious society, how much more so could we average and regular people, who are lacking this background, be influenced by our environment.

During much of our history, Jews adhered to this Rabbinic principle of not associating with those who could influence them negatively and adversely. For nearly eighteen-hundred years, we used certain criteria to determine whether or not to move into a new neighborhood. We made certain that the community had well-functioning and vibrant shuls with *rabbanim* who were *Talmidei Chachamim* and a very structured lay leadership. We carefully examined the existing religious schools and made certain that they would instruct our children in only the most effective and positive manner.

Much of this time, whether voluntarily or involuntarily, we worked and lived solely among our fellow Jews. Our social relationships, likewise, were confined only to those who shared our religious and social beliefs. However, around two-hundred and fifty years ago, the ghetto walls which served to separate Jew from non-Jew were broken down both physically and ideologically. From that moment, Judaism has never been the same.

Many Jews the world over left their all-Jewish communities, first to work, then to socialize, and eventually to live. They began to adopt the lifestyles of the non-Jews. Ever since, there has been an almost complete breakdown in the observance of Jewish traditions and commandments in many segments of our population. The lifestyle, the *halacha*, the laws, and traditions for which many of our ancestors gave their lives have now been considered by these groups as antiquated, obsolete, and merely relics of the past.

Unfortunately, many of our brethren believe that what is most important and absolutely necessary is that they become intimately involved in the development and growth of our overall, general, non-Jewish society. Jews, they feel, must strive to better our cities, work to improve our governments, and help rid the world of the evils of discrimination, hunger, poverty, and war.

While all these acts are fine and wonderful examples of *Tikun HaOlam,* making the world a better place, we dare not do this at the expense of our Jewish values. Jews, both young and old, have been at the forefront of almost every movement to help ameliorate the world's problems for the past one-hundred years. Jews are and have always been involved in the fight for equal opportunity and equal rights for persons of all colors. However, in the early 1960's when Soviet Jews cried out for our help, when they desperately desired an opportunity to live and worship as Jews, when they literally begged us to help them immigrate to Israel, their voices initially fell on deaf ears.

Many of our non-religious brothers and sisters marched for peace in Vietnam but not for peace in the Middle East. They have aided the poor, the hungry, and the sick in Biafra, Bangladesh, and throughout the world, but have not even recognized that there are thousands of infirmed, aged, and poverty-stricken American Jews – mostly Holocaust survivors – who also need our help and assistance.

There have also been and continue to be some very misguided, uninformed, and ignorant Jews who have given political, financial, and moral aid and support to the Palestinian people and even to some of the terrorist groups who threaten the very existence of Medinat Yisrael. However, they have never once even considered aiding and supporting our brothers and sisters in the State of Israel.

The question which we must address is, when will we begin to work for our own house? When will we begin to recognize that if we do not help our own people, no one else will? Haven't we learned any lessons from history? Our non-religious brethren have become so worldly and secularized that it is almost impossible to detect any Jewish identity within them.

Today, we are facing the same dilemma that Yaakov Avinu faced. His fear was that he was losing his own identity and assuming the identity of Lavan and those around him. Yaakov, however, had the *mesorah*, the traditions of his fathers – Avraham and Yitzchak – so ingrained in him that he was able to recognize his problem and to rediscover his own identity before it was too late.

The question for our generation is, will it be too late for so many of our fellow Jews? Will they realize that they have assumed the identity of the world around them and have enough time to change? Will our generation be able to leave their children an everlasting heritage, a real and genuine *mesorah* which reflects the uniqueness and the extraordinary and exceptional aspects of *Am Yisrael*?

If we follow the example set so beautifully by each of our *Avos*, especially Yaakov Avinu, we will bring genuine satisfaction and complete happiness to *HaKadosh Baruch Hu*.

Let us hope and pray that Jews the world over will soon awaken from their slumber and from their dreams. Hopefully, they will arise with sufficient time to realize that the destiny of Judaism and the future of *Am Yisrael* depends, in no small measure, upon each of our actions and our deeds. Let us do what we can to make a real and everlasting difference, *Amen*.

6. Shalom, Peace that Reigns Supreme
Parshas Vayigash

One of the most essential purposes and major aims of a family unit is to serve as a nest of love and a breeding place for trust and loyalty. Parents try to instill positive values and timeless ideals in their children which will help guide and direct their lives. They teach them to recognize the individuality of man and the sanctity of human life. They instruct them to contribute their share toward the betterment of society. First and foremost, however, they teach them to love, respect, and defend at all costs, the members of their immediate family.

Some parents are blessed with children who are completely and totally devoted and dedicated to the other members of their family. Unfortunately, all too often, many parents' ardent prayers go unanswered. Some families do not live in peace and harmony and instead are embroiled in intrafamilial disputes. In many cases, brothers turn on brothers and sisters attack sisters. Unwarranted animosity is generated between certain members of a family. It often spreads malignantly throughout the household, until the entire family structure is eventually weakened and then, subsequently crumbles. The initial cause for such

Parshas Vayigash

enmity and hostility is very difficult to detect, and the reason for the dispute is often forgotten.

Throughout Jewish history, many parents were saddened as they observed their family structure weakened through fraternal disputes. Adam, the first father in the Torah, was also the first to lose a son during his lifetime. His son Kayin murdered his other son, Hevel, due to Kayin's intense jealousy of his brother.

The first of our *Avos*, Avraham Avinu, was renowned universally for his practice of *Hachnosas Orchim,* deeds of hospitality and kindness towards all of his contemporaries. However, Avraham was forced to expel his oldest son Yishmael from his home after Yishmael continually taunted and attempted to corrupt the character of his younger brother, Yitzchak.

The second of our *Avos*, Yitzchak Avinu, was also not spared the pains of family feuding. His two sons, Esav and Yaakov, were diametrically opposite in every possible way. Esav was a hunter, an outdoorsman, and a dilettante in the immoral polytheistic society in which he lived. Yaakov, on the other hand, was a יושב אוהלים, a dweller in the tents of Torah and service to Hashem. He lived within the monotheistic society advanced by his grandfather and practiced by his father.

Yaakov spent his time learning about *HaKadosh Baruch Hu*, Who created Heaven and Earth and Who rules the universe. It was, however, after Yaakov replaced Esav as the recipient of Yitzchak's *berachos* that Esav's true hatred and envy of Yaakov came to the surface. The Torah states (Bereishis 27:41):

וַיִּשְׂטֹם עֵשָׂו אֶת יַעֲקֹב עַל הַבְּרָכָה אֲשֶׁר בֵּרֲכוֹ אָבִיו וַיֹּאמֶר עֵשָׂו בְּלִבּוֹ יִקְרְבוּ יְמֵי אֵבֶל אָבִי וְאַהַרְגָה אֶת יַעֲקֹב אָחִי:

And Esav was hostile to Yaakov because of the blessing wherewith his father blessed him. Esav said in his heart, "The days of mourning for my father are approaching; I will kill my brother Yaakov."

Thus began the millennia-long feud between the descendants of Yaakov and of Esav; it is the origin of the hatred and animosity between *Am Yisrael* and *Edom*.

However, of all the Torah's recorded incidents of family feuding, the most widely known was the conflict between Yosef and his brothers, the sons of Yaakov Avinu, the third of our *Avos*. When Yosef was but a mere youngster, his brothers were very envious of him. They were jealous of the fact that Yaakov tended to favor him above all his other children. They also held a great deal of animosity towards him for bearing tales to their father about their conduct. Their hatred was certainly intensified when Yosef began recounting the various dreams he had dreamt. These

Parshas Vayigash

dreams, Yosef said, depicted him as a ruler, and showed his father, his mother, and his eleven brothers prostrating themselves before him as one does before a sovereign ruler.

The brothers seriously contemplated killing him and removing forever this prickly thorn in their side. However, when a situation arose where they could have ended Yosef's life, they were unable to carry out this abominable act. Instead, they sold him into slavery, exposing Yosef to the potential of great physical and psychological harm. Through their actions, they subjected their father to immense mental anguish and years of deep and ongoing personal mourning.

Twenty-two years later, the tables were completely turned. Yosef became the viceroy of Egypt, second only to Pharaoh, the king of Mitzrayim. He was given the power to make policy which determined the fate of the entire Egyptian population. One of his duties required him to be the supervisor over the sale of grain during the seven years of the great famine which plagued the entire Middle East.

This famine also took its toll on Yaakov's family in Eretz Yisrael. After two years, when their food supply ran out, Yaakov sent his ten older sons to Egypt to purchase grain for their starving family. His brothers appeared before Yosef and requested permission to purchase food for their families. They were unaware

Parshas Vayigash

that the Egyptian viceroy before whom they were standing was their younger brother, Yosef.

This would have been the opportune time for Yosef to reveal his true identity to his brothers and demand retribution for their past actions towards him. Fortunately, he was not ruled by a desire for *nekamah*, revenge or retribution. He was instead blessed with the element of compassion and forgiveness. Although he remembered the difficulties, the pain, and the hardships that his brothers had caused him, he did not bear any grudges and he attributed their past actions to the will of Hashem.

Throughout Jewish history we have been taught to follow the example set by Yosef. We have been told to be compassionate instead of cruel, to be forgiving instead of vengeful. Unfortunately, our actions down through the ages have all too often been ruled by the negative aspects of revenge, hatred, and divisiveness.

At the end of the First Commonwealth of Israel in 586 B.C.E., there was an ongoing conflict between the pro-Babylonian and the pro-Egyptian factions in Judea. These two parties were pitted against one another to the point of violence. The internal feuds were so severe that it was said that when Nebuchadnezzar and his Babylonian army approached Jerusalem on its final assault on the city, they found the gates already open; military victory was easily assured.

This same internal dissension occurred during the last days of the Second Jewish Commonwealth in 70 C.E when the second *Bais HaMikdash* was destroyed by the Roman legions. *Chazal* state that Hashem allowed this to occur primarily because of the *sinas chinam,* the unwarranted animosity and baseless hatred which prevailed among the Jews at that time.

Even as the Roman armies were mounting their final assault on Yerushalayim, disastrous party strife and brotherly hatred continued to plague the Jewish citizens. Titus and his Roman legions conquered a nation that was already ruined and destroyed by internal division and baseless hatred. While the Romans were responsible for murdering hundreds of thousands of Jews, many others lost their lives earlier to their own fellow Jews who murdered any of their brethren who disagreed and refused to follow their military initiatives.

Throughout the centuries, the Jewish people have unfortunately continued to be infested with this curse of internal dispute and a lack of *achdus,* unity. During the 8th century, the Jewish community was divided over the Karaite schism. In the 17th century, the Shabtai Tzvi scandal almost split Judaism in two. The 19th century witnessed the dissension between the *chassidim*, the followers of the Baal Shem Tov, and the *Misnagdim,* led by the Gra, the Vilna Gaon and his followers. This was followed a century later by the dispute between the traditional Orthodox *rabbanim* and the Reform leaders of the *Haskalah*, the Enlightenment.

This divisiveness between our people has not ended even during our own century. There are numerous reasons for the overall American Jewish community's lack of any meaningful response during the trying years of the Holocaust. Historians assert that a primary reason was the lack of unity. For example, the American Jewish Committee advocated a policy of silent protests and preferred working through diplomatic channels; the American Jewish Congress, on the other hand, advocated a program of public protests. This dissension resulted in very limited Jewish participation in the anti-Nazi rallies and demonstrations.

Dr. Stephen S. Wise, the President of The American Jewish Congress and the recognized leader of secular American Jewry during the Holocaust era, wrote a letter to Professor Albert Einstein on January 13, 1936. In the letter he said:

> I may say to you in strictest confidence that I saw the President (Franklin D. Roosevelt) yesterday for the first time in a long while. Unfortunately, I tell you with sorrow his first words were, 'Max Warburg wrote to me lately that things were so bad

in Germany. There was nothing that could be done.' You see how this bears out our theory that Max Warburg and his kind do not really desire to help. This is exactly what the Nazi government wants him to do. The President threw up his hands as if to say, well if Max thinks nothing can be done, then nothing can be done. When I saw (Louis) Brandeis (Supreme Court Justice), he told me that the President would have acted in March, 1933, if it had not been for the Warburg family. You see, Professor Einstein, how these great philanthropists are our deadliest enemies and a fatal cause to the security and honor of the Jewish people.

The rich German Jews whom Dr. Wise castigated were the leaders of the American Jewish Committee and the various other groups who advocated a policy of nonintervention. The Committee either opposed or refused to participate in almost every public denunciation of Hitler and his policies. It was not until 1943, when the Committee finally joined the American Jewish Conference (the umbrella organization which encompassed most major American Jewish groups), that they realized that their quiet diplomatic policy was totally ineffective.

However, later that year, in November, 1943, the Committee once again divided American Jewry by withdrawing from the Conference. The results of this divisiveness among American Jewry enabled Hitler to continue to intensify his diabolical plan of annihilating

European Jewry without any significant protests from any major foreign power.

Almost immediately after the ashes of our holy martyrs were buried and the human skeletons who survived the *Shoah* were released from their living hell, world Jewry became involved in yet another battle, the fight to create a Jewish state. Every important Jewish organization utilized men, money, and materials to help their Palestinian brethren create the first sovereign Jewish country in 2,000 years - the State of Israel.

One would have thought that the tragic results of the Holocaust would have finally prompted world Jewry to reassess and reevaluate its ineffective habit of internecine disputes and conflicts. But this, however, was not to be the case. Even within Palestine itself, the Jewish community was divided in its support of the two major underground Jewish defense organizations, the Haganah and the Irgun.

The methods of the Irgun were largely militant and radical in nature. It specialized in the spectacular which often made the headlines. It would attack a British government office (at that time, Britain was the Mandate power ruling Palestine), or the Palestine administration, another symbol of the enemy. The idea behind this was to push the British to the brink of desperation, where they would finally accede to Jewish demands and leave Palestine.

The Haganah, which commanded much wider support of the world community for its more moderate actions, often put some of the Irgun leaders in jail. On one particular occasion, they actually shot and killed some of their fellow Jews. It was only when these two organizations united and joined forces to become the Israeli Defense Forces that they were successful in their struggle against the numerically superior Arab forces in the 1948 War of Independence.

These feelings of animosity and intense hatred have been carried over even to the realm of religion. Since the State of Israel was established, its religious leaders have ardently worked toward bringing religion to the people. They have been striving to make Judaism relevant and meaningful for all Israelis, the observant as well as the non-observant. However, many of the policies, innovations, and statements of the Israeli Chief Rabbinate have been maliciously attacked and maligned.

Is this what *Yahadus* is all about? Were the words of the Navi Yirmiyahu (8:11) שָׁלוֹם שָׁלוֹם וְאֵין שָׁלוֹם – "Peace, peace, and there is no peace," meant also for our generation? If we disagree politically or religiously with other Jews or with anyone else for that matter, should we resort to violence to achieve our aims? Haven't we learned anything from our history?

Unfortunately, it appears that we keep on repeating the same mistakes time and time again.

We apparently are blind to the handwriting on the wall. Do we so easily forget that *sinas chinam,* unwarranted animosity and causeless and baseless hatred, between brothers can only bring destruction and not positive results? We have been witness to the deaths of millions of Jews, the destruction of our national homeland, and the disintegration of individual family units, where ferocity has replaced mercy and punishment has taken the place of pardon.

We must, if we are to survive, grow, and serve as a model for others, follow the example set for us thousands of years ago by Yosef HaTzadik. He made peace with his brothers although they caused him much physical and psychological harm. While he strongly disagreed with their way of thinking and their course of action, he knew that they were his brothers. During the twenty-two years in which he was separated from them, Yosef matured and grew in human understanding and was ready to forgive and forget the past. He dealt with his brothers in a compassionate, kind, and loving manner.

My dear friends, we too must heal our internal rifts. We must realize that כל ישראל ערבים זה בזה – each Jew, no matter how different he may be, is responsible for his fellow Jew. We are all brothers and must therefore act toward one another in a fraternal and amicable manner. Only when we truly begin to put into practice the word "Shalom," peace, will we be able to preach Shalom to others.

I hope and pray that the next prophetic words to be uttered will be, "שלום שלום ויש שלום" – "Peace, peace and there is peace." May peace reign supreme throughout all of *Klal Yisrael*. Amen.

7. Separate but Very Equal
Parshas Vayigash

On May 18, 1896, the United States Supreme Court, in a near-unanimous vote, issued a landmark decision. In the case of Plessy v Ferguson, it ruled that racial segregation laws, which were in effect at that time, did not violate the United States Constitution. It included a proviso stating that as long as the facilities for each race were equal in quality, there could then be two separate areas – one for white people and another for blacks. This doctrine came to be known as "separate but equal."

This edict stood as the law of the land for fifty-eight years until it was overruled in 1954 by Brown v Board of Education. That verdict determined that the "separate but equal" doctrine was unconstitutional.

L'havdil, in *Yahadus*, we also have a "separate but equal" concept in regards to the different roles played by Jewish men and women. Fortunately, our approach on separate but equal has not been overturned nor has it been abandoned (although many people and various non-traditional Jewish groups have made efforts over the past half century to do so). In this essay, I would like to discuss the different roles which Jewish men and Jewish women play in Jewish life.

Throughout our lives we pay a great deal of attention to the different stages of development of the male gender. When a baby boy is eight days old, he is given a *bris*. It is accompanied with many people in attendance who enjoy a sumptuous feast. When, in certain circumstances and depending upon one's lineage, a male firstborn child is thirty days old, we celebrate his *Pidyon HaBen,* the "redemption of the firstborn son" ceremony. We rejoice at his bar mitzvah when he is thirteen years old, and we congratulate him on becoming a *chassan* at his *aufruf* on the Shabbos prior to his marriage.

Some have wondered about the seeming superiority of men over women in Jewish life. Why, they ask, do we not afford girls the same privileges that we do boys? Why shouldn't we celebrate a girl's birth and her development in the same fashion as we do her male counterpart?

On the surface, by observing the woman's role in traditional Jewish life, one would think that she is indeed considered inferior to man. Women are not counted in the quorum for a *minyan* of ten. Women do not have the obligation of davening thrice daily or of learning the Torah. Throughout Jewish history, they appeared to have taken a back seat to men in the molding and development of Judaism. If, however, we were to investigate much deeper, we would discover that the woman's role in Jewish life is of primary importance and is indeed very significant.

In this week's *sedra*, Parshas Vayigash, Yaakov Avinu learns that his beloved son Yosef, whom he thought to be dead for twenty-two years, was alive and was actually the viceroy, the second most important person in Egypt. After revealing himself to his brothers, Yosef sent word to his father to move his entire family to Egypt and avoid suffering during the remaining years of the Great Famine.

Yaakov was quite perplexed. He very much wanted to live with Yosef and spend his last remaining years with his beloved son and family. However, he feared leaving Eretz Yisrael and moving to Egypt, which was one of the least ethical and most immoral areas in the ancient world. He also knew that this move would begin the fulfillment of the Divine promise made by Hashem many years earlier to his grandfather Avraham. G-d said (Bereishis 15:13):

יָדֹעַ תֵּדַע כִּי גֵר יִהְיֶה זַרְעֲךָ בְּאֶרֶץ לֹא לָהֶם וַעֲבָדוּם וְעִנּוּ אֹתָם אַרְבַּע מֵאוֹת שָׁנָה:

Know of a surety that your descendants shall be foreigners in a land that is not theirs. They will enslave them and oppress them for four hundred years.

Parshas Vayigash

Yaakov was not as concerned for his children's physical enslavement. He was confident that they would be able to withstand those potentially great dangers. What he mostly worried about was their eventual spiritual and religious decline. He knew that Mitzrayim was not only the most powerful and most cultured country in the ancient world. It was also the capital of licentiousness and the seat of depravity. He feared that his descendants, through close involvement and contact with Egyptian society, would be influenced by them. Yaakov correctly worried that his future descendants would become enmeshed in the Egyptian culture and forsake their Jewish heritage and tradition. As a result, the way of life that he had taught them would be forgotten as they, instead, would follow in the paths of the Egyptians.

Yaakov's fears and concerns were only assuaged through the intervention of Hashem Himself Who appeared to Yaakov prior to his descent to Mitzrayim. Hashem told him (Bereishis 46:4):

אָנֹכִי אֵרֵד עִמְּךָ מִצְרַיְמָה וְאָנֹכִי אַעַלְךָ גַם עָלֹה...

I will go down with you into Egypt, and I myself will also surely bring you up again...

With this guarantee, Yaakov continued on his journey. It was, however, not until he reached the very gates of Egypt that he was completely assured of his family's future. The *Midrash Rabbah* (94:9) relates

Parshas Vayigash

that as soon as his entourage approached Egyptian soil, Yaakov witnessed the birth of a granddaughter, a daughter born to his son, Levi. This was no coincidence. The commentary *Nezer HaKodesh* on the Midrash explains that Hashem always provides the remedy before the illness. As Yaakov and his children were taking their first steps into the Egyptian exile, a baby girl was born who would be the source of the Jews' eventual redemption from Egypt. Yaakov's new granddaughter was none other than Yocheved, the mother of Moshe, the future גואל ישראל. The seed of Hashem's promise to Yaakov was, even now, beginning to be fulfilled. Yaakov was optimistic and hopeful for the future of his progeny.

Our *mesorah* relates that it was through the deeds of the נשים צדקניות, the righteous Jewish women in Egypt, led by Yocheved and her daughter Miriam, that our forefathers were redeemed and brought out of bondage. The men had grown apathetic and despondent. They had practically abandoned any hope of ever being freed. They therefore refused to conceive any additional children for fear of exposing them to the same hardships of slavery and persecution to which they were subjected.

The women, though sharing their husbands suffering and agony, encouraged them to hope, aspire, and look to the future. They sought out their husbands' love and were responsible for the birth of a new generation, one that was fit to be redeemed. The same has been true of our people in every generation and in every country. When all seemed hopeless, Jewish women have sweetened their husbands' lives, consoled them in times of adversity, and kindled the spark of hope for better times.

When *Klal Yisrael* sinned with the Golden Calf at the foot of Har Sinai, the women resisted and tried to discourage their husbands from this apostasy. When Haman threatened to destroy the Jews in the Persian Empire, Esther played a leading role in saving her people. When the Syrian-Greek ruler Antiochus sought to put an end to the practice of many basic areas of *Yahadus,* Chanah set an example for her people through her courageous death and that of her seven sons. She thereby was מקדש שם שמים, she sanctified the Holy Name of Hashem. Yehudis was another heroic woman who arose during the Syrian-Greek persecution. Her courage led to the downfall of one of the great Greek generals and laid the groundwork for the revolt of the Maccabees, led by Matisyahu and his sons.

Throughout our history, in ancient as well as in modern times, Jewish women have played a very important and significant role in helping mold and develop our people and our faith. Nevertheless, we

Parshas Vayigash

must understand that there is a great difference between their activities. While men and women are, in essence, equal in nature, each has different tasks and different responsibilities.

Men have always been considered to be the conquerors and the aggressors (Rashi to Bereishis 1:28), while it is wives and mothers who provide love, strength, and the wherewithal for their husbands and sons to carry on. Men's responsibilities, as dictated by the *Kesubah* which every husband must give his wife, have been to provide for and protect their families. Women carry the role of managing their households and rearing their children. Most importantly, women have a primary role in educating their children, as Shlomo HaMelech (Mishlei 1:8) teaches, וְאַל תִּטֹּשׁ תּוֹרַת אִמֶּךָ – *do not abandon the teachings of your mother.*

It is in this light that the *Avudraham* explains why a woman is not mandated to daven with a *minyan* and learn Torah. In fact, a woman is not responsible to fulfill any positive commandment which has a time limit. For example, women are not obligated to take the ד' מינים or sit and eat their meals in a Sukkah during the Yom Tov of Sukkos as are men. And women need not hear the sound of the Shofar on Rosh Hashanah while men are commanded to do so. Parenthetically, it has become a *minhag,* an old established custom, that women, while exempt from these *mitzvos*, have taken

Parshas Vayigash

it upon themselves to fulfill the different obligations of Sukkos as well as to listen to the *Tekias Shofar* on Rosh Hashanah.

Some halachic authorities explain that the reason women cannot be considered part of a *minyan* is because they are exempt from מצוות עשה שהזמן גרמא, positive Mitzvos which have a time limit. Thus, the fact that a woman is not counted as part of a *minyan*, nor is she allowed to serve as the *baal tefillah* during the davening, does not stem from her inferiority, but rather it reflects her different position and role as well as taking into account the realities of a woman's life.

Our commentaries' interpretation of the *Birchos HaShachar* can best illustrate this point. The text which men recite daily is:

בָּרוּךְ אַתָּה ה' אֱלֹקֵינוּ מֶלֶךְ הָעוֹלָם שֶׁלֹּא עָשַׂנִי אִשָּׁה.

Blessed are you Hashem, our G-d, King of the universe, who has not made me a woman.

Our *chachamim* do not, G-d forbid, explain this *beracha* in a derogatory or disparaging manner. Rather, they explain that man is forever grateful and thankful to the *Ribono shel Olam* that he did not impose a woman's obligations and responsibilities on him. Had He done so, we certainly would not be able to manage them. The burdens and obligations of a woman are far more difficult and complex than those of a man. Indeed. A woman's versatility and power of endurance are much greater than a man's. It is for this reason, therefore, that men bless G-d and thank Him each morning for not creating them as a woman.

    This morning, we have the honor and the great merit of welcoming two newly born girls into our *shul*. To their parents go our sincerest wishes of congratulations and *mazel tov*. We offer our *tefillah* that both girls grow up in the tradition of our beloved אמהות, *Sarah, Rivka, Rachel* and *Leah*. May they become great Jewish women and be a source of pride and *nachas* to their parents, their families, and to all of *Klal Yisrael. Amen.*

8. To be a Man
Parshas Shemos

The late senator and 1968 presidential candidate, Robert F. Kennedy, often said, "Some men see things as they are and say, 'Why?' I dream things that never were and say, 'Why not?'"

Man has constantly been plagued by the dilemma of whether after observing the evils of society he should silently accept the status quo, bitter as it may be, or whether he should attempt to improve life, and by doing so, cause old and established customs and traditions to be completely uprooted.

For thousands of years, most people have unfortunately chosen the easier and less controversial path. They may have decried certain contemporary inequities and oppressions. They have, however, generally acquiesced and given in to the wishes and strong arm of the ruling authorities. And with that decision, their dreams and ideals for the future have often come to naught.

There have been only a handful of individuals throughout history who have had the courage, the fortitude, the valor, as well as the backbone to challenge the balefulness of their society and the wickedness of their times. They were not solely concerned with their own welfare and future. They were far more interested in the establishment of justice and equality for all and the granting of freedom to each and every person. They publicly espoused their proposals and programs which were far ahead of their times.

The נביאים, men like Eliyahu, Elisha, Yeshayahu, Yirmiyahu, and Yechezkel, were the most famous and best known of the numerous prophets who chastised *Am Yisrael* and caused them to take stock and reevaluate their lives as well as their interpersonal relationships. They paid no attention to the threats made against their lives. Their sole concern was to help man raise himself just a little closer to G-d and to carry out His principles of love and concern and the ultimate brotherhood of all men.

There was one man who stood up and cried out against the evils of his day many years before our nation was even established. During the harsh and burdensome *shibud Mitzrayim,* Egyptian servitude, the first of the Jewish נביאים rallied his people. The man who is considered to be the greatest Jewish prophet aroused his fellow Jews to action. He strengthened their all but broken backs and breathed a spirit of independence into those who had lost all hope for the future. That man was our leader and teacher, the incomparable Moshe Rabbeinu.

For many years after the deaths of Yosef and his brothers, our ancestors were subjected to every kind of physical and mental cruelty. They were mercilessly beaten, and they were forced to work both day and night. However, they never gave up the hope of being rescued from their torturous hell. They used their period of enslavement advantageously and grew in strength and number. They increased in population from a small tribe of less than one hundred persons – the children and grandchildren of Yaakov Avinu – to a nation of almost two million individuals.

The Egyptian rulers became paranoid. They were concerned lest the Hebrew people grow in number and in strength and eventually lead and direct a revolt against their tyrannical, autocratic, and oppressive rule; or they may perhaps join together with other groups who would be fomenting a revolt and an insurrection. The higher echelons of the Egyptian government therefore forced *Bnei Yisrael* to continuously work in order to minimize the time that husbands and wives could be together. The astrological advisors of King Pharaoh also forecast that a son would be born who would eventually lead his people out of bondage. Pharaoh therefore decreed that every male baby born be cast into and drowned in the Nile River.

However, all of these harsh decrees and deeds of oppression did not completely break the spirit or decrease the number of the Jews. In fact, the opposite occurred. It seemed that the more severe the decree, the more the Jews appeared to multiply and gain strength and determination. Many of the sons who were condemned to die were miraculously saved. One son, Moshe, indeed became his people's redeemer and led them out of Egypt.

Moshe, the future leader of *Am Yisrael*, was saved by Pharaoh's daughter Basya and was adopted by her. He, in fact, spent his formative years in the royal Egyptian palace. There he was introduced to the cultures of the country and was trained to become a member of the Egyptian elite. He could have spent the rest of his life living in a carefree, complacent manner, unburdened and untroubled by the ills and sufferings of his people. However, this was not to be his trajectory. While his people's customs and traditions were not yet a significant part of his life, Moshe threw his lot in with his enslaved brethren.

The Torah tells us that when Moshe was grown, he went out of the palace to his people to observe and internalize their sufferings. He came upon an Egyptian taskmaster mercilessly beating a Hebrew man, one of

Moshe's own brethren, without any reason or provocation. The Torah then says (Shemos 2:12):

וַיִּפֶן כֹּה וָכֹה וַיַּרְא כִּי אֵין אִישׁ וַיַּךְ אֶת הַמִּצְרִי וַיִּטְמְנֵהוּ בַּחוֹל:

And he turned this way and that way, and when he saw that there was no man, he smote the Egyptian to death.

Our *Chachamim* offer diverse commentaries on this verse. Some suggest a purely literal interpretation and say that Moshe looked around, and when he saw that no one was present who could testify against him, he slew the Egyptian. Others maintain that Moshe used his gift of prophecy and foresaw that no worthy progeny would issue from this evil man, and thus his life was not worth sparing. However, two latter-day *meforshim* offer interpretations which I feel truly exemplify the extraordinary character of Moshe Rabbeinu.

The *Netziv*, Rav Naftali Tzvi Berlin, says that Moshe sought a way to bring the Egyptian to justice for his criminal act. וַיַּרְא כִּי אֵין אִישׁ וַיַּךְ אֶת הַמִּצְרִי – "And he saw that there was no man." He saw that there was no one to whom he could appeal for justice. The Egyptian jurists conveniently looked the other way. Moreover, they were quite pleased with the overzealous manner in which their countryman carried out Pharaoh's ruling. When Moshe saw that the Egyptian judicial system was corrupt and would not protect the Jews, he took the law into his own hands.

Rabbi Yaakov Tzvi Mecklenburg, the 19th century author of *HaKsav v'HaKabalah,* explains that Moshe thought that perhaps one of the Jewish bystanders would come to the rescue of his inflicted brethren. Moshe looked from side to side. However, "He saw that there was no man." He saw that there was no one among the Jewish people who was physically able to intervene in his brother's misfortune. There was no man who was even willing to risk his future to help his fellow Jew who was downtrodden, in trouble, and in distress. Moshe just could not bear this sight and he, therefore, slew the Egyptian.

Thus, our great lawgiver, the father of the נביאים, began his aid and assistance to his people through violent means. He disproved the theory which argues that insurrection and rebellion against the established order is always unacceptable and unwholesome. His actions contradicted the view that extremes of violence are always unacceptable and unwholesome. Moshe had hoped that his actions would be a springboard, that it would serve as an inducement and incentive to the Jews. He thought that after seeing his public denunciation of Egyptian tyranny, it would bring forth a response from his fellow Jews. His aim was that the Jewish slaves would mobilize and attempt to throw off their yoke of oppression.

While Moshe's action did not have the immediate effect he had desired, it taught us a most important principle which was later incorporated into our tradition. In *Pirkei Avos* (2:6) we are told:

ובמקום שאין אנשים, השתדל להיות איש.

And in a place where there are no men, strive to be a man.

When you find yourself in a situation where courage, decisiveness, and forthright determination are required, you must stand up and be counted regardless of the repercussions. At a time when action is necessary, do not be a fence straddler, for those who straddle the fence usually end up falling off. While the lesson of Moshe and the principles which he developed have become part of our religious tradition, we have all too often conveniently forgotten them. Throughout our two thousand years of Diaspora history, there have been many situations which required us to be an איש, but relatively few times when we actually rose to the occasion.

We have seen our brothers in extreme difficulty in Europe during World War II and in present day Russia. We look "from here to there and see no man." Nonetheless, we still do not accept the challenge. We don't become the איש that Moshe became nor the איש that he pleaded with us to be.

However, there is one group of our people who lifted this sacred banner high and have enabled us all to hold our heads up very proudly. Three thousand five hundred years after Moshe, his people, the citizens of the State of Israel, put into action the words that Moshe preached. When surrounded by seven belligerent and bellicose nations in 1967 who threatened her with wanton destruction and the murder of her citizens, Israel turned to the world community for help. " וַיִּפֶן כֹּה וָכֹה." They looked this way and that way; they beseeched one capital after another to find a peaceful solution to the impending hostilities. However, as hard and as long as she looked, Israel could not find any איש. Not one country was willing or able to risk its status in the community of nations and assure Israel of its total support. Therefore, when one finds himself in a situation where there are no men, he himself must strive to be a man. Israel herself thus became that איש. She did as *Moshe* did thousands of years ago and slew the Egyptians as well as the Syrians and the Jordanians.

Nineteen years before that historic and memorable war, Israel was faced with its first great challenge. After the horrors and tortures which were inflicted upon the Jewish people during the Hitler era came to an end, world Jewry then began picking up the pieces and planned for the future.

Parshas Shemos

After a Holocaust, the magnitude of which had never before been seen, the only logical place for Jewry to begin anew was in Palestine, its ancient homeland. Jewish leaders pleaded with country after country and president after president for their help and assistance. While we received a great deal of sympathy and pity and many words of support, very little concerted action was apparent. In a period where no one wanted to become a "man", one person stood alone and accepted the mantle of leadership. He became the true איש in the tradition of Moshe Rabbeinu and single-handedly helped Israel become, for the first time in two thousand years, a nation among nations. This giant of men – the thirty-third President of the United States – Harry S. Truman, was laid to rest this past week.

President Truman will be remembered in the annals of history for the Truman Doctrine, the Marshall Plan, and many other acts which aided the world community. However, to Jews the world over, he will best be remembered for the role he played during the critical years of the fight to establish a Jewish State in Palestine. In an era when his British allies were against Jewish statehood, when the Departments of State and Defense and his own military leaders balked at the idea of granting independence to Palestine, Truman stood alone. He acted with courage, fortitude, and determination. In a time when there were no men to be found, Harry Truman acted as an איש, he acted as a man.

In his memoirs he wrote:

> I was always aware of the fact that not all my advisors looked at the Palestine problem in the same manner as I did. The military kept talking about two things, our inability to send troops to Palestine if trouble should break out there and secondly, the oil resources of the Middle East. Secretary Forrestal spoke to me repeatedly about the danger that hostile Arabs might deny us access to the petroleum treasures of their countries. The Joint Chiefs of Staff on several occasions submitted memoranda to show me that we could not afford to send more than a token force to the area. The Department of State's specialists on the Near East were, almost without exception, unfriendly to the idea of the Jewish State. If the Arabs are antagonized, they will go over to the Soviet Camp. There were some men in the State Department who held the view that the Balfour Declaration could not be carried out without offense to the Arabs. Like most of the British diplomats, some of our diplomats sided with the Arabs on account of their numbers and because of the fact that they controlled such immense oil resources; thus, they should be appeased. I am sorry to say that there were some among them who were inclined to be antisemitic

These and other arguments never swayed President Truman. In fact, on May 14, 1948, just moments after the State of Israel was established, President Truman recognized the provisional government as the de facto authority of the new State of Israel. Thus, America became the first country to do so.

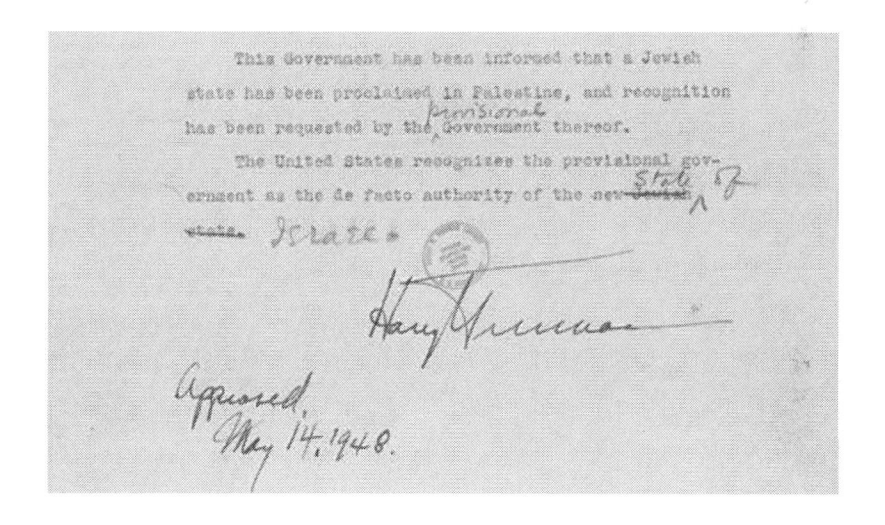

> This Government has been informed that a Jewish state has been proclaimed in Palestine, and recognition has been requested by the provisional Government thereof.
>
> The United States recognizes the provisional government as the de facto authority of the new State of Israel.
>
> Harry Truman
>
> Approved,
> May 14, 1948.

About a year after he recognized the State of Israel, President Truman was visited by the late Chief Rabbi of Israel, Rabbi Isaac Herzog, *zt"l*. Harav Herzog told him: "G-d put you in your mother's womb so you would be the instrument to bring about the rebirth of Israel after 2,000 years. The President was reported to be so overcome by these words that tears were running down his cheeks.

Harry Truman was, indeed, a true man. His entire life exemplified this fact. When decisions were necessary, he made them regardless of political consequences or repercussions. He often made unpopular judgments for which he was strongly censured but which he knew were right. Historians have only recently begun to agree with him and to appreciate what a truly great leader he was.

It is most ironic that President Truman once said, "I am the best friend that the Jews have had since Moses." As Moshe Rabbeinu set an example of bravery and valiance for ancient Israel when it underwent the pangs of development and growth, so too did President Truman set an example of courage and heroism for modern Israel in its infant and formative stages. Harry Truman was a president, a statesman, and a world leader. Most of all, he was an איש par excellence. He was a real and true man. To him, a grateful Jewish community says thank you and *Shalom*. Goodbye, and may you rest in peace.

Postscript:

This essay was written in 1973, over fifty years ago. Since then, the world community has, by and large, constantly, and continuously been against and opposed to almost all Israeli actions. Led by the rabidly antisemitic United Nations, they have been a thorn in the side of the State of Israel.

With the exception of a few special and heroic individuals such as Lyndon Johnson, Ronald Reagan, and Donald Trump, we have not had a President of the United States who was as dedicated, devoted, and as forceful for Am Yisrael and especially towards Medinat Yisrael as President Harry Truman,

Now, especially during the current and most difficult existential war in which the State of Israel finds itself, I wish we had a Harry Truman as our President. The entire Jewish community in the Diaspora as well as our brethren in Medinat Yisrael would feel a great deal more secure and safe.

RHG - February 2024

9. A Time to Act
Parshas Beshalach

Throughout Talmudic literature, there has been an ongoing debate among *Chazal* as to whether study or action – לימוד or מעשה – is of primary concern. The final decision is that the art of learning and studying is more important to *Yahadus* than specific individual actions. However, what our *chachamim* actually meant was that one is unable to properly live a total Jewish life if he is not well prepared and learned. Subsequently, they stressed the primacy of education and scholarship *vis á vis* performance and action. Study, however, should only be a means to an end. It should eventually lead to one's performing the *Mitzvos* properly and one's service and assistance to humanity in general and to *Am Yisrael* in particular.

There are far too many people who act rashly and impetuously without any thought or consideration. Their actions, instead of aiding society, actually harm it. On the other hand, there are some people who spend their entire lives pursuing study for their own intellectual growth and development. They do not attempt to aid anyone other than themselves. In *Pirkei Avos, Ethics of The Fathers*, we are taught to combine the elements of both study and action in our personal lives. Rabban Shimon ben Gamliel said (*Avos* 1:17):

ולא המדרש הוא העיקר אלא המעשה

Study is not the most important thing but rather practice and performance.

According to the *Shelah HaKadosh*, while one's performance and actions are a priority, one must first study all that he can and then use this knowledge to contribute to and assist society. There are times when study and scholarship and *tefillah* should be the order of the day. But there are other occasions which require immediate action and performance. One such experience occurred thousands of years ago at the *Yam Suf*, the Red Sea.

The recently liberated Jewish people found themselves pursued by their former Egyptian taskmasters. They were sandwiched in between the rushing waters of the Red Sea on one side and the Egyptian army who were swiftly attempting to tighten the noose around their necks. They were panic stricken, and thus urged Moshe Rabbeinu to take some immediate and forceful action. Moshe began to fervently pray; he began to *daven* to *Hashem*.

The *Ribono shel Olam* then responded to *Moshe* (Shemos 14:15):

וַיֹּאמֶר ה' אֶל מֹשֶׁה מַה תִּצְעַק אֵלָי דַּבֵּר אֶל בְּנֵי יִשְׂרָאֵל וְיִסָּעוּ:

Hashem said to Moshe, "Why do you cry out to Me? Speak to the children of Israel that they may go forward.

Rashi explains:

למדנו שהיה משה עומד ומתפלל אמר לו הקב"ה לא עת עתה להאריך בתפלה שישראל נתונין בצרה.

From this we learn that Moshe was standing and davening to Hashem. G-d said to Moshe, "Now is not the time to pray at length, for the Jewish people are in distress."

This was not a time for study, contemplation, or even prayer. It was a time for personal involvement and total and complete commitment. *Bnei Yisrael* adhered to the advice of Hashem and took that first plunge into the Red Sea. The waters then miraculously split apart, allowing them to cross on dry land and escape forever from their oncoming Egyptian pursuers. Following *Am Yisrael's* completed journey to the other bank of the sea, their Egyptians pursuers were swallowed up in the gulf tide of the onrushing waters.

Upon their final deliverance from the yoke of oppression and servitude to which they were subjected in Mitzrayim, our ancestors offered their thanks and appreciation to the *Ribono shel Olam*. Led by Moshe and his sister Miriam, they sang the *Shirah, Song of the Sea*. This *Shirah* is the main theme and central portion of this week's *Parshah, Parshas Beshalach*.

Parshas Beshalach

Chazal, commenting on the singing of the *Shirah* at the *Yam Suf,* are puzzled. They say that while it was most appropriate and correct for the Jewish people to praise Hashem after He completely obliterated their enemies at the Red Sea, they, however, sang no song of thanks, nor did they offer any public acclaim to Hashem when they left Egypt just seven days earlier. Wasn't their delivery from two hundred and ten years of enslavement and tyranny reason enough for the Jews to express their appreciation and thankfulness to G-d? Why was their gratitude to Hashem first expressed at the Red Sea and not before?

This question has also been asked concerning two other events in our history. In the *Haftorah* that we read this week from *Sefer Shoftim* we are told of the great military victory of the Jews led by the Prophetess Devorah and her Chief of Staff, Barak, over the Canaanites in the early days of ancient Israel.

Following their resounding triumph over an enemy far more numerous than they and certainly better prepared for battle, the Jews thanked and offered their praise and appreciation to Hashem. Led by Devorah and Barak, the people expressed their gratitude to G-d by singing a *shirah* – *Shiras Devorah.*

However, many centuries later, towards the latter part of *Bayis Rishon*, the Assyrian hordes were besieging Jerusalem, the capital of the kingdom of

Yehuda. They were planning for one final thrust against עיר דוד. Inside the city walls, King Chizkiyahu and his subjects were panic-stricken and anticipated the worst. However, the night before the final assault, a *Malach*, a heavenly angel, descended upon the Assyrian camp, wrought havoc in its midst, and slew hundreds of thousands of its soldiers.

After witnessing this miraculous victory over his enemies, King Chizkiyahu and the entire Jewish nation were deathly silent. They offered no thanks and appreciation to G-d.

Our *Chachamim* were critical of Chizkiyahu's apparent lack of recognition and acknowledgement of the work of Hashem. In fact, *Chazal* felt that he had the opportunity to become the *Melech HaMoshiach*. However, following his lack of public acknowledgment of Hashem's intervention on his behalf, they observed that he lost his chance.

What is the difference between these two incidents? In both episodes, a great and miraculous victory was had. Nevertheless, the responses to these events were diametrically opposed. Why did Devorah feel the need to sing *Shirah* while Chizkiyahu did not?

The *meforshim* tell us that Devorah, Barak, and their followers, played an active, personal, and significant role in their decisive battle with the Canaanites. Therefore, following their phenomenal

Parshas Beshalach

and prodigious triumph and their overwhelming victory, they were exultant and expressed their great appreciation to Hashem.

King Chizkiyahu and his subjects on the other hand, took no active role in their battle against the Assyrians. They put their complete and absolute trust and faith in *HaKadosh Baruch Hu* and in His Divine promise to keep, protect, and defend the Jewish people. They subsequently played a completely passive role. They did not participate in any aspect of the war. They did not experience any of the sorrows and defeats of battle, nor did they savor the triumphs of success. Thus, when their enemy was completely vanquished and their conquest was assured, the Jews did not publicly thank *HaKadosh Baruch Hu*. They remained completely silent.

When our ancestors left Mitzrayim, they too were not instrumental in overthrowing their autocratic and despotic oppressors. They passively stood by. They acted as mere spectators and observed as Hashem, בכבודו ובעצמו, utterly destroyed the very backbone and total resistance of the great Egyptian military might. Thus, following *Yetzias Mitzrayim*, the Jews did not sing praise or offer public thanks unto G-d.

However, at the *Yam Suf*, just one week later, the *neis*, the miracle of the splitting of the waters did not occur until *Am Yisrael* actively became involved. Only when they went forward and personally jumped into the waters, only when Shevet Yehudah, led by Nachshon ben Aminadav, took the first plunge did the sea split for them. Only after their personal and direct involvement, when *Am Yisrael* risked their own lives and the lives of their families to fulfill G-d's wish, did they jubilantly express their thanks and appreciation to Hashem.

  This distinction that is made between active participation and passive onlooking as a criterion for public expression of praise to G-d is most fascinating but quite obvious. There is a great deal more ebullience, exuberance, and joy following one's personal efforts and labors than after one is merely a passive spectator to an historic event. Certainly, one who has sacrificed of his time, energy, and person toward a specific goal is more apt to break out in song and share in the ecstatic moment of ultimate triumph.

  Each of us in our own private lives as well as in our interpersonal relationships must make the same decision. We can, if we wish to, passively sit by while others are involved in the great events which can change the world. We can take a back seat and observe as our friends and relatives are actively involved in feeding the hungry and the poor and alleviating the misery of millions of the world's unfortunate souls. Or else, we can rise to the occasion and join in this great struggle. We can ascend to the challenges of the day and personally make the world a little better for all.

On the Jewish scene, the most ambitious and most important cause today is that of Soviet Jewry. It will take many years of long and arduous work on the part of thousands – perhaps millions – of Jews until we will be able to finally free our enslaved brethren. The only way that our brothers and sisters will be allowed out of their imprisoned society and be given the opportunity to leave will be the public pressure that must be exerted upon the Soviet authorities.

For too many years, most of the major Jewish organizations have been content with merely writing and disseminating articles about the condition of Soviet Jewry. While the world community became appraised and enlightened and perhaps even sympathetic to their plight, nothing significant was done to help them. Today, however, all that has changed. While there are still certain groups whose major purpose remains to write and issue eloquent statements about the Russian Jews, this too is changing. Fortunately, there are a number of organizations such as the Student Struggle for Soviet Jewry and the Jewish Defense League, as well as countless individuals who dedicate much of their time to work for and try to ameliorate the plight of their incarcerated brothers and sisters.

The *Atlanta Constitution* recently reported a story about an Illinois woman, Mrs. Corel Pollack, who rings up a $300 phone bill each month. The calls she makes are to Jews in the Soviet Union. Her purpose is to offer encouragement to them and let them know that they are not alone. She is fully aware that her calls are all monitored, and the Russian Secret Police constantly listen in on her conversations. But they too have become aware that world Jewry will not silently sit by and allow their Soviet brethren to be religiously, psychologically, and physically tortured.

Mrs. Pollack said that she remembers that when she was growing up, "Jewish children my age were going up in smoke in Germany, and no one was doing anything. I don't want this to happen again, so I have to do my share; I must act."

Mrs. Pollack is not alone. There are countless numbers of Jews all over the Western world who make calls to Russia weekly. Thousands of others write letters to the Soviet Authorities, members of the Congress, and the President, asking them to give the Russian Jews the chance that the victims of Hitler's Holocaust were not given. These individuals are totally committed to the cause of Soviet Jewry.

I have a very good friend, Dr. Howie Shaw, who recently shared with me a letter which he wrote to the Soviet Premier Kosygin. In it he describes his personal care and concern and his feelings of ערבות, solidarity, with his brothers and sisters in the Soviet Union. This letter was written a few years ago, on the afternoon just prior to his wedding. It reads as follows:

> Dear Premier Kosygin,
> On a day when my spirits should be completely uplifted, at a time when my heart should be pounding with joy and I should be filled with happiness and exultation, I find, unfortunately, that I am instead quite sad and disconsolate. For when I look around and see my brothers and sisters in Russia enslaved, persecuted, and undergoing all forms of discrimination, I am terribly depressed. It is for this reason, Mr. Premier, that I have decided to write to you on this afternoon, just prior to my wedding.

My friends, when the day comes, and it certainly will, when *HaKadosh Baruch Hu* will perform another miracle for our people, when our enslaved Soviet brethren will be freed, another *Shirah* will be sung and another *Hallel* will be recited. However, only those who actively participated in helping bring about this miracle will be at the forefront in jubilantly singing the *Shirah* and praising Hashem.

Will we be among them? Will we share in this future great moment of ecstasy and ultimate triumph? Will we act in the tradition of our ancestors at the *Yam*

Suf and personally take the plunge? The decision, my friends, is ours to make, and the future depends in no small part on our choice.

<u>Postscript</u>:

This drasha was delivered in the early 1970's. A number of years later, due to international political pressure and to the yeoman efforts of many Orthodox Jews, everything changed. The Soviet authorities allowed hundreds of thousands of their Jewish citizens to immigrate to Israel and the United States.

In December, 1991, the Soviet Union was disbanded. It was replaced by the newly independent Russian State. This new entity gave permission to the remaining Jews to practice all aspects of their faith. RHG.

10. A Friend at All Times
Parshas Yisro

"A friend in need is a friend indeed," goes the old English adage. While this statement may be considered trite and hackneyed, it contains a great deal of truth. Many people pride themselves on the vast array of friends and acquaintances which they have managed to accumulate over the years. At many affairs – weddings, Bar-Mitzvahs, etc., it is not only the elegance of the occasion, nor the importance and sanctity of the moment which most people remember. Rather, the number of individuals who have been invited to participate serves as the superficial criteria which many of us use to judge another's success in life. Perhaps, more than on any other occasion, one's own funeral is frequently an indicator of his popularity. All too often, we judge a person's accomplishments or failures in life by the number of mourners who pay homage to him and the number of automobiles which slowly accompany the deceased to his final resting place.

I remember most vividly the newspaper reports in 1962 of the funeral of Rav Aharon Kotler *zt"l*. Rav Kotler was the undisputed leader of American

Orthodox Judaism. He was considered by all as the *Gadol HaDor*. His contribution to Torah Judaism on this continent and throughout the world was heralded and appreciated by Jews from all walks of life. The press reported that on the day of his funeral, 25,000 people paid him their final respects. This honor, said the newspapers, was the greatest ever accorded any Jew in this country. These reports seemed to imply that because of the huge crowds which bid him farewell, Rav Kotler's eminence and his distinguishing accomplishments were evident. And had fewer people turned out, would his contribution to Judaism have been diminished? How childish, how immature, but yet how true this is of all human beings. And how guilty we all are of this desire to be loved by all during our lives and buried by all when we die.

Most of us who do not achieve world fame and glory must be content with the few true friends we make during our lifetime. In fact, as the historian Thomas Fuller said in 1732, "If you have one true friend you have more than your share." We each have many acquaintances whom we categorize as friends, people with whom we share professional and business concerns and others with whom our relationship is extended into the realm of personal and social interests.

However, the true mark of friendship is commitment and sacrifice, one friend giving of himself to help his comrade. A truer perspective leads one to the conclusion that the distinguishing characteristic that differentiates the true friend from the casual acquaintance is that the former is present in your moments of need and crisis while the latter is absent. It is all well and good to help celebrate one's happy occasions and be a fair-weather friend. However, to be with one in his most trying circumstances, when he is in need of a shoulder to cry on, or someone to whom he can confide in is, in essence, the real acid test of comradeship and loyalty. As the English writer Owen Feltham remarked in *Resolves* in 1620, "To find friends when we have no need of them and to want them when we have, are both easy and common. In prosperity who will not profess to love a man? In adversity how few will show that they do indeed?"

If we analyze this concept closely, however, we will see that to be present in times of adversity alone is insufficient to be defined as true brotherhood and friendship. Far too often, those who are present in our times of need are not genuinely sharing our grief or experiencing our sorrow. True, they may express anguish and perhaps even shed a tear or two over our loss. Mostly, they come to appreciate what they still possess. How many times have we heard about people who attend the funeral of a "friend of many years" and express their sadness over the loss but never once do they later visit his widow or loved ones. They do nothing to help try to fill the void in the mourners' lives or share in the future joys of the distraught family. To merely show sympathy and pity is not a real sign of true and genuine friendship. True friendship is to be present in both moments of joy and happiness and also to be available to offer help and assistance in moments of grief and sorrow.

With this thought in mind, we may perhaps help solve a problem which has perplexed our *meforshim* for some time. The main theme of this week's *Parshah,* Yisro, is מעמד הר סיני, the transmitting by Hashem to *Bnei Yisrael* of the *Aseres HaDibros*, the Decalogue, the very foundation of *Yahadus*. The *Sedra* is named "Yisro" after the Midianite father-in-law of Moshe. Why, our Rabbis ask, was this, perhaps the most significant and meaningful of all the weekly *Parshiyos*, named after a non-Jew? Even our *Avos*, Avraham, Yitzchak, and Yaakov, did not warrant such an honor. Even the incomparable Moshe Rabbeinu, who led his people and who labored for forty years teaching the Torah to *Klal Yisrael*, did not merit such a distinction. What worthy deeds did Yisro perform to deserve this revered and dignified honor?

Some of our *meforshim* maintain that he warranted this distinction and fame because of his suggestion to Moshe of the establishment of a

Parshas Yisro

legislative system. For some time after *Yetzias Mitzrayim*, all *halachic* issues, both major and minor, were brought to Moshe. He was swamped from morning to night with the almost impossible task of solving the religious perplexities and personal differences of his people. Immediately upon arriving in מחנה ישראל, Yisro recommended that Moshe set up a system of lower and higher courts that would deal with the regular disputes and differences of *Am Yisrael*. Moshe would serve as a Supreme Court, the highest court of appeal. He would not have to be involved in deciding each and every dispute.

Other *meforshim* feel that this *Sedra* was named for Yisro because of his great admiration and love for *HaKadosh Baruch Hu* as well as for *Am Yisrael*. The *Midrash Rabbah* says that when Amalek heard of all the miracles, all the נסים ונפלאות which *Hashem* had performed for *Klal Yisrael*, they immediately and without any provocation attacked the Jewish people. On the other hand, when Yisro heard of the prodigious and wonderous works of G-d for the Jewish people, he traveled to the Sinai Desert, cast his lot together with *Am Yisrael*, and converted to Judaism. Yisro was a truly righteous person whose belief in Hashem was genuine and sincere. Thus, according to many of our *Chachamim*, he was deserving of having a *Parshah* named for him.

Parshas Yisro

However, while these may have been most noble and certainly important attributes of Yisro, these explanations alone are not sufficient to merit the naming of so important a Torah portion for him. The primary reason was that *Yisro* exemplified the principle ascribed to, unfortunately, far too few people. He was a real and *bona-fide* righteous gentile. He was a true member of an altogether very small group of חסידי אומות העולם. He was a genuine member of the righteous of the nations of the world.

The *Midrash Rabbah* discusses the early stages of שעבוד מצרים, when the *Mitzriyim* were just beginning to enslave the Jews. Yisro, as one of Pharoah's main advisors, attempted unsuccessfully to intercede on their behalf with the Egyptian monarch. He defended the loyalty and the fealty of the children and grandchildren of Yaakov Avinu. He vouched for their allegiance toward their Egyptian hosts. He fought against his fellow advisor and Jew hater, Bilam, who advocated that Pharoh deal rather harshly with the small but ever-growing Hebrew minority. Yisro suffered the anguish of the Jews and tried to alleviate their distress. When the *Bnei Yisrael* were eventually freed from Egypt and celebrated their independence, we are told that Yisro rejoiced with them. The Torah says (Shemos 18:9):

וַיִּחַדְּ יִתְרוֹ עַל כָּל הַטּוֹבָה אֲשֶׁר עָשָׂה ה' לְיִשְׂרָאֵל

Parshas Yisro

And Yisro rejoiced at all the good that Hashem did for Israel.

Yisro was a friend at all times. He was real and genuine. He was with Israel in its trying moments of need, adversity and difficulty. He was also with our people during our greatest triumphs and exaltations. He was a faithful, loyal, and devoted friend who never let us down. He was a friend for all seasons.

Throughout Jewish history, there have been many non-Jewish world leaders who, in moments of Jewish misfortune and tragedy, have expressed their sorrow and compassion. They were sympathetic to our plight but consistently claimed to be unauthorized and unable to help the downtrodden Jews. During the tragic and bitter years of the Shoah, world leaders were almost unanimous in their condemnation of the atrocities perpetrated by the Nazis. They issued many statements and resolutions calling upon Hitler to end his policy of extermination. They threatened the Nazi leaders with retribution, punishment, and reckoning. However, when it came to specific actions, the world leaders were deadly silent. When world Jewry literally begged the allied powers to bomb the railways to Auschwitz and the other concentration camps, our purported friends and allies recoiled and reneged on their promises of help. They were all deadly silent.

Similarly, in the weeks preceding the 1967 Six-Day War, the world community was aghast at the thought that Israel, that tiny bastion of democracy in the Middle East, was being threatened with complete destruction by her Arab neighbors. However, when the United States desperately attempted to unite the members of the United Nations to help preserve peace and avert war, our professed friends again became helpless and remained deadly silent. And when Israel overwhelmingly defeated Egypt, Syria, and Jordan, she suddenly was changed from a pitied underdog to an "aggressive and imperialistic" power. These same United Nations members, who just weeks before claimed concern and worry about her very survival, now began to condemn Israel, a policy which has continued until today.

Yisro's true friendship for Israel was expressed in both times of joy and in moments of despair and distress. He promised little and performed magnificently. Our sometimes-friends, on the other hand, sympathized with us when we were down and out but were no longer present when the difficult times were over and the time for rejoicing was at hand.

Last week, America lost one of its truly great leaders. At the age of 64, Lyndon Baines Johnson, the 36th president of the United States, passed away very prematurely. From a purely Jewish perspective,

Lyndon Johnson could best be compared to Yisro. While no Torah portion will be named after him, and while no Jewish community will probably unveil a monument to him in the near future, he was as important to our people in our times as was Yisro 3,500 years ago.

Throughout his public life, President Johnson was totally committed to the preservation of a strong, safe, and viable Israel. One need only read through Abba Eban's latest book, *My Country*, to see how many times Johnson publicly and privately came to Israel's defense.

In 1956, after the victorious Sinai Campaign, the world powers, led by President Dwight Eisenhower, attempted to force Israel to retreat from its "conquered territories." After much pressure from the United States and the Soviet Union, Israel acceded to the coercion. She stipulated, however, that the major powers, especially the United States, give her guarantees of free access to the Gulf of Aqaba and freedom of navigation through the Straits of Tiran. While these negotiations were taking place, President Eisenhower delivered a speech in which he strongly hinted that he might support United Nations sanctions against Israel if she did not withdraw from the territories. This evoked a mass protest from the American public and especially from the Senate

Parshas Yisro

Majority leader, Lyndon Johnson. Mr. Johnson insisted that America bring about an arbitrated solution with Israel.

It was, however, in his position as President that Mr. Johnson's true friendship for Israel really shone forth. He became the first U.S. President to officially invite an Israeli Prime Minister to visit Washington. In 1964, the late Levi Eshkol made his first trip to the White House. One major result of this meeting was an agreement that led to the American sale of tanks and other military equipment to Israel. This 1964 agreement was subsequently expanded by Mr. Johnson to include planes, initially the Skyhawks and later Phantom jets. It was largely due to these modern weapons that Israel was able to achieve her swift and overwhelming victory in the Six-Day War.

In the weeks before that war, President Johnson urged Israel to use restraint in her response to the Egyptian mobilization of troops in the Sinai Desert and the illegal closing of the Straits of Tiran. He also exerted pressure and called for United Nations action in response to Arab aggression and warlike behavior. He assured Israel that the United States would carry out its commitments to her to maintain and protect her security. He informed Israeli Foreign Minister Abba Eban that he would use any or all possible measures to

Parshas Yisro

keep the Straits open. "Israel would not be alone," he said, "unless it decided to go alone."

In his Presidential Memoirs, *The Vantage Point*, President Johnson wrote that on June 10, 1967, for the first time since its installation, he and Soviet Premier Kosygin used the hotline telephone between the Kremlin and the White House. Kosygin accused Israel of ignoring U.N. resolutions and warned that if Israel did not pull back from its conquered territories and end the war, Russia might use military action against her. Johnson immediately ordered the United States' Sixth Fleet to move within fifty miles of the Syrian coast, cancelling previous orders that the Fleet stay one hundred miles away. In addition, he informed the Soviet Premier that if he would even think of attacking the State of Israel, the United States would retaliate to such an extent that the Soviet Union would be completely destroyed.

Johnson later wrote: "The Soviets had made a decision. I had to respond. The United States was prepared to resist any Soviet intrusion in the Middle East." On June 19, 1967, President Johnson made a broadcast to the special session of the General Assembly of the United Nations. He said that while he favors withdrawal of Israeli forces, it should only be to secure borders, not to fragile and often-violated

Parshas Yisro

armistice lines. He called for direct negotiations between Israel and the Arabs:

"Clearly the parties to the conflict must be the parties to the peace. Sooner or later, it is they who must make a settlement in the area. It is hard to see how it is possible for nations to live together in peace if they cannot learn to reason together." This very pro-Israeli statement became the basis of the continuing United States position at the United Nations.

President Johnson, as Yisro before him, was always a friend of Israel and the Jewish people. He was with us in our times of need, when we required a strong, sincere, and genuine comrade. He was also at our side in victory and in triumph. He never at any time let us down.

Only time will tell how history will record Lyndon Baines Johnson. However, as far as Jewish history is concerned, he has carved out a very important and everlasting niche. To paraphrase the eulogy given by former presidential aide Marvin Watson: "The future will be very lonely without you Mr. President. We will certainly miss you, but we are ever grateful for the opportunity to have had you as our leader and as 'a friend at all times.'" A grateful Jewish nation thanks you for all you have done. May you rest in peace.

11. Donating Funds; Preparing for Freedom

Parshas Mishpatim – Parshas Shekalim

The opening words of this week's *Sedra*, Parshas Mishpatim are (Shemos 21:1):

וְאֵלֶּה הַמִּשְׁפָּטִים אֲשֶׁר תָּשִׂים לִפְנֵיהֶם:

And these are the commandments which I have set before you.

Rashi is troubled by the use of the 'ו, the addition of the conjunction "and" to the word אלה. It is unusual for a *Parshah*, he says, to begin with a letter which is generally used to connect two separate ideas and thoughts. Rashi explains:

ואלה המשפטים - כל מקום שנאמר אלה פסל את הראשונים, ואלה מוסיף על הראשונים...

The purpose of the 'ו is to teach that this section, which deals with civil laws, is very much connected to and affiliated with last week's *Sedra*, Yisro. The main theme in that *Parshah* was the *Aseres HaDibros*, the Decalogue, the Ten Commandments.

Rashi continues:

מה הראשונים מסיני, אף אלו מסיני.

The use of the additional 'ו comes to teach us that just as the *Aseres HaDibros* were revealed by Hashem and transmitted to *Bnei Yisrael* at Har Sinai, so too were all the following civil laws found in Parshas Mishpatim. These rulings that pertain to man's relationship with his fellow man were also given by G-d at Har Sinai and must be observed by all Jews.

This is the normative explanation. However, if we were to examine a little further, we could perhaps come up with yet an additional interpretation. The first section of Parshas Mishpatim describes the concept of slavery and the Jewish attitude toward it. In the second *posuk* of this week's Parshah (Shemos 21:2) we read:

כִּי תִקְנֶה עֶבֶד עִבְרִי שֵׁשׁ שָׁנִים יַעֲבֹד וּבַשְּׁבִעִת יֵצֵא לַחָפְשִׁי חִנָּם:

If one buys a Hebrew slave, he shall serve for six years. However, in the seventh year he shall go out free without any liability.

The Torah then sets down a complete set of laws and regulations which were intended to make the life of a Jewish slave as humane and as decent as possible. The fact that the first part of this week's portion deals with slavery is most apropos. The major theme of last week's Parshah was Hashem's giving the Torah to *Am Yisrael*. It was the transmitting of a Divine set of moral and ethical values as well as the transforming of a group of former slaves and idolators into an *Am Kadosh* and an *Am haNivchar*, a sanctified and chosen nation totally dedicated to G-d. Thus, this week, when we read of the Mitzvos of obeying civil laws, the obligations which man has to his fellow man, we are first told about the proper treatment of the slave.

This Shabbos, in addition to learning about the necessity of treating slaves humanely, we also begin preparing for the Yom Tov of Pesach. The *Shulchan Aruch* (או"ח סי' תרפ"ה סעיף א') rules that around Rosh Chodesh Adar, about seven weeks prior to the onset of Chag HaPesach, all Jews must be reminded about the Halacha of giving a half-*Shekel*. This was done in the days of the Beis HaMikdash to help facilitate the purchase of animals which were to be brought as communal sacrifices for the coming year.

This Shabbos is known as "Shabbos Shekalim" because the *Maftir* this week, taken from Parshas Ki Sisa, is about the half-Shekel donation. It is one of a series of four Shabbasos set aside to prepare us for the coming of the holiday of freedom and liberty. Without proper preparation for this great Yom Tov, the entire message of self-determination and independence would not be the same. In addition, the many long, hard, and arduous years which our ancestors spent in servitude would have little meaning or real significance.

We have all too often seen nations or minority groups fight many long years for the right of freedom and equality, only to be totally unprepared and unready when this right was finally granted. One such example was the Republic of Congo. For many years, this Belgian colony tried to force their Motherland's army to leave their land and grant them independence. Eventually, the Congolese people succeeded in obtaining their independence on June 30, 1960. However, they were completely unprepared for self-rule and self-government. Unfortunately, a period of turmoil, revolution, and bloodshed was ushered in. The first Prime Minister was Patrice Lumumba; Joseph Kasavubu became President. He was then succeeded very soon after by Joseph Mobutu, while Lumumba was assassinated shortly after. It took that country almost an entire decade to form some semblance of self-rule.

    This same problem of unpreparedness for freedom affected the American Black community. After being emancipated from slavery by President Abraham Lincoln in 1863 with the Emancipation Proclamation, the Black community was not prepared to enter into American social and economic life. More significantly was the fact that white Americans throughout the United States were not ready or willing to accept the new Back citizens as equals and peers. It took many decades and countless acts of legislation by Congress until real and genuine progress was achieved. Unfortunately, while race relations in the United States have certainly made great strides in the past 150 years, it has, unfortunately, not been totally resolved even to today.

One of the lessons of the giving of the *Shekel* is the method of using money properly. A basic difference between a free man and a slave is that one who is free may own and control his own property, while a slave has no ownership rights at all. In fact, the Gemara in Meseches Kiddushin (*daf* 23a) says about an עבד כנעני, a non-Jewish slave: מה שקנה עבד קנה בעלו – "Whatever possessions a non-Jewish slave owns is automatically owned by his master."

In addition, when *Am Yisrael* left Egypt, Hashem gave them great wealth which was taken from their former Egyptian taskmasters. However, just twelve weeks later, the *Eigel HaZahav*, the Golden Calf, was formed and worshipped by *Am Yisrael*. Hashem then contemplated destroying the entire nation. Moshe continuously pleaded on their behalf. One of the arguments that he used was, "*Ribono shel Olam*, You cannot really blame Your people for making this calf. The fact of the matter is, You, gave them too much wealth, and they did not know what to do with it. Unfortunately, instead of using it for good and proper projects, they used it to create the Golden Calf." The lesson that this special Shabbos Shekalim teaches is the proper usage of the money which Hashem has given us.

Parshas Mishpatim – Parshas Shekalim

The Chasam Sofer quotes the *Midrash Tanchuma* on Parshas Ki Sisa (#9). The Midrash says: זה יתנו אמר ר' מאיר כמין מטבע של אש הוציא הקדוש ברוך הוא מתחת כסא הכבוד והראהו למשה וא"ל זה יתנו כזה יתנו.

The Midrash explains that Hashem drew forth a coin of fire from beneath His Throne of Glory and showed it to Moshe saying, "In this manner shall they give."

The Chasam Sofer explains this Midrash in the following manner. Moshe was very concerned about the future unity of *Klal Yisrael*. He was worried that they would stand apart and be divided. A community that is split and unattached, one which lacks a particular unifying force and a cohesiveness can eventually disintegrate and lead to discord and enmity.

Am Yisrael had just been redeemed from their Egyptian bondage. They had spent over 200 years enslaved by the great Egyptian empire. They were 12 disparate and divided tribes. Could they be joined together? Was there a common purpose, a united goal, which could bind and make them as one?

In response to Moshe Rabbeinu's concern, Hashem used the example of a מטבע של אש, a fiery coin. It demonstrated in a very dramatic way that the basic nature of the Jewish people is essentially one of unity, solidarity, and harmony. For while our physical bodies may be separate and divided, our fiery *neshamos* coalesce towards one spiritual goal. This showed Moshe Rabbeinu that we do indeed have a common goal and a united purpose.

The Chasam Sofer continues and explains that this is why Hashem commanded that we use the half shekel as opposed to the full shekel coin. This Halacha was intended to promote harmony and solidarity amongst *Bnei Yisrael*. No one person has the capability to complete all his objectives by himself. When one realizes that he is only half of a complete whole, he will diligently work together with others in order to achieve his objective.

There is another message that can be learned by the symbolic use of a fiery coin. Fire, in essence, possesses two very different and distinct qualities. On the one hand, it has the capacity to burn and cause much damage and destruction. On the other hand, it can also provide much needed warmth and comfort to those who are cold and frigid. In a similar way, money, which is represented by a coin, also possesses both qualities. It can also be used for both positive and negative acts.

Money used for *tzedakah*, for charitable and worthwhile causes, can indeed be a great benefit to mankind. However, if it is squandered, if it is used for profane and unseemly purposes, it has the potential to

Parshas Mishpatim – Parshas Shekalim

cause ruin and destruction. This is comparable to a fire that is allowed to burn out of control.

Rav Asher Weiss – the great Rosh Yeshiva and *Poseik* in Eretz Yisrael – explains another facet of the remarkable nature of the *Machatzis HaShekel*. In his sefer *Minchas Asher*, Rav Weiss explains the *posuk's* guarantee that by using a coin when counting *Am Yisrael*, a devastating plague is prevented from occurring. A plague may stem from discord and divisiveness. In order to prevent this, the Jew must at all times think of himself as only half a person. He needs to connect to and associate with his fellow Jew. By himself, a Jew is merely half a coin.

Therefore, when we are commanded to give, we do not give a full shekel. Rather, we each donate a half *shekel* to inspire within ourselves the importance of the unity and synthesis of all Jews.

This Shabbos therefore, is entitled "Shabbos Shekalim." We remind all of our brethren that Pesach is rapidly approaching, and we should seriously begin preparing for it. It has become a *minhag Yisrael* that on Purim, just prior to the reading of the *Megillah*, each Jew donates one half dollar in commemoration of the half *shekel* required of each Jew in ancient times. Now that we no longer have a Beis HaMikdash, and the need to purchase animals for *korbanos* no longer exists, the money is then distributed to the poor, the needy, the widowed, and the orphaned. This, together with the mandatory *Matanos l'Evyonim* helps them in their preparation for Purim and then for Chag HaPesach. Let us all participate in this very important act of kindness and altruism. By so doing, we will begin our preparation for the holiday of freedom, liberty, and autonomy, our very special and beloved Yom Tov of Pesach. We will then be able to transition from עבדות לחירות, from the nadir, the low point of slavery and oppression, to the zenith of independence and self-determination. Amen.

12. The Mishkan in Our Heart
Parshas Terumah

This Shabbos, the weekly *Sedra* which we read is Parshas Terumah. The main theme of this Sedra deals with the construction of the Mishkan, the Tabernacle. That was where Hashem's *Shechinah* rested while *Bnei Yisrael* travelled in the *Midbar.* This portable *Mishkan* remained an integral part of *Bnei Yisrael* for hundreds of years until it was subsequently replaced by a more permanent structure, the *Beis HaMikdash* in Yerushalayim.

Hashem commanded *Am Yisrael* (Shemos 25:8):

וְעָשׂוּ לִי מִקְדָּשׁ וְשָׁכַנְתִּי בְּתוֹכָם:

They shall build for me a sanctuary, a Mikdash, so that I may dwell among them.

The Ramban, the great 13th century commentator and philosopher asks: why did the building of the *Mishkan* not precede *Ma'amad Har Sinai*? Why was the command to construct it not given to *Am Yisrael* immediately following their emancipation from Mitzrayim? He says that it was only after *Am Yisrael* said *"Na'aseh v'nishma,"* only after they completely and totally accepted all the laws of the Torah and

Parshas Terumah

attained a level of *kedusha v'taharah*, only then was it necessary and meaningful to command them to build the Mishkan which would house Hashem's *Shechinah*. The Ramban explains that we became an *Am Kadosh*, a holy nation, only through our observance of the Mitzvos of Hashem. It was only at that time that it became imperative to construct a *Mishkan*, a home for Hashem.

The Ramban, for that matter, was not the first Torah authority to voice this opinion. It was declared more than 1,500 years before by Yirmiyahu HaNavi. He lived towards the end of the First Jewish Commonwealth and constantly chastised the hypocritical behavior of the Jews of his time.

The people of his generation acted unjustly and cruelly toward their fellow Jews. They oppressed the downtrodden. They robbed the poor, the widowed, and the orphaned. However, to appease their consciences, they would bring *korbanos*. They would offer sacrifices to Hashem in the *Beis HaMikdash*.

Yirmiyahu said (Sefer Yirmiyahu 7:22-23):

כִּי לֹא דִבַּרְתִּי אֶת אֲבוֹתֵיכֶם וְלֹא צִוִּיתִים בְּיוֹם הוֹצִיאִי אוֹתָם מֵאֶרֶץ מִצְרַיִם עַל דִּבְרֵי עוֹלָה וָזָבַח: כִּי אִם אֶת הַדָּבָר הַזֶּה צִוִּיתִי אוֹתָם לֵאמֹר שִׁמְעוּ בְקוֹלִי וְהָיִיתִי לָכֶם לֵאלֹקִים וְאַתֶּם תִּהְיוּ לִי לְעָם וַהֲלַכְתֶּם בְּכָל הַדֶּרֶךְ אֲשֶׁר אֲצַוֶּה אֶתְכֶם לְמַעַן יִיטַב לָכֶם:

For neither did I speak with your forefathers nor did I command them on the day I brought them out of the land of Egypt concerning a burnt offering or a sacrifice. But this thing I command them saying: Obey me so that I may be your G-d and you may be My people and you will walk in all the ways that I command you so that it be well with you.

If one refrains from work on Shabbos, if one observes the laws of Kashrus, if he upholds the laws of *Taharas HaMishpacha*, if he follows and observes all the מצוות עשה and the מצות לא תעשה, if one fulfills all the מצות בין אדם למקום as well as those בין אדם לחבירו, Hashem will be happy. He will be much more satisfied through these deeds and acts than by receiving sacrifices and gifts from those who are hypocrites and imposters.

The *Haftorah* which we read this week from *Sefer Melachim* beautifully sums up this idea. Hashem tells Shlomo HaMelech (Melachim I 6:12-13):

הַבַּיִת הַזֶּה אֲשֶׁר אַתָּה בֹנֶה אִם תֵּלֵךְ בְּחֻקֹּתַי וְאֶת מִשְׁפָּטַי תַּעֲשֶׂה וְשָׁמַרְתָּ אֶת כָּל מִצְוֹתַי לָלֶכֶת בָּהֶם וַהֲקִמֹתִי אֶת דְּבָרִי אִתָּךְ אֲשֶׁר דִּבַּרְתִּי אֶל דָּוִד אָבִיךָ: וְשָׁכַנְתִּי בְּתוֹךְ בְּנֵי יִשְׂרָאֵל וְלֹא אֶעֱזֹב אֶת עַמִּי יִשְׂרָאֵל:

This Temple that you build, if you follow My decrees, perform My statutes, and observe all My commandments to follow them, then I shall uphold My word that I spoke to Dovid, your father. I shall dwell among the children of Israel, and I shall not forsake My people, Israel.

Our *Meforshim* explain that Hashem said to Shlomo: "Do not think that the house which you have built can become a *Makom Kadosh* just because you made generous use of gold and silver in its construction. It will be holy and will endure only if you walk in the path of My statues and execute My ordinances. Only then will you be able to build a home in which My *Shechinah*, my very presence, will dwell. And only then will it be turned into a real and genuine *Beis Elokim*."

It is the duty of each and every Jew to build his own personal *Mishkan*, his own sanctuary, a *Makom Kadosh*. We must try to forge a holy and sanctified area within our own hearts. We must designate a specific place in which Hashem's *Shechinah* is welcome and can dwell at all times.

My dear friends, if we each internalize this most important message, if all of *Am Yisrael* can build such a Mishkan, a Tabernacle within their hearts, Hashem will be happy and will indeed dwell within the hearts of each of us. Let us do what we can to transform this dream into a reality, Amen.

13. Purifying the Impure
Parshas Ki Sisa/Parshas Parah

This Shabbos we read in the Torah about two of the most puzzling events in Jewish history. The first was the building and the worship of the *Eigel HaZahav*, the Golden Calf, at the foot of Har Sinai. The second is the commandment of the *Parah Adumah*, the Red Heifer.

Immediately following Hashem's revelation to Bnei Yisrael, right after *Ma'amad Har Sinai*, the great and momentous Theophany, Moshe Rabbeinu ascended Har Sinai. He stood at the zenith of this mountain for forty days and nights. He did not drink water nor did he partake of any food. He spent the entire time learning the complete Torah, both תורה שבכתב and תורה שבעל פה from *HaKadosh Baruch Hu*. However, while Moshe was involved in the most important face to face, so to speak, dialogue in the history of man, his fellow Jews immersed themselves in matters of apostasy and heresy.

Am Yisrael, just 40 days after the greatest and most momentous event in human history, almost caused their own self-destruction. They were led by the *Eruv Rav*, the mixed multitude of Egyptians who accompanied the Jewish people on their journey

Parshas Ki Sisa/Parshas Parah

through the Sinai Desert. They made a monumental and almost catastrophic mistake. The Jewish people were convinced that Moshe Rabbeinu had died while in the presence of Hashem and would never return. Without their leader, their protector, and their link to *HaKadosh Baruch Hu*, the Jewish people felt lost, confounded, and bewildered.

All the religious exuberance that they had experienced just a short time before at *Ma'amad Har Sinai* was now gone. The Jewish people had linked their religious observance and especially their belief in Hashem with Moshe. He was there to lead them in the desert and then again when they agreed unquestionably to accept the Torah. At that time, they said, *"Na'aseh v'Nishma,"* "We will do and then we will listen." However, now, many doubts and uncertainties entered their minds.

The people beseeched Aharon HaKohen, Moshe's brother, to make them something physical and tangible so that they would always be able to see and believe that it was Moshe's replacement. Aharon attempted to postpone the inevitable; however, he eventually succumbed to their pleas and demands. He requested that they bring him the gold jewelry from their wives, sons, and daughters. The *nashim tzidkaniyos*, the righteous women of that time, refused to go along with this nefarious plan. Undeterred, the men simply removed their own golden earrings and brought them to Aharon. He took all their valuables and threw it all into a burning cauldron. It miraculously formed into an עגל הזהב, a golden calf. When they observed this miraculous creature, the *Eruv Rav* proclaimed (Shemos 32:8):

אֵלֶּה אֱלֹהֶיךָ יִשְׂרָאֵל אֲשֶׁר הֶעֱלוּךָ מֵאֶרֶץ מִצְרָיִם:

"These are your gods, O' Israel, who brought you out of the land of Egypt."

Aharon, still attempting to push off the inevitable, began to build a *mizbeach*, an altar. He was hoping that Moshe would return at any moment and stop their heretical behavior. He therefore said: חַג לַה' מָחָר – *"Tomorrow shall be a feast to G-d."*

Hashem, meanwhile, observed this blasphemous and sinful act and told Moshe to descend the mountain unto the camp of *Am Yisrael* (Shemos 32:7-8):

וַיְדַבֵּר ה' אֶל מֹשֶׁה לֶךְ רֵד כִּי שִׁחֵת עַמְּךָ אֲשֶׁר הֶעֱלֵיתָ מֵאֶרֶץ מִצְרָיִם: סָרוּ מַהֵר מִן הַדֶּרֶךְ אֲשֶׁר צִוִּיתִם עָשׂוּ לָהֶם עֵגֶל מַסֵּכָה וַיִּשְׁתַּחֲווּ לוֹ וַיִּזְבְּחוּ לוֹ וַיֹּאמְרוּ אֵלֶּה אֱלֹהֶיךָ יִשְׂרָאֵל אֲשֶׁר הֶעֱלוּךָ מֵאֶרֶץ מִצְרָיִם:

Your people, whom you brought out of the land of Egypt, have dealt corruptly. They have turned aside quickly from the way which I commanded them. They have made for themselves a molten calf and have worshipped it and have sacrificed unto it. They said, "These are your gods, O' Israel, which brought you up out of the land of Egypt."

G-d then proceeded to tell Moshe of His plan to annihilate the Jewish people and form a chosen people from Moshe himself. However, before descending the mountain and exhorting his people, Moshe passionately and lovingly pleaded with Hashem. He urged *HaKadosh Baruch Hu* not to destroy the Jewish people. Subsequently, Hashem agreed to cancel His guilty verdict and eventually forgave them.

This entire episode is filled with many disturbing questions. This morning, I would like to discuss a few of the problems. Firstly, how many Jews were involved in the actual construction and, especially, in the worship of the calf? Second, how did our ancestors forget *Ma'amad Har Sinai*, the Divine Revelation, which occurred just forty days before, when Hashem commanded them (Shemos 20:2):

לֹא יִהְיֶה לְךָ אֱלֹהִים אֲחֵרִים עַל פָּנָי:

"You shall have no other gods before Me."
Third, if *Am Yisrael* was indeed guilty of actually desecrating the name of G-d by constructing and then worshipping idolatry, then they certainly did deserve to die. Why did Moshe intercede on their behalf? Fourth, what is the significance of the *Parah Adumah*, the Red Heifer, and why is that Parsha, which is found in Sefer Bamidbar in Parshas Chukas, read today as our *Maftir*?

With just a superficial and a cursory reading of the *pesukim* by themselves, without any *meforshim*, it would appear that the entire Jewish people did indeed participate in the worship of the Golden Calf. However, if we study this *perek* very closely, we will determine that no more than three thousand out of one and one half million Jews participated in this form of idolatry.

Rav Zalman Sorotzkin, the early 20th century Rav and head of the Vaad HaYeshivos in Europe, in his masterful *Sefer* on Chumash, *Aznayim laTorah*, provides us with an answer. He says that the individuals who led this revolt against Hashem and who actually built and worshipped the *Eigel HaZahav* were not the rank and file of *Am Yisrael*. Rather, they were the *Eruv Rav*, the mixed multitude of non-Jews who left Egypt with *Am Yisrael*. In fact, he says, it was these individuals whom Shevet Levi were commanded to kill after Moshe's return to the camp.

If this be the case, if only a handful of individuals, mainly the *Eruv Rav*, participated in the construction, the desecration, and especially in the worship of the calf and the abominations which followed, why did Hashem wish to destroy all of *Klal Yisrael*?

Rav Nissan Alpert *z"l*, a former beloved Rebbe at Yeshiva University and a *talmid muvhak* of HaRav Moshe Feinstein *zt"l*, in his sefer, *Limudei Nissan*, provides us with an answer. He said that while only a handful of Jews actually desecrated the name of G-d, all the other Jews were equally as guilty. They received this verdict because they stood by silently and did not protest this most egregious and abominable act of treason. Their silence, says Rav Alpert, was tantamount to their tacit approval of these immoral acts. It was this great *chillul Hashem* which caused them to also deserve the death penalty. And it was for these people, the rest of *Klal Yisrael*, that Moshe fervently and continuously davened to Hashem.

The Jewish people had recently been redeemed from their long and difficult bondage in Egypt. They had spent almost two hundred years under the whip of their Egyptian taskmasters. While they certainly feared their oppressors, they eventually began to imitate some of their ways as well. The *Midrash* notes that on the one hand, *Am Yisrael* refrained from changing their language, their Hebrew names, or even their distinctive clothing; it was in the merit of these acts that they were redeemed. On the other hand, however, they were still greatly influenced by the Egyptians. Many worshipped their gods and engaged in behavior unbecoming a great and noble people. They had sunk to almost the lowest level of *tumah* from which it might have been nearly impossible to be extricated.

For this reason, even after *Ma'amad Har Sinai*, the Revelation of the Torah at Har Sinai, our ancestors were still not yet a completely holy and sanctified people. They were unable to resist or oppose the negative influences of the *Eruv Rav*.

Moshe realized the gravity of their transgression. He understood that there was no question that they certainly deserved death. However, he appealed to Hashem to deal with them compassionately and not with strict justice. He pleaded with Him to judge them with forgiveness instead of with vengeance. He begged Hashem to be the G-d of *Rachamim*, of mercy and compassion and not the G-d of pure and strict *Din*, complete and objective justice.

This episode, say *Chazal*, shows Moshe at his greatest. He was not interested in having a chosen people emerge from him and his family. He certainly did not desire power and honor for himself. Rather, he saw his destiny, his fate, and his very future as only that which was interwoven and interconnected with the Jewish people. He was able to meet פנים אל פנים, "face to face" with Hashem, not because of his own uniqueness or his extraordinary qualities but because he represented the *Bechor* of Hashem, the first-born of *HaKadosh Baruch Hu*, *Klal Yisrael*. Without the Jewish people, Moshe felt unimportant and insignificant.

When he appealed to Hashem, he did not do so on his own *zechusim* or his spiritual strengths. Rather, he did so on the greatness of the *Avos* and the promise that Hashem made to them (Shemos 32:13):

זְכֹר לְאַבְרָהָם לְיִצְחָק וּלְיִשְׂרָאֵל עֲבָדֶיךָ אֲשֶׁר נִשְׁבַּעְתָּ לָהֶם בָּךְ וַתְּדַבֵּר אֲלֵהֶם אַרְבֶּה אֶת זַרְעֲכֶם כְּכוֹכְבֵי הַשָּׁמָיִם וְכָל הָאָרֶץ הַזֹּאת אֲשֶׁר אָמַרְתִּי אֶתֵּן לְזַרְעֲכֶם וְנָחֲלוּ לְעֹלָם:

Remember Avraham, Yitzchak and Yisrael Your servants to whom You swore by Your Name and said to them, 'I will multiply your seed as the stars of heaven, and the entire land that I have spoken of, I will give to your seed and they shall inherit it forever.'

Moshe used three arguments to plead with Hashem to forgive *Am Yisrael*. Upon the conclusion of his beseeching, he threw his lot completely with *Bnei Yisrael*. He said (Shemos 32:32):

וְעַתָּה אִם תִּשָּׂא חַטָּאתָם וְאִם אַיִן מְחֵנִי נָא מִסִּפְרְךָ אֲשֶׁר כָּתָבְתָּ:

"Yet now, if You will forgive their sin, and if not, then blot me out from Your book, the Torah that You Have written."

Rashi explains that Moshe said "It should not be said of me that I was not worthy enough to ask for mercy on their part."

After listening to all these arguments and especially to this last and most courageous and compassionate plea, Hashem set aside His decree of death. It was only on the following Yom Kippur that He completely forgave them

This Shabbos, we also observe the third of four special Shabbosim before Pesach, "Parshas Parah," "the Shabbos of the Red Heifer." The Torah in Sefer Bamidbar, Parshas B'ha'aloscha (9:2-3) commands each Jew to participate in the *Korban Pesach*. As the story continues there (9:6-7), however, we learn that only individuals who are *tahor*, those who are spiritually pure, may take part in this most important Mitzvah. Those who have come in contact with the highest form of spiritual defilement - a dead body – must remove their defilement before partaking of the Korban Pesach.

Sefer Bamidbar, Parshas Chukas (19:1-22) explains that this impurity may be removed with the ashes of a burned Red Heifer. The Kohen Gadol was to take this *Parah Adumah*, the Red Heifer, slaughter it, and then burn it. Those who were *tamei* would be sprinkled with the ashes of the heifer and their impurity would be removed. They then would be able to participate in the fulfillment of the Mitzvah of eating the *Korban Pesach*.

This is one of the most difficult Mitzvos in the Torah to comprehend. It doesn't seem logical nor is there any explanation offered. This law is entitled a *Chok*, a statute, a Mitzvah without a reason. It carries however, the same weight as a Mitzvah with a reason and must be equally observed.

Parshas Ki Sisa/Parshas Parah

Today, we unfortunately no longer have the Bais HaMikdash. We also have no Kohen Gadol, and *Korbanos* - animal sacrifices - have been eliminated. Nevertheless, we read about this Mitzvah of becoming pure. We do this in order to help us prepare for the very special Yom Tov of Pesach. Rashi cites Rav Moshe HaDarshan who maintains that the reason for the service of the Red Heifer is that it was to serve as an atonement for the sin of the *Eigel HaZahav*. It was a golden calf that caused the Jews' spiritual defilement; the Red Heifer is a cow, symbolizing the mother of that calf, as the reddish hue resembles gold. Just as a mother is called upon to clean up the mess of her child, so is a cow called upon to rectify the sin caused by her offspring, the calf, changing the Jewish people from their state of *tumah* to *taharah*.

It is thus most appropriate on this Shabbos, when we read about the first great transgression committed by Bnei Yisrael as a nation, that we also read about Hashem's forgiveness. The *Ribono shel Olam* is not a vengeful and hateful G-d. He is, rather, full of *Rachamim*, compassion and forgiveness. He gives his children, *Am* Yisrael, every opportunity to not only repent, but also to attain a level of *kedusha v'taharah*, holiness and purity. Only if we, in our time, try our best to purify our hearts and attempt to reach our highest degree of holiness and sanctity, will we be ready to participate in the most beautiful Yom Tov of redemption - Pesach. Let us not miss this most propitious opportunity.

14. What will Israel Say?
Parshas Ki Sisa

For two thousand years, one of the guiding principles of Jewish political and social decisions has been מה יאמרו הגוים – "What will the gentiles say?" "How shall the nations of the world react to this or that choice which we make?" This was of primary concern to all Jewish communities in the Diaspora being that we were merely alien residents of the various countries which we inhabited. We were not afforded first or even second-class citizenship. Rather, we dwelled in a particular area solely due to the goodwill of its ruler. Our forebears were a minority who were tolerated and were given the tenuous right to live in a specific country so long as they contributed to its welfare and deemed not to be negatively impacting its citizens.

When the rulers so wished, be they of France or England in the 13th and 14th centuries, or of Spain and Portugal in the 15th and 16th centuries, the Jews were forced or coerced to leave these countries. The citizens of these nations who were the recipients of the Jews' enormous contributions stood silently by as their former friends and neighbors were led away into exile into the unknown. The Jews always knew, however, that if forced to flee from one country, they would always find a refuge and haven in another location, one where other Jews had already begun residing. Therefore, they wandered from nation to nation, always willing and able to serve their new adopted country faithfully and without any reservations.

In most of the lands they inhabited, the Jews were given the right to determine their internal religious affairs. When conflicts would arise between two Jews, whether they were in business transactions, social matters, and especially in regard to religious and Halachic issues, Jewish law prevailed. Jewish self-rule and self-government became highly developed throughout most of the Middle Ages and down even to modern times. All the internal decisions which our ancestors made, however, contained one underlying question: Will the gentiles object? Will this regulation or that decision be offensive to the ruling authorities? Will they respond with a pogrom or with an inquisition? Will they expel or exile us? These were the prevailing questions which were involved in making each decision.

Thus, while this internal self-rule was most beneficial in developing a very highly structured style of self-government, these overriding considerations forced us to be afflicted with what is so aptly called, the "*Golus* Mentality" or the "Exile Psychology." This concern of מה יאמרו הגוים – "What will the nations of the world say?" was prevalent throughout all of Jewish history.

Many years before the Jews were ever exiled from their homeland and dispersed to the four corners of the world, before they even had their own independent country, this fear was first expressed. In Parshas Ki Sisa, the Torah records the incident of the *Eigel HaZahav*, the Golden Calf. Forty days after *Ma'amad Har Sinai*, after the Theophany, after the Revelation of the *Aseres HaDibros* on Har Sinai, the Jewish people revolted against the word of Hashem. While Moshe Rabbeinu stood at the apex of that historic mountain, learning the Torah from the *Ribono shel Olam*, his brethren took their newly acquired gold and created an *Eigel HaZahav*, a Golden Calf. When they saw this *Avodah* Zarah they proclaimed (Shemos 32:4):

וַיֹּאמְרוּ אֵלֶּה אֱלֹהֶיךָ יִשְׂרָאֵל אֲשֶׁר הֶעֱלוּךָ מֵאֶרֶץ מִצְרָיִם:
These are your gods O' Israel who brought you out of the land of Egypt.

Almost all of *Klal Yisrael* stood by silently, without even a word of criticism, as the *Eruv Rav*, the mixed multitude of Egyptians who left Egypt with our ancestors, behaved in a most immoral and promiscuous manner. They offered sacrifices to and worshipped this calf of gold. They appeared to have forsaken the G-d

Parshas Ki Sisa

of their fathers and the commandment which they heard with their own ears from Hashem (Shemos 20:2):

לֹא יִהְיֶה לְךָ אֱלֹהִים אֲחֵרִים עַל פָּנָי:

"You shall have no other gods before me."

After observing their blasphemous and profane conduct from on high, Hashem wished to destroy the entire Jewish people. He informed Moshe of His plan to extinguish the Jewish people and to form the new "Chosen People" from Moshe's seed. Hashem said (Shemos 32:10):

וְעַתָּה הַנִּיחָה לִּי וְיִחַר אַפִּי בָהֶם וַאֲכַלֵּם וְאֶעֱשֶׂה אוֹתְךָ לְגוֹי גָּדוֹל:

And now, leave Me be and let My anger be aroused over them, and I will exterminate them and I will make you into a great nation.

However, in language which reached sublime heights of self-sacrifice and devotion, Moshe prayed for his apostate people. He admitted the guilt of all the Jews but nevertheless sought to save each and every one. He did not rest until *HaKadosh Baruch Hu* informed him that He had indeed forgiven the Jewish people.

Moshe offered two basic *tefillos* to Hashem. The first was a fervent plea for general mercy and compassion. The second was a remorseful confessional to attain complete and total forgiveness. In his first *bakasha*, he used three arguments:

Parshas Ki Sisa

He began (Shemos 32:11):
וַיְחַל מֹשֶׁה אֶת פְּנֵי ה' אֱלֹקָיו וַיֹּאמֶר לָמָה ה' יֶחֱרֶה אַפְּךָ בְּעַמֶּךָ אֲשֶׁר הוֹצֵאתָ מֵאֶרֶץ מִצְרַיִם בְּכֹחַ גָּדוֹל וּבְיָד חֲזָקָה:
Moshe implored before the presence of Hashem, his G-d and he said, "Hashem, why should Your wrath blaze against your people whom You brought out from the land of Egypt with great power and with a mighty hand?"

The *Midrash Tanchuma* explains that Moshe said:

> Of all countries in the world, You found no other area to enslave Your children than Egypt. There, they were greatly influenced by the form of cattle idolatry; so much so that now they too made themselves a golden calf. They need training and guidance; they need Your helping hand to transform them into a true *Am Kadosh LaHashem,* a holy nation, completely dedicated to You.

His second argument was (Shemos 32:12):
לָמָה יֹאמְרוּ מִצְרַיִם לֵאמֹר בְּרָעָה הוֹצִיאָם לַהֲרֹג אֹתָם בֶּהָרִים וּלְכַלֹּתָם מֵעַל פְּנֵי הָאֲדָמָה שׁוּב מֵחֲרוֹן אַפֶּךָ וְהִנָּחֵם עַל הָרָעָה לְעַמֶּךָ:
Why should the Egyptians say, "He brought them out of Egypt to kill them in the mountains and to annihilate them from the face of the earth." Please turn from

Your blazing wrath and reconsider the intent of doing evil to Your people

One of the great medieval *meforshim*, HaRav Don Yitzchok Abarbanel, the 15th century Portuguese philosopher, scholar, and religious leader, questions the purpose and motive of this argument. "Did Moshe," the Abarbanel asks, "expect to convince Hashem that He should not use the principle of *Din*, strict and stern justice, because of some confounded fool's malicious remarks?" This question is answered by the Ramban, Nachmanides. He says that Moshe expressed great fear and trepidation over the possible *Chillul Hashem*, the desecration of the Holy Name of the *Ribono Shel Olam*. He says that even when *Am Yisrael* truly deserves to be punished, the *Umos HaOlam*, the nations of the world, may attribute it to a limitation of the Divine powers of Hashem. Therefore, the pardon, the forgiveness, and the ultimate well-being of Israel will amount to a *bracha* and a *Kiddush Hashem*, a blessing and consecration of G-d's Holy Name. This argument, while forceful and powerful, was not effective in convincing Hashem.

Hashem was persuaded only when Moshe invoked the memory of the *Avos HaKedoshim*, Avraham, Yitzchok, and Yaakov and Hashem's promise to them (Shemos 32:13):

Parshas Ki Sisa

זְכֹר לְאַבְרָהָם לְיִצְחָק וּלְיִשְׂרָאֵל עֲבָדֶיךָ אֲשֶׁר נִשְׁבַּעְתָּ לָהֶם בָּךְ וַתְּדַבֵּר אֲלֵהֶם אַרְבֶּה אֶת זַרְעֲכֶם כְּכוֹכְבֵי הַשָּׁמָיִם וְכָל הָאָרֶץ הַזֹּאת אֲשֶׁר אָמַרְתִּי אֶתֵּן לְזַרְעֲכֶם וְנָחֲלוּ לְעֹלָם:

Remember Avraham, Yitzchak and Yisrael, Your servants to whom you swore by Your Self and said to them, 'I will make your descendants as numerous as the stars of the heaven; and all this land of which I have spoken, I will give to your descendants and they will inherit it forever.'

When Moshe focused his *tefillos* for the survival of Israel not on the basis of what others would say but rather upon the memory of the *Avos* and Hashem's pledge to them, only then did G-d pardon and forgive *Am Yisrael*.

Moshe later said (Shemos 32:32):

וְעַתָּה אִם תִּשָּׂא חַטָּאתָם וְאִם אַיִן מְחֵנִי נָא מִסִּפְרְךָ אֲשֶׁר כָּתָבְתָּ:

If You, Hashem, will forgive them, I will be saved, but if not, blot my name out of the book of the living.

Moshe felt it was his sacred duty and obligation to tie himself together with the fortunes of his people. He wanted to survive and lead them only if they were forgiven. If, however, they were doomed to die, he did not want to continue living. It was only at that moment that Hashem completely forgave *Am Yisrael*.

We thus see that even at the beginning of our national existence, the argument and fear of מה יאמרו הגוים was invoked. While at Har Sinai it was used exclusively to avoid any desecration of G-d's Holy Name, it in itself was insufficient to alter Hashem's decree. Nonetheless, until Jews were given full citizenship and equal opportunity with all other members of their adopted countries, the concern for the gentile's opinion was of paramount importance. However, once any and all forms of discrimination were removed, once the ghetto walls that separated Jew from gentile were destroyed and all barriers to Jewish advancement were broken down, there was no longer any need to be afraid of what the ruling authorities would think.

Jewish organizations and especially Jewish leaders were now free to make decisions for their people without any fear or concern that their judgments would backfire and adversely affect their fellow Jews. They now had the opportunity and the possibility to decide matters on the basis of whether it was good or bad for the Jews alone. The determining factor should have been whether we will benefit from these judgments and how as Jews we will react.

In the Western democracies – and especially in the United States during the early years of the twentieth century – this unfortunately was not the case. In the very difficult and bitter years of the Shoah, European Jewry was faced with the prospect of complete and total extermination. The secular Jewish leaders, especially in this country, should have been concerned with one thought and nothing else – the rescue of their condemned European brethren. All other considerations should have been secondary. Yet, this was not the case.

They were concerned, almost to the point of schizophrenic fear, of 'מה יאמרו הגויים?'. "How will society's reaction to the Holocaust affect the Jews' very insecure and tenuous positions in the United States and elsewhere?" In 1933, the year that Hitler came to power in Germany, the American Jewish Congress and other leading secular organizations launched an economic boycott against all German products. This was to last until such time that all persecution against German Jews would end. This proposed boycott had great potential. If effective, it might have possibly forced Hitler to alter his planned murder of Jews and other minorities. However, from the very beginning, the boycott was doomed to failure.

Judd Teller, in his very informative historical book *Strangers and Natives,* wrote that the major benefit of the Boycott Council was that it made headlines, but in actuality, it did very little. The American Jewish Community failed to produce even a minimum of the required funds. The Council did not receive the support of Jewish importers, film distributors, bankers, and department stores. R. H.

Macy, a Jewish owned firm, one of the largest department stores in the country, stated that the boycott was un-American and in advertisements in the press stated its desire to continue to carry German products.

On December 2, 1942, after learning that the extermination of European Jewry was in full swing, 50,000 Jewish workers in New York observed a ten-minute work stoppage in protest of the atrocities. They were joined by non-Jews who participated in shop meetings at which resolutions condemning the Nazi massacre of Jews were adopted. This work stoppage was made up later in the day in order "not to retard the war effort."

Had these Jews and hundreds of thousands more stopped work for more than one complete day and not have made it up, had they been more concerned with the murder of their brothers and sisters and less concerned with themselves, perhaps then, the Roosevelt Administration would have taken notice and may have offered its help.

It was perhaps the fear of the impending rise of antisemitism in America which caused American Jewry to be too concerned with their own personal well-being. In the years immediately preceding the United States' entry into World War II, there was a great deal of sentiment for U.S. neutrality in this European War. In 1939, the American First Committee was created. It included many organizations that had Nazi and Communist fronts, as well as some which were very sincere and patriotic. Among the members of the board were ostensibly distinguished Americans. One of them was Charles Lindberg, the famous aviator, who gave the anti-Jewish forces its greatest impetus.

On September 11, 1941, he addressed a rally of the American First Committee in Des Moines, Iowa. He claimed that the three most important groups responsible for stirring the United States towards the impending war were "the British, the Jews, and the Roosevelt Administration." He accused the Jews of being the most dangerous because of their "large ownership and influence in motion pictures, the media, the press, and government."

Certain Jews, especially those in the higher echelons of American society, became so concerned that antisemitism would spread throughout this country that they resorted to all sorts of apologies. Judge Samuel Frank, a former Harvard Law School professor and member of the United States Circuit Court, wrote the major defense of the Jews which appeared in the Saturday Evening Post. He said that a majority of Jews in the United States were isolationists until 1940. The Zionists were only a "minority among the Jews" and that most of the "ancient Jewish traditions were

Parshas Ki Sisa

rejected by a majority of American Jews who were not immigrants."

In the darkest period of Jewish history, when our leaders could have possibly helped change the course of human events, they failed to act in any meaningful way. They were not concerned with what our slain brethren would say about their inaction. They worried more over what the non-Jews would think of their "rabble rousing and warmongering tactics." They thought that they could try to save their doomed relatives through quiet and diplomatic methods. However, they were so unfortunately and deadly wrong.

This attitude of "?מה יאמרו הגוים" did not help sway *HaKadosh Baruch Hu* from His original decision to punish the Jewish people for their most egregious transgression of serving the *Eigel HaZahav*. It also did not help move our allies and our so-called friends to save the innocent victims of Hitler's madness. It was only when Moshe Rabbeinu completely threw his lot in with his people for better or for worse and was willing to accept all the consequences that the *Ribono shel Olam* completely forgave *Am Yisrael*. Similarly, it was only when American Jewry was no longer concerned with "מה יאמרו הגוים", that the Vaad Hatzalah was created with the implicit declaration that "We are no longer concerned with what you think of us or our actions. We will continue doing whatever we consider right and just." Only then, when American Jewry stood up to the world community, did they begin to have a modicum of respect for the Jewish people.

While the other nations have continued to disagree and often condemn Jewish and Israeli actions, they no longer ignore us or write us off as non-entities. I believe that Israeli Prime Minister Golda Meir put it most appropriately when, upon reporting on her historic meeting with Pope Paul VI on January 15, 1973, she said:

"The Pope said to me at the outset that he found it hard to understand how the Jewish people, which should be merciful, behaves so fiercely in its own country. So I said to the Pope: 'Your Holiness, do you know what my earliest memory is? A pogrom in Kiev. When we were merciful and when we had no homeland and when we were weak, we were led to the gas chambers.' I felt that I was saying what I was saying to the man of the cross, who heads the church whose symbol is the cross, under which Jews were killed for generations. I could not escape this feeling."

Israel has learned through hard and bitter experiences that she cannot worry about world opinion. For almost all of her seventy-six-year existence, the State of Israel has, time after time, been condemned for starting hostilities, perpetrating atrocities, and for

Parshas Ki Sisa

killing and maiming innocent Palestinian men, women and children. Whether it be in the forums of the United Nations, the press, or in the capitals of the world community, most of Israel's actions have been disapproved of and castigated.

Initially, this bothered her leaders. They tried to act in a manner which would be acceptable to all and condemned by none. However, when they saw that whatever action they undertook, whatever policy they advocated, they were constantly criticized and condemned, Israel was no longer pre-occupied with "מה יאמרו הגוים?". Her actions and deeds were decided based on what was best for Israel and for the Jewish people.

Israel, I believe has always attempted to act in a just and proper manner. She has shown the world and has especially taught the Jewish people throughout the world that, while it is often beneficial to have world opinion on your side, it certainly cannot and should not determine the implementation of actions which you consider right and correct.

Israel's new manner of thought, her mantra, her very philosophy, has become "מה יאמרו ישראל?" – "What will Israel say?" "What is best for the State of Israel?" "What is good for *Am Yisrael*, the Jewish people?" And especially, "What is best for the future of Yiddishkeit?" That should always continue to be our guide, our ideal, and our national slogan, Amen.

15. Building Our Own Mishkan
Parshas Pekudei

In the past decade and a half, a great impact has been made on America and on the entire world by the activities of students and other young people in the fields of Civil rights, consideration for individual dignity, and the Vietnam War. This was first exemplified by the student participation on the University of California, Berkely Campus, in 1965.

Their quest for peace showed the tremendous change in the attitudes of the students from that of the 1940's and 1950's when foolish activities were more important to our youth than those beneficial to society.

A question is often raised by our Rabbanim, communal organizations, and individual Jews as to what the position of Jews should be on these present-day activities. All without exception have said that Jews must participate as Jews. This was seen when many Jewish leaders took part in the Civil Rights demonstrations in Selma, Alabama, in 1963 and in various other parts of the South. It was also the case in the latter part of the 1960's when many Rabbis participated in rallies and demonstrations representing both spectrums of political thought on the Vietnam war

Parshas Pekudei

— those favoring the continuation of American participation and those who were opposed.

In the area of Civil Rights, there is absolutely no question that we must support the dignity of the individual and the alleviation of all types of oppression and racial injustice. However, we must do so as Jews, not just as members of our general society. The Torah is replete with sources to this effect:

In Sefer Shemos (23:9) the Torah writes:

וְגֵר לֹא תִלְחָץ וְאַתֶּם יְדַעְתֶּם אֶת נֶפֶשׁ הַגֵּר כִּי גֵרִים הֱיִיתֶם בְּאֶרֶץ מִצְרָיִם:

Do not oppress a stranger; you should know the feelings of a stranger for you were strangers in the land of Egypt.

In the same vein, the Torah states in Sefer Devarim (10:19):

וַאֲהַבְתֶּם אֶת הַגֵּר כִּי גֵרִים הֱיִיתֶם בְּאֶרֶץ מִצְרָיִם:

You shall love the stranger, since you were strangers in the land of Egypt.

And in Sefer Bamidbar (15:29) we are given the Mitzvah:

הָאֶזְרָח בִּבְנֵי יִשְׂרָאֵל וְלַגֵּר הַגָּר בְּתוֹכָם תּוֹרָה אַחַת יִהְיֶה לָכֶם לָעֹשֶׂה בִּשְׁגָגָה:

For the citizen among Bnei Yisrael and the stranger who lives with you, there shall be one law for all, for he who sins unwittingly.

In the Gemara in Meseches Bava Metzia (59b), it is taught in a *Braysa*:

תניא, רבי אליעזר הגדול אומר: מפני מה הזהירה תורה בשלשים וששה מקומות, ואמרי לה בארבעים וששה מקומות בגר - מפני שסורו רע.

Why did the Torah warn us in thirty-six places, and another version says forty-six places, against the oppression of a stranger, a person who finds himself in an inferior position? It is because he has a tendency to revert to his old ways.

Halacha requires and makes demands upon us to treat oppressed individuals well – both verbally and through our deeds and actions. However, authentic Jews, aware of their tradition and faithful to it, are disturbed that the same movement which preaches equal opportunity and complete civil rights for all people, regardless of color or race, also had a spokesman who said that "Hitler's big mistake was that he did not kill enough Jews."

Jews are upset that the same organizations which support the development and wellbeing of the new nation-states and sovereign countries of the so-called "Third World," constantly condemn the State of Israel. They give moral support and financial aid to the Arab nations and the Palestinian terrorists in their struggle with Medinat Yisrael. They not only refuse to help Israel develop into a self-sufficient country but even insist that she does not have the right to exist.

Dedicated Jews are appalled that the same movement which protested the American role in causing violence in Vietnam also attempted to break down and destroy the universities and even our entire governmental structure with the most violent possible methods. (It appears that nothing has changed in the past 60 years - RHG).

We are reminded of the example brought from the Midrash Rabbah on this week's *Sedra*, Parshas Pekudei (Shemos Rabbah 51:8):

משל לבחור שנכנס למדינה. ראה אותם גובין צדקה ואמרו לו תן והיה נותן עד שאמרו לו דייך. הלך מעט וראה אותם גובין לתיטרון. אמרו לו תן והיה נותן עד שאמרו לו דייך.

A young man who entered a certain country. As he approached one area, he noticed that the people were collecting money for a good and just cause. The local inhabitants asked him to contribute, and he did so until they informed him that he had given enough. He went on a little further and found citizens of another locale collecting for a 'Tiatron,' an unimportant and insignificant thing. They asked him to contribute, and without even thinking of the merits or qualities of this cause, he continued to give money until the collectors told him that he had given enough.

It is obvious that this kind of childish enthusiasm is not a new phenomenon. Immature individuals of this sort lack the understanding of the importance of individual actions. Each deed is considered as important as the next. It is accepted among these people that one need merely conform with or rebel

Parshas Pekudei

against others if the majority of one's peers are doing so, no matter what form the conformity or rebellion takes. Can immaturity and juvenility show itself more clearly than in such activities?

A few years ago, Rabbi Arthur Hertzberg, the President of the American Jewish Congress, published an article. In it, he said that many American rabbis eagerly identified with the Civil Rights struggle. They believed that it would bring the college aged Jewish men and women back to Judaism. It would give them an opportunity to participate in demonstrations and actions for social justice, a concept which is at the very heart of Jewish religious tradition. This was also eloquently expressed centuries ago by the *Nevi'im* of old. They constantly called for justice to the poor, aid to the fatherless, assistance to the widowed, and support for the oppressed.

These rabbis, unfortunately, were quite disappointed. They found, however, reports Rabbi Hertzberg, that the many Jewish men and women who did participate did so largely unaware of anything Jewish in this struggle. Their participation stemmed only from an appeal to general humanitarian and liberal principles. They remained distant and unmoved by any of the Rabbanim or their messages of spirituality.

It is quite clear from this experience, that we will not arrive at Jewishness from these activities. If we are to take part in these movements, we must come to them specifically as authentic and dedicated Jews.

This week's Parsha, Pekudei, deals with the building of the *Mishkan* in the *midbar*, as well as the auditing of its accounts. We may say metaphorically that each generation, regardless of the place or age in which it lives, should build its own *Mishkan*, its own sanctuary. This expresses its highest ideals and noblest principles. Ultimately, however, it must give a complete accounting of the materials which went into the building.

There are some generations who, in their struggle for great principles, debase and corrupt them through adulteration with things of little worth. A struggle for civil rights is accompanied by blatant anti-Semitism. A quest for peace turns into a violent fracas filled with plunder, injury, and occasional death. These are the immature generations which see as great a value in the debased qualities of the "Tiatron," as they do in the concept of Tzedakah.

On the other hand, there are other more mature and more venerated generations who do not confuse the noble with the ignoble. They will not place the same value on things of little worth as they do on matters which are basic to human civilization. They will not confuse Tzedakah with "Tiatron." They will work diligently to build their own individual *Mishkan*.

Parshas Pekudei

My dear friends, how will history recall our generation? Will it be said that we indiscriminately went along with every cause and every concern solely because it was popular and fashionable? Or, will it be said that we differentiated and distinguished between unimportant and worthless causes and those which were righteous and just? Will our generation be known for having espoused interests which appeared on the surface to be honorable and virtuous but were in actuality hollow and even reckless? Or, will we be known and remembered for taking up only matters which were thorough, and completely bona fide, authentic and genuine, those which were completely infused with *kedusha* and *taharah*? The decision is ours and ours alone. How history will look upon American Jewry of the mid-twentieth century will largely be determined by the alternative which we choose.

If we decide to become involved in only those causes which are completely and unequivocally just, we must come to them only as Jews. Our commitment to the Torah and Halacha must be total and complete. Before we become involved in programs designed to help mankind in general, we must first find solutions to the problems which afflict the Jewish people. As our great *Tana* Hillel taught in *Meseches Avos*:

אם אין אני לי, מי לי. וכשאני לעצמי, מה אני.

"If I am not for myself, who will be for me? However, if I am only for myself, what am I?" Just as it is wrong to be centered solely with oneself, it is equally incorrect to be completely unconcerned with oneself.

Therefore, before we join organizations that memorialize and eulogize the millions of murdered individuals throughout the world, we must internalize the memory and "Never forget" our own six million קדושים וטהורים, our holy and precious martyrs who were brutally and barbarically killed in the Shoah.

Before we condemn the persecution encountered by the citizens of different countries and before we try to aid and assist them, we must alleviate the suffering of our oppressed brethren in the Soviet Union. And before we aid the poor and the downtrodden throughout the world and even in this country, we must do whatever we can to help the Jewish poor and the elderly in the United States and throughout the Jewish world.

The Gemara in Bava Metzia (71a) says:

אם כסף תלוה את עמי את העני עמך, עמי ונכרי - עמי קודם, עני ועשיר - עני קודם, ענייך ועני עירך - ענייך קודמין, עניי עירך ועניי עיר אחרת - עניי עירך קודמין.

"The poor people of your household should be helped before the impoverished of your city, and the poverty stricken of your city must be aided before the destitute of another locale are helped." This law is codified by the Rambam in *Hilchos Tzedakah*.

It is our duty and obligation to help so many of the poor and unfortunate elderly Jews who are living throughout the country. We must find ways of supporting them in their struggle against loneliness and in their desire to feel wanted, loved, and important. We must help restore to these elderly Jews a sense of dignity, worth, and value.

By helping alleviate the burdens and oppressions of the Jewish poor, by eliminating the loneliness of the Jewish elderly, our young people will be identifying with these causes as authentic and genuine Jews. Our actions and our deeds will speak ever so loudly. We will then have truly fulfilled the Torah's requirement of Tzedakah – charity and true and genuine righteousness. We will then be properly prepared to help all the oppressed and downtrodden of the world and make their lives more humane and worth living.

May the Mishkan of our generation be not a building of a "Tiatron" but rather one composed of deeds of Tzedakah and of *Gemilas Chasadim* – charity, righteousness, and specific actions of kindness and altruism. May it be permeated with virtue, integrity, and the lofty principles of the *Melech Malchei HaMelachim, HaKadosh Baruch Hu* Who is the Father of us all. Amen.

This Drasha was delivered on Shabbos Parshas Pekudei in March, 1966, at the Young Israel of Boro Park. It was the first formal address I ever gave. I want to thank my late and beloved uncle, Rabbi Hyman Tuchman z"l for helping me write, formulate, and edit this speech – RHG.

16. Transforming a Desert into a Paradise, a *Midbar* into a *Gan Eden*
Parshas Bamidbar

Each year on the Shabbos just prior to the Yom Tov of Shavuos, the *Sedra* which is read is Parshas Bamidbar, the first section of Sefer Bamidbar, the fourth Book of the Torah. The fact that this Parshah is read just before Shavuos is no coincidence or accident. It was planned by *Chazal*, and we often double up on some of the preceding *Sedras* in order to read Bamidbar just before this Yom Tov.

What, my friends, is the connection between the Fourth Book of the Torah and Shavuos? In fact, if we were to analyze the actual meanings of both Bamidbar and Shavuos, our difficulty would be even more compounded. The root of the word "Bamidbar" is "midbar," which means desert, a wasteland, an uninhabited area in which nothing can grow or bring forth life.

Shavuos, on the other hand, is called "Chag HaBikurim," the Festival of First Fruits. It is the season of early summer, a time of blossoming and growth, expansion and germination. Thus, these two concepts – Shavuos and Midbar seem not only to be

Parshas Bamidbar

dissimilar but appear to even be contradictory and antithetical. If this is the case, why then do we tend to link these two together at all?

However, with a much deeper and closer observation, we can readily see the intention of our *Chachamim*. A world without Torah, they say, is a barren, unproductive, sterile and infertile wasteland. It is a place where man cannot grow spiritually in stature and in knowledge. If, however, Torah and Mitzvos are introduced into the world, this *"midbar,"* then this uninhabited land can indeed be converted into a ground which can produce *Bikurim*. It can become a paradise, a utopia where man can develop and grow to the loftiest of spiritual heights.

The first man, Adam HaRishon, was placed by Hashem in a paradise, in *Gan Eden*. This was intended to be his permanent domain. His surroundings were superb and most conducive to great achievements and advancements. However, without Torah and by not carrying out his responsibilities, by disregarding and disobeying the one and only Mitzvah given to him by Hashem, this Divine abode was transformed into a barren and unforgiving wilderness. Man was no longer able to live in peace and tranquility. Rather, he was forced to survive only through hard work and בזעת אפך, by the sweat of his brow.

In the ensuing generations and centuries, Adam's descendants behaved in a most corrupt and evil manner. Their actions resulted in bringing the world to complete and total destruction and annihilation. However, two thousand years later, on a small mountain amidst the wasteland of the Sinai desert, the Torah was given.

The world was now given a new opportunity, another chance to cultivate their wilderness, their inhospitable region, and transform it into a paradise. The Yom Tov of Shavuos thus not only commemorates the giving of the Torah, the great Theophany, it also recalls the re-creation of the world.

Our *Chachamim* saw the giving of the Torah as the completion, the re-enactment of *Brias* HaOlam". It was the fulfillment and the spiritual realization of the empty physical structure created thousands of years before. In fact, *Chazal* say that Hashem made the entire creation of the world, the total *Brias HaOlam*, contingent and dependent upon Klal Yisrael's acceptance of the Torah, for without Torah and Mitzvos, the world is incomplete and worthless. It would thus be incapable of surviving.

On this Shabbos just prior to Shavous, the anniversary of the giving of the Torah, it behooves each and every one of us to strive to learn and study the Torah and to internalize all of its teachings. We should then try to impart its rich heritage and traditions to our children and our grandchildren, our families and friends. Only in this way will we be assured that we will continue our beautiful *mesorah*, our chain of tradition. We will also help make certain that the world will continue to be transformed and altered from a *Midbar* to *Bikurim*, from a desert into a paradise. Let us do our share in fulfilling this dream. Amen.

17. Controversies
Parshas Korach

One of the most fascinating and thought-provoking statements in Pirkei Avos is found in the fifth chapter, Mishnah 17:

כל מחלוקת שהיא לשם שמים סופה להתקיים ושאינה לשם שמים אין סופה להתקיים. איזו היא מחלוקת שהיא לשם שמים זו מחלוקת הלל ושמאי, ושאינה לשם שמים זו מחלוקת קרח וכל עדתו:

Any argument which is for the sake of Heaven will endure. Any dispute, on the other hand, which is not for the sake of Heaven will not last. Which controversy was in the name of Heaven? The disputes between Hillel and Shammai. And which argument and controversy was not in the name Heaven? The controversy of Korach and his company.

Rabbi Dr. Norman Lamm *z"l*, the late president and Rosh Yeshiva of Yeshiva University, comments on this *posuk* in his outstanding *sefer* on the Torah, *The Royal Reach*. He says that the most important *beracha* which Jews pray for is the plea for shalom, peace. In the *Shemoneh Esrei*, we recite the *tefillah* of *Sim Shalom*. שים שלום טובה וברכה. We ask the *Ribono shel Olam* to "Grant peace, goodness, and blessing onto us and on all of Israel." Prior to that *tefillah*, we recite the

Parshas Korach

Birchas Kohanim, the *beracha* recited by the Kohanim, which concludes with the words וישם לך שלום – "And Hashem will give you peace."

However, the peace which we request, says Rabbi Lamm, is certainly not a "unanimity of ideas, nor is it that many should relinquish their opinions so that there be only one mode of thought." Indeed, he says: "*Yahadus* has always respected and encouraged differences of opinions and a great diversity of views and ideas."

The prime example which illustrates this thought is the Gemara itself. Each of its many *Mesechtos* contains countless pages of debates between different Rabbanim. Each of the *Tana'im* in the Mishnah and the *Amoraim* in the Gemara offers and defends his opinions and attempts to refute those of his colleague. Eventually one Rav's approach and view is judged to be correct and is accepted as Halacha.

What *Chazal* did warn us about, however, was to distinguish between מחלוקתים, arguments or controversies, which are not considered good and beneficial and which will bring on bitterness, dissension and even hatred.

Hillel and Shammai were two of the early *Tana'im*. They are viewed as the fathers of תורה שבעל פה, the Oral Tradition. The debates of their *talmidim* center around interpretations of the *pesukim* and *halachos* of the תורה שבכתב and their application to everyday life. They debated, discussed, and fought over each and every halacha, but nevertheless, maintained the highest regard and had the greatest respect for each other. In fact, the Gemara tells us that they actually married into each other's families.

Each one was totally committed to his position and argued it to its conclusion. There are several instances in *Shas* where one realized that the others views were more logical and tenable than his, and he yielded his position and accepted that of his colleague's. These arguments, the Mishnah says were, *L'sheim Shamayim*, for the pure sake of Heaven. They were concerned with matters very sacred and even vital to Judaism. Even though the outcome of these disputes has long since been decided, usually in Hillel's favor, *Am Yisrael* still refers to Shammai's position as examples of the divergence and diversity of Halacha.

On the other hand, the rebellion of Korach and his associates, which is the main theme of this week's *Sedra*, Parshas Korach, was the very opposite. Korach rebelled against the very authority of Moshe and Aharon. He attempted to remove Aharon from his lofty position of *Kohen Gadol,* and he questioned Moshe's appointment of his cousin, Elitzafan ben Uziel, as leader of the Kehas family of Levites.

This controversy, say *Chazal*, was the classic case of a *machlokes* that was not *L'sheim Shamayim*, not for the sake of Heaven. This abortive revolt failed, and the controversy did not endure. Rather, it ended quite quickly and was buried together with the rebels who were miraculously swallowed up in the ground.

The questions that we must address is who really was Korach, and why did he choose to cause a rift with Moshe and Aharon specially at this time?

The Torah tells us that Korach was from Shevet Levi and that he, together with Dasan and Aviram of Shevet Reuven, took 250 men and challenged the leadership and authority of Moshe and Aharon. Korach said (Bamidbar 16:3):

וַיִּקָּהֲלוּ עַל מֹשֶׁה וְעַל אַהֲרֹן וַיֹּאמְרוּ אֲלֵהֶם רַב לָכֶם כִּי כָל הָעֵדָה כֻּלָּם קְדֹשִׁים וּבְתוֹכָם ה' וּמַדּוּעַ תִּתְנַשְּׂאוּ עַל קְהַל ה':

"You take too much upon you, seeing all the members of the congregation are holy, every one of them, and Hashem is among them. Why do you lift yourselves above the congregation of Hashem?"

The Ramban ask, why did Korach, one of the elites of Shevet Levi, a wise and wealthy individual, decide at this particular time to rebel against the authority of Moshe and Aharon? What prompted him to take action against their authority now?

The Ramban answers that until that moment, the time was not yet propitious for any type of revolt or insurrection. From *Yetzias Mitzrayim*, the Exodus, until *Matan Torah* and the building of the Mishkan, anyone who would dare pose a challenge to the leadership of Moshe and Aharon would have certainly been killed. *Am Yisrael* had unreserved love and unquestionable obedience to them. Korach thus kept silent and waited for the opportune and right time to strike.

However, after the calamities in Parshas B'ha'aloscha, Korach saw his fortune about to change. First there was the devastating fire at Taveirah which consumed the מתאוננים, those who complained. This was followed by the tragedy of Kivros HaTa'avah where those who lusted for the quail were stricken and died. Korach sensed that even the survivors of these events were very bitter and disillusioned. Insult was added to injury in Parshas Shelach when, after believing the report of the Spies, the *Meraglim*, the entire generation of Jews who left Mitzrayim were informed by Hashem that they would not enter Eretz Yisrael. Rather, most of them would die in the desert.

These disastrous events combined to create a situation where even the average Jew became very resentful and began to even have doubts about the leadership ability of Moshe and Aharon. It was only at that point in time that Korach felt secure enough to begin his mutiny and his rebellion.

Parshas Korach

The fact that Korach had to rely on the political winds before initiating his revolt is a clear indication that it was not conducted for noble or altruistic reasons. It was instead promoted for the personal advancement of Korach and his followers. Such a *machlokes*, such a controversy, says the Mishna in Meseches Avos, cannot ever be sustained and certainly will not endure. In fact, after only a very short interval, the insurrection came to a very sudden end. The earth miraculously opened its mouth and swallowed up Korah and his band of rebels, burying forever this attempt to defy the ציווי, the command of Hashem.

The lesson that we learn from this incident is that we must always carefully examine our motives when pushing for change lest we be guilty of acting like Korach and his followers. We must be wary of engaging or joining in any controversy, especially one whose purpose – even if not immediately apparent – is ultimately to downgrade peace and harmony simply to advance one's own ambitions. Nothing positive will result, and the only accomplishment of such actions will be to sow the seeds of contention and disunity. Instead, if we ever become involved in any form of controversy, we must do so in the spirit of Hillel and Shammai, with love and kindness, with genuine concern and affection for our opponent. This requires wisdom, integrity, and moral strength. It demands גבורה and חכמה.

If we use these resources properly, we would certainly help fulfill the *tefillah* of ה' עוז לעמו יתן ה' יברך את עמו בשלום - "G-d will give His people strength; G-d will bless His people with peace." Amen.

18. Shalom – Aharon HaKohen's Legacy

Parshas Chukas

One of the main themes in Parshas Chukas is the death and burial of Aharon HaKohen, the *Kohen Gadol* and the older brother of Moshe Rabbeinu. Both he and Moshe were punished at Mei Merivah for not obeying Hashem's command of speaking to the rock (Bamidbar 20:8):

...וְדִבַּרְתֶּם אֶל הַסֶּלַע לְעֵינֵיהֶם וְנָתַן מֵימָיו...

"Speak to the rock in the presence of Bnei Yisrael so that it may give forth water."

For their transgression of not listening to Hashem's ציווי and instead striking the rock, both Moshe and Aharon were informed by Hashem that neither of them would fulfill their lifetime dream of leading Bnei Yisrael into Eretz Yisrael. Instead, they would both die and be buried in the desert, as the *posuk* says (Bamidbar 20:12):

...לָכֵן לֹא תָבִיאוּ אֶת הַקָּהָל הַזֶּה אֶל הָאָרֶץ אֲשֶׁר נָתַתִּי לָהֶם:

A short while later, we read of the death of Aharon, as the *posuk* says (Bamidbar 20:29):

Parshas Chukas

וַיִּרְאוּ כָּל הָעֵדָה כִּי גָוַע אַהֲרֹן וַיִּבְכּוּ אֶת אַהֲרֹן שְׁלֹשִׁים יוֹם כֹּל בֵּית יִשְׂרָאֵל:

And the entire congregation saw that Aharon died, and the entirety of the House of Israel cried for Aharon for 30 days.

Rashi draws attention to the phrase "כל בית ישראל" – "the entirety of the House of Israel."

כל בית ישראל - האנשים והנשים, לפי שהיה אהרן רודף שלום ומטיל אהבה בין בעלי מריבה ובין איש לאשתו:

Both the men and women cried over Aharon, for Aharon pursued peace and caused there to be peace between quarreling parties and between husbands and wives.

Rashi emphasizes this point again when speaking of the passing of Moshe Rabbeinu at the end of V'Zos HaBeracha. The *posuk* says (34:8):

וַיִּבְכּוּ בְנֵי יִשְׂרָאֵל אֶת מֹשֶׁה בְּעַרְבֹת מוֹאָב שְׁלֹשִׁים יוֹם וַיִּתְּמוּ יְמֵי בְכִי אֵבֶל מֹשֶׁה:

And the Bnei Yisrael cried over Moshe in the Plains of Moav for 30 days...

Rashi states:

בני ישראל - הזכרים, אבל באהרן מתוך שהיה רודף שלום ונותן שלום בין איש לרעהו ובין אשה לבעלה נאמר (במדבר כ, כט) כל בית ישראל, זכרים ונקבות:

The verse states that the <u>Bnei</u> Yisrael cried over Moshe, indicating that only the males cried. In regards to Aharon, however, since he pursued peace and he caused there to be peace between man and his fellow and between a woman and her husband, the posuk *states* "כל בית ישראל" – *that the entire House of Israel cried, both male and female.*

I feel we can elaborate on this Rashi in the following manner. While Moshe's leadership and his contributions to *Klal Yisrael* were extraordinary and unparalleled, Aharon's relationship with *Am Yisrael* was on a different and more personal level. While Moshe taught them the Torah, while he judged them and provided for all their physical requirements, Aharon took care of their emotional and individual needs. While Moshe's superior degree of *kedusha*, caused most of *Am Yisrael* to hold him in awe and reverence, Aharon came down to their level. He treated them with tremendous love and affection. He demonstrated his care and his concern for each and every member of *Klal Yisrael*. Thus, it was for Aharon alone that each and every member of *Klal Yisrael* mourned and cried.

In addition, and perhaps most important, Aharon's entire modus operandi was to bring peace and harmony to each and every Jew. He was the quintessential איש שלום. He was the supreme man of peace. He was completely devoid of selfishness and exemplified the trait of selflessness. As such, he was at peace with himself and was therefore able to devote his entire life to making peace among others. His mission statement was to be an אוהב שלום and a רודף שלום. Everyone claims to be a lover of peace; only Aharon, however, mastered the art of pursuing peace. His raison d'être was to make peace between two enemies, between two quarrelling friends, and between a husband and a wife. For that, he was beloved and admired by all and mourned by the masses when he was *niftar*.

What is most fascinating is that immediately after the Torah discusses the death of Aharon, it tells of the attack on Bnei Yisrael by the king of Arad. The *posuk* says (Bamidbar 21:1):

וַיִּשְׁמַע הַכְּנַעֲנִי מֶלֶךְ עֲרָד יֹשֵׁב הַנֶּגֶב כִּי בָּא יִשְׂרָאֵל דֶּרֶךְ הָאֲתָרִים וַיִּלָּחֶם בְּיִשְׂרָאֵל וַיִּשְׁבְּ מִמֶּנּוּ שֶׁבִי:

And the Canaanite king of Arad who lived in the south heard that the Israelites had come the way of Asarim; and he waged war against the Israelites and he captured captives.

Rashi says:

וישמע הכנעני - שמע שמת אהרן ונסתלקו ענני כבוד וכו', כדאיתא בר"ה (דף ג א). ועמלק מעולם רצועת מרדות לישראל, מזומן בכל עת לפורענות:

When the king heard that Aharon died and the Clouds of Glory dissipated, he then attacked Bnei Yisrael.

While the king of Arad may have been one of the first to attack *Am Yisrael* when they were vulnerable, he certainly was not the last. Over the millennia, many

Parshas Chukas

of our enemies have understood that when Bnei Yisrael are lacking *shalom* and *achdus*, when *machlokes* and strife become the order of the day, it is then a most propitious time to attack us. With the death of Aharon HaKohen, the individual who personified peace and harmony, love and respect, *Am Yisrael* was bereft and was in mourning. They no longer had their leader who was able to motivate them towards peaceful interactions. They then reverted back to their old ways. Thus, when there is dissension, quarrelling, and disagreement, we are indeed quite vulnerable to all external attacks.

This concept has certainly been a focal point of our history. Both *Batei Mikdash* were destroyed primarily because of inner strife and internal dissension. While the generation of the first Beis HaMikdash was guilty of the most heinous crimes, there was also a lack of *achdus* between the leaders. A conflict broke out between two different factions – those who favored aligning themselves with the Egyptians and those who supported the Babylonians. This helped contribute to the dissension in the country which preceded the final attack by the Babylonians in 586 BCE. At that time, they destroyed the Bais HaMikdash, ended the first Jewish Commonwealth, and sent multitudes of our brethren into exile.

The Second Beis HaMikdash, say *Chazal*, was destroyed exclusively because of the sin of *sinas chinam*, causeless and baseless hatred between different segments of the populace. Each individual group had only disdain and contempt for the other group.

This, unfortunately, has been the case for the past two thousand years of our *golus*. When we were divided, when we had division and strife, we were vulnerable to our enemies. Over the years, we suffered tremendous losses. However, when we stood together, when we fought shoulder to shoulder, when we did not descend to discord and disagreement, no power on earth was able to defeat us.

One example of this occurred in June 1967. Prime Minister Levi Eshkol established a national unity government. He brought into his government the Honorable Menachem Begin and his Likud party. They joined together with Moshe Dayan, Abba Eban, and the Labor party. They acted with one mind and with one heart. Because this national unity government worked together with *achdus* and *shalom*, they were able to soundly defeat the militarily superior countries of Egypt, Syria, and Jordan in just six days. That was, perhaps, one of the greatest and most significant military victories of all time.

However, as recently as just a year and a half ago, during 2022-2023, the State of Israel descended into strife and dissension. Each different group, each political party was fighting for its own agenda, for its own cause. Their primary concern was not the overall well-being of Medinat Yisrael. Eretz Yisrael turned into a State filled with rancor and selfishness, enmity and hatred. There was genuine antipathy of one person for another. The acrimony and alienation that permeated the Jewish people was so intense that they were almost on the verge of a disastrous civil war. They were so consumed with disdain and contempt for each other that they totally forgot about their real enemy, their adversary from without. They let their national defense down.

When there is no *shalom*, when there is a lack of harmony and comradery, our enemy seizes the opportunity. Our brothers and sisters in Eretz Yisrael were brutally and barbarically attacked by Hamas on Simchas Torah. On October 7, 2023, that surprise assault resulted in the greatest calamity to affect *Am Yisrael* on one day since the end of the Shoah in 1945. When we forget the traditions and teachings of Aharon HaKohen, when we abandon his guidance and his advice, we then fall prey to our enemies.

For a short time after the start of the war in Gaza there was *achdus* and *shalom* amongst all segments of

Am Yisrael. We were all unified and united in support of Israel in its hour of need. However, after only a few months, we returned to our same dissension and our lack of togetherness and peace. Thus, this war continues and has become the longest, most costly, and most divisive in the history of the State of Israel.

This same idea also applies to other nations and to other peoples. Even here in the United States, for the past twenty years, and especially for the past eight years, the hatred, the animosity, and the abhorrence between the Democrat and Republican parties has deteriorated and reached its lowest point since the Civil War in the 19th century. Neither party has been able to say anything positive about the other. This is especially true of the leaders of these parties. The sense of *shalom* and a real unity of purpose is unfortunately completely missing from our national scene.

The situation has deteriorated so badly that just this past Shabbos, on Parshas Chukas, on July 13, 2024, an assassination attempt was made on the former president and the current Republican presidential candidate, Donald Trump. But for the grace of Hashem, Mr. Trump would have been killed. In fact, he publicly thanked G-d for saving him and keeping him alive.

When, my friends, will we once again follow the example of Aharon HaKohen? When will we, both in

Eretz Yisrael and throughout the world, begin to realize that only through real and genuine peace and harmony can we truly experience a world that is secure and productive? When will we finally understand that hatred and animosity will only lead to continuous wars, bloodshed, and destruction? When will we finally comprehend that only when we incorporate the concept of real and genuine *shalom* into our lives can we then live in peace and tranquility? Only at that time will we truly witness the ushering in of the messianic era. We will dwell in peace and accord. We will then see the coming of Moshiach ben Dovid, במהרה בימינו אמן.

19. Battling Two Different Enemies
Parshas Ki Seitzei

This past Shabbos, 11 Elul, 5784, September 14, 2024, the *Sedra* which was read was Parshas Ki Seitzei. That day marked a most memorable and momentous occasion in my life, for it was the 65th anniversary of my Bar Mitzvah which occurred on September 12, 1959. It also commemorated the last Shabbos that Rivkie and I spent in Elizabeth, New Jersey. After living in that wonderful community for 41 years, we relocated to Lakewood New Jersey, five years ago to be closer to our children. As such, I feel it appropriate to share a few thoughts on the Parshah and its significance for our times.

Parshas Ki Seitzei begins and ends with a discussion about war. In addition, it consists of seventy-four Mitzvos – twenty-seven positive and forty-seven negative commandments. In the first *posuk* the Torah says (Devarim 21:10):

כִּי תֵצֵא לַמִּלְחָמָה עַל אֹיְבֶיךָ וּנְתָנוֹ ה' אֱלֹקֶיךָ בְּיָדֶךָ...

When you go out to war against your enemy, Hashem will deliver him into your hands...

Rashi says:

Parshas Ki Seitzei

במלחמת רשות הכתוב מדבר.
The Torah is speaking about an optional, non-obligatory battle.

Hashem assures us that if we go out to war against our enemy, Hashem will help and assist us, and we will be successful.

Many of the *mefarshim*, most notably, the Magid of Mezeritch, my illustrious ancestor, as well as the *Chasam Sofer*, explain that the war which the Torah is discussing is man's internal and very personal war with his own *Yetzer Hora*, his personal evil inclination. The *Yetzer Hora* is a very sly, cunning, and deceitful creature. He is constantly attempting to ensnare us and convince us to violate and abrogate our commitment and allegiance to the *Ribono shel Olam*.

The *Shem MiShmuel*, Rav Shmuel Bornstein, the early 20th century Chassidic master, says that this optional battle which we are waging is indeed a war against an actual external enemy. This war was first mentioned in last week's *Sedra*, Parshas Shoftim. There, the Torah delineates a number of different people who are exempt from engaging in this war. They are told to take leave of their comrades and – יֵלֵךְ וְיָשֹׁב לְבֵיתוֹ – "Let them go and return to their homes" (Devarim 20:8).

Rav Bornstein says that in describing this kind of war, the Torah gives the directive in *lashon yachid*, in the singular (כי תצא למלחמה) rather than in the plural (כי תצאו למלחמה). He explains that when the Jewish nation goes out to war, when they attack their enemy, there must be אהבה ואחוה ושלום ורעות. There must be love and comradery, friendship and peace. There must be a unanimity of purpose. We must be כאיש אחד בלב אחד. We must be of one mind and one heart; we must have a unity of spirit. He continues that if we go to battle with that perspective, with that mindset, and with that purpose, then – וּנְתָנוֹ ה' אֱלֹקֶיךָ בְּיָדֶךָ וְשָׁבִיתָ שִׁבְיוֹ – "Hashem will give over your enemy to you." You will be victorious, "and you will even take prisoners." In other words, if there is Jewish unity, if we and our fellow Jews are on the same page, if we are one with Hashem, then the *Ribono shel Olam* will guarantee our complete and total success.

The last part of the Parshah, the *Maftir*, talks of another war, a different battle. This war is a *Milchemes Mitzvah*, it is an obligatory battle for which every Jew is mobilized and obligated to participate in. It involves every member of *Klal Yisrael*. It is our eternal battle against our archenemy, Amalek. This section seems to challenge the Jew to forego his usual degree of mercy and compassion towards his fellow man. Instead of forgiving our enemy for his misdeeds, the Torah commands *Am Yisrael* to remember and never forget the heinous and destructive actions of Amalek.

We are directed to destroy and wipe out any and all vestiges of this vengeful and vindictive nation. We are commanded to destroy and kill every man, woman, and child who emanates from this miserable people.

Harav Zalman Sorotzkin in his masterful commentary on the Torah *Aznayim L'Torah* says that Amalek's attack on the recently liberated Jews was unfounded and unwarranted. It was fought on both a physical and spiritual level. It was provoked and stirred on by the heavenly representative of Eisav – he who stood for everything that was evil in this world. This *Malach* attempted to cause *Am Yisrael's* spiritual decline along with its physical destruction.

Klal Yisrael had just been redeemed from their long and torturous enslavement in Egypt. They were on the road to Har Sinai to receive the Torah and become the *Am HaNivchar*, the Chosen People and an *Or LaGoyim*, a light unto the nations of the world. Then came Amalek.

Amalek attempted to block this road and thwart our upward spiritual ascent. Amalek is unlike any of our other enemies. They attempted to oversee the complete and total annihilation and destruction of the Jewish people. Therefore, we have an eternal command at all times, in every era, and in each generation, to destroy and wipe out any and all vestiges of this uncivilized and vicious foe.

Parshas Ki Seitzei

The Rav, HaRav Yosef Soloveitchik *zt"l* says:

> Amalek is obviously more than a nomadic tribe. He is more than a particular nation or people. He is every man gone berserk who has shed his divine image for that of Satan. Any nation which declares that her policy is to destroy the Jewish people is Amalek. It has emblazoned on its banner the slogan of impersonal hatred. This is the persistent villainy that Hashem bids us to combat and against which He has sworn eternal enmity. It is for this reason that there is a מצות עשה, 'You shall always remember what Amalek did to you. Do not forget.' Amalek is a historic phenomenon. *"Lo Tishkach,"* the lesson must never be forgotten."

Am Yisrael, and especially Eretz Yisroel, has been in a seemingly endless battle with the current embodiment of Amalek, Iran and its main proxies – Hamas and Hezbollah – for many years. There appears to be no letup in the new Amalek's attempt to obliterate and destroy our people. The worldwide antisemitism which has manifested itself in this modern-day Amalek seems to grow with every passing day. The Jewish world certainly has every reason to be frightened and concerned for the future.

The battle today is as it was with Amalek of old. It is not just a war with *Bnei Yisrael*; it is also a battle against *HaKadosh Baruch Hu*. Rav Soloveitchik says,

Parshas Ki Seitzei

"When the battle is against the Jews, Hashem will do the fighting. When, however, it is waged against Hashem, then the Jewish people must be the ones to do the fighting."

Today, the war is a two-fold battle both against the Jewish people and against Hashem. We therefore should be comforted in knowing that while we must do our *hishtadlus*, we must take our own initiative and go to battle, we will ultimately have the help and assistance of our only real and true ally, the *Ribono shel Olam* Himself.

My friends, we must stand united as one. We must maintain our strength and our fortitude in our battle against our eternal enemy. We must also be aware that in the final analysis, we will prevail. We will ultimately succeed in destroying Amalek and its many allies. As we defend the honor and sovereignty of *HaKadosh Baruch Hu*, we are assured that Hashem Himself בכבודו ובעצמו will come to our assistance and destroy all our enemies.

Let us hope and pray that this will occur very soon. We will *im yirtzeh Hashem* bear witness to the coming of Mashiach Ben Dovid. He will usher in a period of peace, harmony, and tranquility, במהרה בימינו אמן.

20. Our Three Pillars
Pirkei Avos

Pirkei Avos, *Ethics of the Fathers*, is divided into six chapters, one of which is read each Shabbos between Pesach and Shavuos. In fact, it has become a *minhag Yisrael*, a well-established custom to continue this study even after Shavuos, every week until Rosh Hashanah.

Perek Aleph begins:

משה קבל תורה מסיני ומסרה ליהושע ויהושע לזקנים וזקנים לנביאים ונביאים מסרוה לאנשי כנסת הגדולה...
Moshe received the Torah from Sinai and gave it over to Yehoshua, and Yehoshua to the Elders, and the Elders to the Prophets, and the Prophets gave it over to the Men of the Great Assembly.

The "Torah" that the Mishnah speaks of does not refer specifically to the תורה שבכתב, the Written Torah, i.e. the *Chamishah Chumshei Torah*. That was given to Moshe directly by *HaKadosh Baruch Hu* in written form and did not require a *Mesorah*. Rather, it primarily refers to the תורה שבעל פה, the Oral Torah, namely the Mishnah and the Gemara.

Our *Mesorah* maintains that both the Written Torah – תורה שבכתב – and the Oral Law – תורה שבעל פה – were Divinely given at *Ma'amad Har Sinai*. The Oral Law was, as its name implies, transmitted verbally from generation to generation, from father to son, from teacher to student, until the third century of the Common Era. Then, following two traumatic and difficult centuries after the destruction of the Beis HaMikdash and the end of Jewish sovereignty, after the Jewish people were defeated twice by the mighty Roman legions, Judaism was at a great crossroads. Many of our great *Talmidei Chachamim*, our outstanding scholars and teachers, were killed by the Romans. With their passing, the תורה שבעל פה, our oral tradition, was in danger of being lost forever.

Rabbi Yehudah HaNasi, Rabbi Judah the Prince, who was the spiritual leader at the time, felt that a change in the transmission of תורה שבעל פה was absolutely vital in order to preserve the future of *Yahadus*. תורה שבעל פה, which had for centuries been orally passed down from one generation to another, had to, out of necessity, be written down and codified in order that it not be forgotten and, G-d forbid, lost forever.

Thus, approximately in the year 200 C.E., Rebbe, as he was affectionally called, with the assistance of many of his colleagues, wrote down the

Mishnah. This now gave added dimensions and explanations to the Written Torah in a format that was accessible to all. It was this single heroic act which, in essence, ensured the faithful continuation of *Yahadus*. We now had a foundation, a basis from which our oral tradition would continue to survive, grow, and flourish.

Subsequently, about 150 years later, the Talmud Yerushalmi was written down. This was followed approximately in 500 C.E with the transcribing of the Talmud Bavli, the Babylonian Talmud led by Ravina and Rav Ashi. This has become the basis, the very foundation, from which all Halachos and traditions were developed and formulated throughout the centuries.

I would like this morning to study the second Mishnah of the first Perek in *Pirkei Avos*. The text begins:

שמעון הצדיק היה משירי כנסת הגדולה. הוא היה אומר: על שלשה דברים העולם עומד - על התורה, ועל העבודה, ועל גמילות חסדים:

Shimon the Righteous was one of the survivors of the Great Assembly, the Anshei Kneses HaGedolah. He used to say: The world stands upon three pillars – upon Torah, upon service to Hashem, and upon acts of lovingkindness.

Shimon the Righteous was the leader of the Jewish community as well as the Kohen Gadol. He lived approximately in the 3rd century B.C.E., during the early days of *Bayis Sheini*, the Second Commonwealth. He was well aware that not all of *Klal Yisrael* lived in Eretz Yisrael. Most of the Jews living during that period were dispersed to different areas of the world. He wanted to provide all Jews, no matter where they may be, with a key, an understanding, and an overriding principal to *Yahadus*. He therefore chose these three pillars, the three main components which make up the essential elements of *Yiddishkeit*. They are: לימוד התורה, the study of Torah; עבודת ה', the service to G-d; and גמילת חסדים, deeds and acts of lovingkindness toward one's fellow man.

Judaism thus resembles a structure which rest on three legs. In order to maintain its balance, all three parts of this tripod are of vital importance. If any of the limbs are removed, if any of these posts or supports are missing, the entire structure may very well fall apart. In order for one to experience a totally religious life, he must internalize and incorporate all these three elements of *Yahadus*.

In his commentary to this Mishnah, the Chida, Rav Chaim Yosef Dovid Azulai, cites the *Zohar* which states that these three pillars of the world are best exemplified by our *Avos HaKedoshim*, our great forefathers, Avraham, Yitzchok, and Yaakov.

Avraham was the epitome of *Gemilas Chasadim*, deeds and acts of lovingkindness. He was the quintessential friend and champion to all members of his society. When his nephew Lot was captured, he waged an all-out war to rescue him. When Hashem revealed the impending destruction of Sedom and Amorah, Avraham appealed to Him to save these cities, despite the fact that most of their inhabitants were guilty of capital crimes. Most famously, Avraham Avinu constantly kept the doors of his tent open throughout the day, so that he could be of service to all weary travelers, no matter what their religious beliefs were. He continually and at all times attempted to aid, provide comfort, and assist his fellow man.

    Yitzchok represented the highest form of *Avodah* – worship, sacrifice, and service to Hashem. It was he who offered his life on the *Mizbeach* at Har Moriah at the *Akeidah* because Hashem requested it. All his life he was the true representative of the *Eved Hashem*, G-d's loyal and devoted servant.

    Yaakov, while combining the main characteristics of both his father and grandfather, also exemplified and personified the concept of Torah at its best. He is described in Sefer Bereishis as a יושב אהלים, as the man who dwelled in the tents of learning Torah. There, he daily absorbed the words of the Torah, internalized and incorporated its teachings from the *Yeshiva Shem v'Ever*, and passed them on to each of his twelve sons and to his extended family.

Although all three principles are most important and absolutely necessary for one to become a complete Jew, we begin with the pillar of Torah. Before we are able to serve *HaKadosh Baruch H*u appropriately, or before we can help our fellow man, we must familiarize ourselves with our life's manual - the Torah. We must learn and absorb all elements of both תורה שבכתב as well as תורה שבעל פה.

If we truly understand the teachings of the Torah, if we become familiar with all the specific and intricate *dinim* and *mishpatim* of the Torah, we will know how to properly conduct our lives. We then will be able to serve the *Ribono Shel Olam* in a most appropriate and exemplary way. Only through the prism of the Torah will we be able to successfully and righteously perform true acts of lovingkindness and benevolence toward our fellow man. If we combine all these three essentials, we will be assured that *Yiddishkeit* will continue to grow and develop and will endure forever. Amen.

21. Who Will be for Me? Will I Only be for Myself?

Pirkei Avos

In the first chapter of Pirkei Avos, we find a number of statements from the great *Nasi*, Hillel HaZakein. In the fourteenth Mishnah, Hillel presents us with a unique formula:

הוא היה אומר: אם אין אני לי מי לי, וכשאני לעצמי מה אני, ואם לא עכשיו אימתי:

He used to say: If I am not for myself, who will be for me? And if I am only for myself, what am I? And if not now, when?

Hillel appears to present a very perplexing situation. To what extent should a person be focused on his own welfare? On the one hand, the answer is quite obvious. Each person is a world unto himself. Only he can experience and know himself best. No one, not even one's spouse, parents, or his dearest friends can completely embody his pains and anxieties. Nor can anyone else know the full extent of his frustrations or rejoice in his happiness and pleasure as he himself can. Thus says Hillel, "If I am not for myself, who will be for me?"

On the other hand, if one becomes consumed solely with himself, with his own personal predicaments and crises, and, in the process, he ignores those around him and their many difficulties – what really is he?

Can one alone, by himself, without any outside help or assistance, solve all of his own problems? If we take this approach of not relying or depending upon anyone for anything, we will become completely wrapped up in ourselves. We will become self-centered and self-absorbed. We become concerned only with our own problems while neglecting the difficulties of our peers.

In this light, I would like to share a *pshat* of the Chiddushei HaRim, the first Gerrer Rebbe. The Rebbe made the following comment regarding the ninth plague, *Choshech*, darkness, which Hashem inflicted upon Mitzrayim.

החשך הגדול הוא כשאין איש רואה את רעהו ואינו משתתף בצער הזולת.

"The worst darkness that one can experience is the blindness in which one person will not see or empathize with another's problems or vicissitudes." True *choshech* occurs when we care only about ourselves, when we are only concerned with our own needs and our own happiness. אור, light, on the other hand, includes being concerned with and caring for other people and their problems.

Hillel in this Mishnah is thus expressing two contrasting thoughts and ideas. He first discusses each human being's need for independence – to be an individual and unique. He then dwells upon the virtue of interdependence – how we need others and others need us.

These contrasting ideas are also mentioned in *Sefer Tehillim*. Dovid Hamelech wrote (Tehillim 8:5-6):

מָה אֱנוֹשׁ כִּי תִזְכְּרֶנּוּ וּבֶן אָדָם כִּי תִפְקְדֶנּוּ:
What is man, that you are mindful of him?

This *posuk* represents Hillel's idea of וכשאני לעצמי מה אני – that alone and selfish, we are unworthy of being remembered. The next *posuk*, however, draws a contrast:

וַתְּחַסְּרֵהוּ מְּעַט מֵאֱלֹקִים וְכָבוֹד וְהָדָר תְּעַטְּרֵהוּ:
Yet You have made man but a little lower than angels.

This *posuk* recalls Hillel's injunction of אם אין אני לי—*if I am not for myself.* This is the fundamental Jewish principle of בשבילי נברא העולם – "The whole world was worth being created for myself alone." It is the importance of a man's own self-esteem and self-worth.

This concept of אם אין אני לי מי לי—of having self-dignity and being independent is underscored in Parshas Mishpatim in the Torah's description of the *Eved Nirtza*. A Jew who had the misfortune of serving as an *Eved Ivri*, a Jewish slave, is allowed to be freed from his servitude after six years. However, if he chooses to remain a slave, he must go through a very degrading and laborious procedure. He is brought to *Beis Din* and has a hole bored into his ear. He then remains as a permanent slave. Technically, he remains a slave until the next *Yovel*, the Jubilee year, and is called an *Eved Nirtza*.

The reason that *Chazal* give for this procedure is that there is something very wrong with a person who voluntarily chooses to be someone else's servant. Each man's ideal is to be free and independent, and when a person has the opportunity to make that a reality and chooses otherwise, he is given a permanent mark on his body to indicate the Torah's displeasure with his choice. Indeed, it is to underscore this message that we make the *beracha* of שלא עשני עבד – "Thank you Hashem for not making me a slave," every single day.

֍

There is another lesson that can be gleaned from Hillel's words in this Mishnah, and that is the necessity of correcting oneself, which requires the prerequisites of being humble and unassuming. Often, even our closest friends are reluctant to correct our deeds and imperfections and to tell us things that we are doing wrong, for fear that we may be hurt or offended.

Thus says Hillel: אם אין אני לי מי לי - "If I am not for myself," if I don't see my own faults and shortcomings, if I refuse to see my inadequacies and my blemishes, leaving them uncorrected, then, מי לי – "Who will be for me?"

On the other hand, וכשאני לעצמי – "If I am only for myself," if I do not try to help and correct others but instead remain silent when rectification and correction are required, then מה אני – "What, truly, am I?"

If one attempts to assist a friend by giving him loving *mussar,* and he is a true and genuine colleague, he will appreciate your overtures; he will not be offended and will realize how it will indeed benefit him.

✡

In Hillel's closing statement he says: ואם לא עכשיו אימתי - "And if not now, when?"

Hillel is teaching us that time is extremely important. If one has a job at hand, or an opportunity to do a specific good deed, he should not procrastinate and put it off. Rather, it should be done as soon as possible. As the proverb states, "Never put off until tomorrow what can be done today."

In *Sefer Tehillim* (90:12) we are told:

לִמְנוֹת יָמֵינוּ כֵּן הוֹדַע וְנָבִא לְבַב חָכְמָה:

Teach us well to number our days so that we may acquire a heart of wisdom.

The usual method of "counting one's days" is by determining how many years a person has already lived, how old the person is today. We should, however, not emphasize the days that have already passed. They are gone forever and can never be replaced. Rather, we should accentuate and highlight the days which we still have ahead – the days in which we can still perform Mitzvos both to Hashem and towards our fellow man. If we could only change our thinking on this fundamental point, we would then be able to plan our lives in a most appropriate and meaningful manner.

When a person becomes aware that his days on earth are limited, he will carefully evaluate his deeds and actions. He will not spend his last days wasting his time. The Gemara in Shabbos (153a) sums this up beautifully. It says:

תנן התם, רבי אליעזר אומר: שוב יום אחד לפני מיתתך. שאלו תלמידיו את רבי אליעזר: וכי אדם יודע איזהו יום ימות? - אמר להן: וכל שכן, ישוב היום שמא ימות למחר, ונמצא כל ימיו בתשובה.

R' Eliezer said, "One should repent one day before his death."

"How," ask his students, "should one know when he will die?" Thus, how then can a person do *Teshuvah* one day before his death?

R' Eliezer responded: "Since one cannot know when he will die, he must constantly repent; he must, at all times, evaluate his deeds and always try to perform the will of G-d."

My dear friends, this should become our mantra, our true way of thinking, our philosophy of life. It should emerge as a most essential and fundamental message for us all. Since we can never really know how much longer Hashem will allow us to live on this earth, we must utilize every moment and every second of each day. We must try to make ourselves and the world around us a little better and safer for all. When each of us fully understands this dictum and realizes the true value of time, we will attempt to manage our life wisely and carefully.

Let us instill these essential and varied lessons of Hillel. In this brief, pithy statement, Hillel has taught us the principle of valuing oneself and the necessity of self-correction. He has taught us to value others and to influence them positively. Lastly, he has taught us that the time for these accomplishments is now.

I pray that we all take these most important lessons to heart, Amen.

THE YOM TOVIM

22. To Reach the Present Day
Rosh HaShanah

There is one question which is posed time and again, and that is: what is the reason that the Jewish people survived as long as we have? To what can be attributed our presence among and yet, at the same time, apart from all the nations of the world? We ourselves are even more astonished with the successful resistance with which our ancestors have turned away every assault upon our distinct identity made by the nations of the world.

The truth of the promise that: נצח ישראל לא ישקר, "Israel is an eternal people," seems to be evident to us all. Shall we ever forget the slaughter in the days of the Roman Empire when the Beis HaMikdash was destroyed when that unique bond between Bnei Yisrael and *HaKadosh Baruch Hu* was diminished? Then, hundreds of thousands of Jews were mercilessly butchered, the best, the noblest, and the most learned among them.

Additionally, so many more were driven into the remotest corners of the globe. They were forced into exile until only a tiny, miniscule remnant remained in Eretz Yisrael, the land of our people. This took place more than 1,900 years ago.

We were dispersed, and we roamed the four corners of the earth, but we were never destroyed. Whatever country the Jew went to, he lived as a proud and practicing Jew. Wherever he emigrated to, he emulated the example set by Avraham Avinu, about whom we read in today's *leining*. Avraham was forced to wander among strangers in strange lands. Yet, whatever land he came to, he refused to be submerged into the mass of idolators, pagans, and barbarians among whom he was fated to move.

Since our dispersion and exile from our homeland, continuous attempts have been made to destroy us. In various countries, throughout our almost two-thousand-year sojourn in Europe as well as in the early years in America, discrimination and prejudice of all sorts – economic, political, as well as social, have been practiced. In many lands we were subjected to violence, torture, murder, and slaughter. The previous generation witnessed the heartrending spectacle of six million Jews cold-bloodedly and calculatedly killed by a nation of unrepentant barbarians, aided and applauded by the moral dregs in every country in the world. Still *Am Yisrael* goes on existing and even growing stronger and more determined.

For centuries we have been the eighth wonder of the world. Where today are the Phoenicians and the Goths? The formerly glorious Greece and the grandeur

Rosh HaShanah

of Rome have also faded and withered, falling, never again to be heard from. Babylon is a pile of bricks and ancient Egypt has been reduced to a handful of curious burial mounds. The seven tribes who previously lived in Eretz Canaan, exist today only in the pages of the Tanach. *Am Yisrael,* however, remain as major actors on the stage of history.

On this day of Rosh Hashanah, which is so important to *Am Yisrael*, we must be more forcibly struck than usual with these puzzling questions. Perhaps in our *Tefillos HaYom*, our prayers for today, we can find a possible answer. On Rosh Hashanah we blow the Shofar and later at the *Seudas HaYom,"* our family meal, we make *Kiddush* over wine. After the *berachos* for both we then recite the *Shehechiyanu*.

We say:

ברוך אתה ה' אלקינו מלך העולם שהחיינו וקיימנו והגיענו לזמן הזה.

Blessed are You G-d, Our G-d, King of the Universe, who has kept us alive and has preserved us and made it possible for us to reach the present day.

This *beracha* contains two ideas – the concept of remaining alive, and that of attaining the present day.

Our *meforshim* ask: why are both ideas needed? If one remains alive, does he not automatically reach the present time? However, our *Chachamim* say that we must take notice that this *beracha* is not worded

שהחיינו וקיימנו לזמן הזה – "Who has caused us to live and has preserved us to the present time." Rather, it says: והגיענו לזמן הזה, "Who caused us to reach the present." The *beracha* does not speak merely of living or of subsisting now. It speaks of reaching, being on a par with the present age. From this approach, we can, I believe, obtain some insights into the mystical and esoteric reasons of our ongoing and continuous existence.

In any analysis of world history, we can observe two approaches which nations have used to deal with threats to their unique identity and culture. The first lies in isolating itself from all other groups by refusing to participate in the life of other nations. By withdrawing entirely and living life exactly as their parents and grandparents before them, they can remain unchanged. They are well described by the statement the non-Jewish prophet Bilam made in Parshas Balak about *Am Yisrael*: (במדבר כג:ט) הן עם לבדד ישכון – "They are a people which dwells alone." There are, in truth, certain nations who live entirely by themselves. They have no real contact with the other people of the world.

We can immediately think of several examples of this kind of nation: the Chinese of the 19th and the early years of the 20th century, the Hindus, and certain African nations. These were, in essence, people who made a religion of complete adherence to the past.

When new or modern ideas were introduced to them, they were never truly accepted by them. Their culture itself remained exactly as before.

The second way of handling challenges to one's identity is by willingly changing customs and institutions. The end result of such progress is that in the course of time the original culture is completely changed. Examples of this are the Greeks and the Romans. Both exist from ancient times. Both were once superpowers and world dominant ancient peoples. Today, both Greece and Italy are relatively modern countries. Yet how completely different they both are from their ancestors. There is today, almost no resemblance to their forbears. The people are different. The language is very much changed. The religion and their way of life are dissimilar and their customs are entirely altered.

The first group, the Chinese of the past and the other nations in its class, have the שהחיינו וקיימנו, they are still living, but have very little to do with our times. They are living a life that goes back a thousand years. The second group - the Italian successors to the Romans as well as the Greeks have the הגיענו לזמן הזה, they have reached our time; they are a part of it, but in the process, they have lost total contact with their past. The first group is fixed and unchanged. The second is part of our life but has no relationship at all with their own past.

Herein lies the great lesson to be learned from this *beracha* which we make on Rosh Hashanah. We praise Hashem who has not only kept *Am Yisrael* alive but has helped us attain the present time. The Jewish people are unique and exclusive in that we have placed great emphasis on both the שהחייני and the וקיימנו as well as on the והגיענו לזמן הזה.

We are not content with a merely static existence. We also insist on being a dynamic part of our present-day life. We cling to our ancient homeland, Eretz Yisrael. Millions of Jews have already helped settle and restore it to its ancient glory. However, the methods used have not been those of our ancestors; they have been the latest and most modern developed by science. In essence, our land is indeed ancient, but our techniques are the most up-to-date.

Our faith in the *Ribono shel Olam* is still the same as it was with our *Avos*: Avraham, Yitzchak, and Yaakov. Our Torah is the same as *Toras Moshe*. Our *Halachos* and traditions are not the product of today. They are centuries upon centuries old. Nevertheless, one merely has to peruse a sampling of modern Responsa to see how the ancient rulings of the Gemara and Shulchan Aruch are applied to the most modern of innovations, whether it be the latest breakthroughs in medicine or how to adapt technological devices to *shmiras Shabbos*. Indeed, we are the most progressive of people. The Jew is never afraid to accept legitimate and proper ideas and truths from the outside world.

Herein lies the secret of the existence of our people. *Am Yisrael* lives with our memories and traditions of the past, but at the same time, we live in a modern and progressive world. We are not only of the present time, we stress not only modern and contemporary knowledge, but we emphasize the primacy of Halacha, the dominance and the authority of Torah.

We ourselves must take to heart the lesson placed so concisely in the most beautiful beracha of שהחיינו. It is no accident that this *tefillah* is recited on all important life occasions, such as at a Bris, a *Pidyon HaBen* etc. as well as on all Yom Tovim.

As we march forward, we must hear the call of the great and incomparable Navi, Yirmiyahu, who in Megillas Eicha said: (5:21):

הֲשִׁיבֵנוּ ה' אֵלֶיךָ וְנָשׁוּבָה חַדֵּשׁ יָמֵינוּ כְּקֶדֶם:

Hashem, please turn us unto You and we shall return; renew our days as of old.

With Hashem always at our side as we live by His Torah, we will march to new heights which have been established on old foundations. Then this day will certainly be the שהחיינו וקיימנו as well as the והגיענו לזמן הזה. Amen.

Postscript:

The theme and the basic structure of this chapter was developed by my late uncle, Rabbi Hyman Tuchman *z"l*. I merely brought it up to date. In addition, this was the first *Drasha* that I gave in the Rabbinate at my Shul, Congregation Sinai Toras Chaim in September, 1973. RHG

23. Remembering the Past; Preserving the Future
Yom *Kippur*

Today, as we gather in our shuls, we join with Jews throughout this country and around the globe. We all daven, we fast, and we afflict our souls. We beseech Hashem to forgive us for all our sins which we committed during the past year, and we ask and beg Him to inscribe us into the *Sefer HaChaim*, the Book of Life, and seal our fate today for a year of peace, for a year of health, and for a year of prosperity. But for a short period this morning, for a brief interlude, we pause and forget about ourselves, about our future, about our fate and destiny. We instead remember, ever so briefly, our loved ones—our fathers and mothers, our husbands and wives, our dear relatives who have departed this world. We will concentrate solely on those who are no longer within our midst, those whose souls have returned to their source and Creator—*HaKadosh Baruch Hu*.

The Hebrew word for remembrance—זָכוֹר—or זֵכֶר—is very much part of the Jew. It is uppermost on his lips throughout the entire year. On the Shabbos which precedes Purim, we read publicly:

זָכוֹר אֵת אֲשֶׁר עָשָׂה לְךָ עֲמָלֵק בַּדֶּרֶךְ בְּצֵאתְכֶם מִמִּצְרָיִם:

Yom Kippur

Thou shall remember that which Amalek did unto you when thou went forth from Egypt.

On Yom HaShoah, one of our newest commemorative days on which we memorialize the six million victims of Hitler's madness, we say over again and again, "We shall not forget. We will always remember."

Just last week on Rosh HaShanah, one of the major sections of *Musaf* was entitled *Zichronos,* "Remembrances." Hashem, we are told, remembers all our deeds and makes an accounting of each and every one of them. And at that segment of the davening, the Shofar was sounded to remind us that each of us still has time to repent for all of our sins and all of our transgressions. We are still able to change our ways. There is yet an opportunity to do *Teshuvah,* to turn over a new, a different, and a better leaf in life.

At all times during the year, the Jew is commanded to remember that Hashem redeemed our ancestors from the yoke of oppression and servitude in Mitzrayim and brought them forth into Eretz Yisrael – the Land of Israel.

The theme of the *Shalosh Regalim* – Pesach, Shavuos, and Succos – centers around the remembering, the *Zichronos,* of G-d's acts of kindness and love toward the Jewish people. Pesach, of course, symbolizes *Yetzias Mitzrayim,* the actual physical

Exodus. After 210 years of unbearable and inhumane torture and bondage, *HaKadosh Baruch Hu* redeemed the Jewish people with a *Yad Chazakah*, with a strong hand, and with a *Zeroa Netuyah,* with an outstretched arm.

On Succos we remember the kind benevolence of Hashem in providing the *Ananei HaKavod*, the Clouds of Glory, which hovered over *Bnei Yisrael* throughout their 40-year sojourn in the Sinai desert.

The Yom Tov of Shavuos recalls that one great historic moment in all of human history when man actually encountered and had communion with Hashem. Shavuos commemorates the revelation of the Holy Torah, the heart and soul of Judaism, by G-d to the Jewish people at Mt. Sinai.

Remembering, however, is insufficient and does not within itself make a major impact upon our lives and the lives of our people. To truly remember, we must be able to link the past with the present and to go forth proudly toward the future.

Twice a year, on Yom Kippur and on Tisha b'Av, our most solemn day and our saddest day, we remember the heroic martyrdom of the עשרה הרוגי מלכות, the slaughter of 10 of our finest and greatest *Tana'im* and teachers who lived during the first and second century, CE.

These 10 leaders and *manhigim* of Klal Yisrael, including the incomparable Rabbi Akiva, died horrific and brutal deaths after *Churban Bayis Sheini* and the Bar Kochba revolt. They were beautiful and bold. They were courageous and defiant. They refused to buckle under to the brutal Hadrianic regime. They were forbidden from teaching Torah. They were prohibited from performing many of the most significant Mitzvos. In spite of the extreme likelihood of being caught and killed, they continued teaching and leading until they were captured and so viciously murdered.

They taught us a most important lesson. No matter where you find yourself, no matter where you are, or who the enemy is, Torah and Mitzvos must always be taught. We must internalize it. This must then be transformed into the constant performance of מעשים טובים. Only in this way will we help, preserve, maintain, and continue the growth of *Am Yisrael.*

The lesson of זכור was taught to us by our leaders, our *Tzadikim*, our *Kedoshim*, in every era and in each century.

We were hated and discriminated against by the countries in which we lived. There was only one reason for this behavior: we were Jewish, and we were different. We were deported from our homes. We faced forced conversions. We were thrown into

Yom Kippur

ghettos. We had to endure the Inquisition. We managed to survive through pogroms. Most heinously, we experienced the worst living hell in human history, the Holocaust, the Shoah.

When we read the stirring account of the *Asarah Harugei Malchus*, when we recall all the atrocities that our people had to endure, when we read about the hardships we faced in every country and in every century, we must ask ourselves a very basic and fundamental question: was it all really worth it? Consider the haughty and disdainful manner with which many of our more recent generations have treated our traditions, our teachings, and our Mitzvos for which millions of our people have given their lives. Pause and reflect on the attitude which leads so many to take the Torah for granted, which leads them to eliminate observances, to forget traditions, and to ignore ancient lessons. The purpose of the Ten Martyrs was to teach future generations that there is no greater vocation than that of Torah study and of Torah practice. To them Torah was life itself—no my friends—it was more important than even life. According to their scale of values, according to their *Cheshbon HaNefesh*, it was indeed worth every ounce of the sacrifice.

A modern story I recently read best reflects the elegy of all the *Kedoshim,* all of our Martyrs down through the ages. There was a recently married young

Yom Kippur

couple, deeply in love and blessed with true understanding and feeling. They had great hopes of raising a large and happy family. However, during the first ten years of married life, in spite of all medical attention, in spite of all prayers, they were not blessed with any children. Suddenly, a miracle occurred and the woman became pregnant. They were soon to become parents. There was much joy and gladness in their home and throughout their families.

The long-awaited day finally arrived. But it was not a day of gladness and joy but rather, one of gloom and grief. Complications arose and the mother's life was endangered. A team of specialists were called in, and they decided that the only action which would save the mother's life was that of a therapeutic abortion. The choice was to be either the mother or the child. The two could not both live. The husband grievously insisted that his wife make the decision. And without a moment's hesitation, she declared, "Let me die, but let the child live." And so it was. As the mother's life slowly ebbed away, the baby's life began. The baby was a boy, and his father never told him the tragic story of his birth.

When the son grew up, he went off to college. There, like so many of his non-observant colleagues and contemporaries, he met a young lady of another faith. One day, he returned home and informed his father of his great love for this girl and of his desire to marry her. Her religion? "That doesn't matter," he said. "We live in the 20th Century. We live in a new and different world. So she isn't Jewish, but we will use a judge anyway—who uses a Rabbi today to perform weddings? And besides, Dad," the son said, "today each of us lives for himself and for no one else. This is my life. I want to lead it as I see fit."

"Yes," said the distressed and distraught father. "It is your life, and you have every right to lead it as you want. But, before you proceed with your plans, just grant me one request." The son agreed, and his father drove him to an older Jewish cemetery. He led him right to his mother's grave. "20 years ago, when a little baby was about to be born, his mother became gravely ill. The doctors, with the father's consent, gave her the choice. 'It could not be both,' they sadly informed her. It was either her life or that of the unborn child. The woman in this grave would be alive today had she not cried out, 'Let me die, but allow the baby to live.' You, my son, are that baby, and this is your mother's grave. Your mother would be alive today had she not given her life so that you could live. Yes, my son, you have your own life to live. But before you go on living it the way you see fit, answer just one question: Did your mother die in vain? Was it worth the sacrifice?"

Yom Kippur

My dear friends, on this holy day of Yom Kippur, we recall the memory of a dear departed parent who sacrificed of himself and herself to give us life. We remember a beloved relative who taught us Torah and authentic values and Jewish education. We recall our ancestors who were at our side both in our joy and happiness and during our sorrows and disappointments. The question to which we must address ourselves is: Was their sacrifice worth it? Were their labors in vain? Were we left with an everlasting and enduring heritage? If we feel drawn closer to the memory of our relatives and to their authentic ideals, then it was worth it. If through them Shabbos becomes a meaningful day of spiritual and physical rest and we have greater devotion to our faith, then we can all say in unison that it most certainly was worth the sacrifice. We thus have a tremendous burden on our shoulders. In order to give meaning to the ultimate sacrifice that our ancestors gave by dying as true and pure Jews, we must commit ourselves to living as faithful and dedicated Jews.

In the memory of our loved ones who are no longer with us, to the millions of our holy and pure Jewish *neshamos* who have given their lives so that Yiddishkeit can remain alive, to these people we loudly say: אלה אזכרה ונפשי עלי אספחה: "To these great heroes I will remember and for them I pour out my soul."

Yom Kippur

It is also quite instructive that when we discuss memory and our need to recall these tragic events, we find it written so clearly in the Torah in Parshas Ki Seitzei. The Torah says:

זכור את אשר עשה לך עמלק.

Reb Bunim of Peshischa, the great Chassidic Rebbe, wonders why the word זכור is in the singular. If the entire Jewish nation has to recall the עמלק experience, should it not say זכרו in the plural?

The Torah, he says, wrote it in the singular to teach us a very important lesson. Amalek, Israel's arch-enemy, cannot attack us successfully if we are as one. Then עמלק – and all her modern successors – have no power over us. However, if we are separate and divided, if we do not act in unison, nor are we as one mind, if we have *machlokes* and divisiveness, then, and only then, will עמלק be able to pierce our veil and attack our nation. When we are united כאיש אחד בלב אחד, he has no power over us at all. Thus, the singular זכור. He says:

סימן הוא לדורות שכל זמן שישראל באחדות אין עמלק שולט בהם.

If we constantly remember our beloved relatives and they remain in everlasting memorial to us, they then will have succeeded. If they propel us to increase our devotion and dedication to Torah and Mitzvos, then we can truly say in the words found in נצח ספר שמואל:

Yom Kippur

ישראל לא ישקר, "The eternity and destiny of Israel will not fail and will not die." It will continue to live and be strong לעולם ועד. Amen.

24. The Holiness and the Special Significance of Chag HaSukkos

This morning, I would like to concentrate on one aspect of the Yom Tov of Sukkos, the "Mitzva" of "Laishev BaSukkah", the Jew's obligation of sitting in the Sukkah.

The Torah in Sefer Vayikra (23:42-43) says:

בַּסֻּכֹּת תֵּשְׁבוּ שִׁבְעַת יָמִים כָּל הָאֶזְרָח בְּיִשְׂרָאֵל יֵשְׁבוּ בַּסֻּכֹּת: לְמַעַן יֵדְעוּ דֹרֹתֵיכֶם כִּי בַסֻּכּוֹת הוֹשַׁבְתִּי אֶת בְּנֵי יִשְׂרָאֵל בְּהוֹצִיאִי אוֹתָם מֵאֶרֶץ מִצְרָיִם אֲנִי ה' אֱלֹקֵיכֶם:

You shall dwell in booths for a seven-day period, every citizen in Israel shall dwell in booths so that your generation will know that I caused the children of Israel to dwell in booths when I took you out of the land of Egypt, I am your G-d."

The Gemara in Meseches Sukkah (11b) brings down a *machlokes*, a debate between two great *Tannaim*, R' Akiva and R' Eliezer. R' Akiva says that following *Yetzias Mitzrayim*, after Bnei Yisrael's exodus from Egypt, Hashem provided huts for them to reside in. This lasted throughout their 40-year sojourn in the desert. To commemorate that kindness, we, their descendants, annually dwell in a sukkah for seven days on the holiday of Sukkos.

Rebbe Eliezer disagrees. He maintains that the miracle which Hashem provided for Bnei Yisrael's shelter was the institution of the ענני הכבוד, the Clouds of Glory which hovered over the Jewish people during their entire stay in the desert.

Rebbe Eliezer bases his position on a *posuk* in Shemos (13:21). There the Torah says:

וַה' הֹלֵךְ לִפְנֵיהֶם יוֹמָם בְּעַמּוּד עָנָן לַנְחֹתָם הַדֶּרֶךְ וְלַיְלָה בְּעַמּוּד אֵשׁ לְהָאִיר לָהֶם לָלֶכֶת יוֹמָם וָלָיְלָה:

Hashem went before the Jewish people by day in a pillar of cloud to show them the way through the wilderness...

Therefore, according to Rebbe Eliezer, the Mitzvah to sit in a frail, temporary hut is done to commemorate that very wondrous and miraculous event of antiquity.

According to Rashi, these Clouds of Glory represented Hashem's *Shechinah* which remained situated above *Am Yisrael* during their entire sojourn in the desert. These *Ananei HaKavod* dispersed all the foes and obstacles which *Klal Yisrael* faced enroute to Eretz Canaan. "It filled in all the crevices, it flattened peaks. It destroyed the very dangerous and foreboding snakes and scorpions that populated the desert."

Our *Chachamim*, however, raise a number of questions concerning this most important Mitzvah. The *Mabit*, Harav Moshe ben Yosef D'Trani, the 16th century scholar and Rav in Tzfas, poses a most interesting query. He says that Hashem performed three *nissim*, miracles, for our ancestors in the *midbar*. He presented our forebears with a באר מים, the well which continuously produced drinking water. He also gave them a daily dose of מן which sustained them and satisfied their hunger. This was in addition to the aforementioned עautomobilesנני הכבוד. He wonders why the Torah commanded that we commemorate only the gift of the ענני הכבוד and ignore the other two great miracles which Hashem performed for our ancestors?

The *Mabit* (*Sefer Bais Elokim, Sha'ar HaYesodos* Ch. 37) answers that while the באר מים and the מן were indeed great miracles in their own right, the ענני הכבוד stood head and shoulders above them in its significance and importance. The reason, he says, is that when Hashem redeemed Bnei Yisrael from their servitude in Egypt, He commanded them to travel via the hot, dry, and parched desert. The Bnei Yisrael only had enough provisions to last them for a few days of travel. Thus, Hashem, had an obligation, an actual *chiyuv*, to provide them with food and drink for the duration of their stay in the wilderness. Therefore, Hashem did not command *Am Yisrael* to memorialize these miracles. Rather, Hashem only emphasized the miracle of the ענני הכבוד.

These Clouds of Glory were not mandatory to protect and preserve the Jewish people. Although some protection was certainly necessary from the blazing sun of the desert, the Chasam Sofer (*Toras Moshe* to Vayikra 23:33) explains that for this purpose, a physical Sukkah-type hut would have sufficed. The gift of the spiritual ענני הכבוד served specifically as an indication of Hashem's great love and care for His special and unique people. Through these ענני הכבוד, Hashem provided our ancestors with an additional layer of protection. For this great and miraculous act, we must show our *hakaras haTov*, our complete and total gratitude and recognition to the *Ribono shel Olam*.

The *Tur*, Harav Yaakov ben Asher, the great 13th century Halachist and commentator, poses a second difficulty. He says that by our sitting in Sukkos on this Yom Tov, it appears that we are commemorating an historical event in the fall season for an incident that actually occurred in the spring. Hashem redeemed the Jewish people from Egypt on the 15th day of Chodesh Nissan, the beginning of the spring season. Immediately after their liberation, Hashem provided them with huts. Why then, asks the Tur, do we celebrate that event only in the autumn period and not during the spring?

He answers that during the spring and summer months, people tend to move their habitat outdoors. They spend a great deal of their leisure time outside their homes. Thus, if the Jewish people were to build and subsequently live in their huts during the spring and summer months, it would not be apparent that they were doing this specifically for a Mitzvah. It would seem to the average onlooker that they were performing these acts merely to enjoy the warm and pleasant weather.

However, says the Tur, when they build and subsequently live in a Sukkah during the fall, at a time when most people are moving back into their homes, it will become quite apparent to all that they are doing this specifically to fulfill a מצות עשה, a Biblically mandated Divine positive command.

This interpretation, say our *Chachamim*, works well if we follow the position of Rebbe Akiva that we sit in the Sukkah to commemorate the fact that our ancestors actually lived in booths in the desert. However, if we utilize the interpretation of Rebbe Eliezer that our sitting in the Sukkah recalls the ענני הכבוד, which preceded and protected the Jewish people as they marched in the desert, there seems to be a problem. These Clouds of Glory began to hover over *Am Yisrael* immediately following the Exodus. As such, why do we not commemorate that miracle in

Chodesh Nissan, during the Yom Tov of Pesach in the spring season, instead of during the Yom Tov of Sukkos, in the fall?

The Vilna Gaon as well as the Baal Shem Tov provide us with an identical answer. They both say that it is true that the ענני הכבוד began protecting *Klal Yisrael* immediately after *Yetzias Mitzrayim*. However, a mere six weeks following *Matan Torah*, after the giving of the Torah, everything changed.

Following the Theophany, after Hashem's revelation of the Torah to *Am Yisrael*, Moshe Rabbeinu ascended Har Sinai. He spent the next forty days and nights learning and receiving the Torah directly from Hashem. He subsequently descended Har Sinai on the 17th day of Tammuz.

Upon his return to the Jewish camp, he witnessed the nation's wild ecstasy and their abominable behavior with the עגל הזהב, the Golden Calf. He then, in the full view of *Am Yisrael*, shattered the *Luchos* which he had brought down from Heaven. At the very moment that this occurred, the ענני הכבוד vanished. They were not seen again for another three months.

Moshe once again ascended Har Sinai and spent the next 40 days and nights beseeching Hashem. He begged and implored the *Ribono Shel Olam* to pardon and forgive *Am Yisrael*. On the tenth day of Tishrei –

Yom Kippur – Hashem finally agreed to Moshe's request. Only then did he descend the mountain and returned to *Machaneh Yisrael*. On that day Hashem finally forgave and totally pardoned *Am Yisrael*.

Consequently, Yom Kippur was established forever as a day in which each and every Jew can achieve total and complete forgiveness for all of the misdeeds and transgressions which he has committed during the course of the year.

On the very next day, the eleventh day of Tishrei, *Klal Yisrael* were commanded to commence building a *Mishkan*, a Tabernacle, which would house Hashem's *Shechinah*. Moshe and *Am Yisrael* spent the next few days raising funds and materials for its construction. Finally, on the fifteenth day of Tishrei, they began to build this home for Hashem.

With that act, the ענני הכבוד, the Clouds of Glory returned and continued to hover over Bnei Yisrael for their remaining thirty-nine-year sojourn in the desert. It was only at the conclusion of their lengthy stay in the *midbar,* upon the death of Moshe Rabbeinu, that these Clouds of Glory finally departed.

Therefore, even according to Rebbe Eliezer, the celebration of Sukkos must, out of necessity, be observed beginning on the 15th day of Tishrei and not in the month of Nissan. For they indeed commemorate a truly historic event, the return of the ענני הכבוד and

Hashem's complete forgiveness of *Am Yisrael* for their sin of the Golden Calf.

The *Sefas Emes*, Reb Yehudah Aryeh Leib, the 19th century holy Gerrer Rebbe, offers a most fascinating approach to this topic. He explains that the period between Rosh Hashanah and Yom Kippur are not just a time for judgement of each and every Jew. It is also, he says, a time of liberation from temptation and from one's evil actions. This is immediately followed by the Mitzvah of Sukkah which is a microcosm of the actual Mishkan. Hashem dwells in each of our personal Sukkahs. Thus, the custom began that immediately following the conclusion of Yom Kippur, we begin to construct our own Sukkah. By so doing, we indicate that we too are quite hopeful that our personal Yom Kippur has brought us סליחה ומחילה for all of our past transgressions.

Therefore, the festival of Sukkos is not an independent Yom Tov. Rather, it is a follow-up and a continuation of the *Yomim Noraim*, the holy and sacred days of Rosh Hashanah and Yom Kippur.

It is therefore understandable that Sukkos is the Yom Tov of pure and complete joy and happiness. It is a זמן שמחתינו, our festival of rejoicing and celebrating. It is only on Sukkos, which also commemorates the beginning of the building of the

Mishkan, that we can each hopefully receive Hashem's complete and total forgiveness.

    Each and every Jew has the capacity to sit and bask in Hashem's glory. We should be grateful that on the fifteenth day of Tishrei, Hashem gave us another chance, another opportunity to correct our ways. We can witness our own personal ענני הכבוד returning to protect us and to provide a most powerful lesson. We can and should work diligently with tremendous effort to enjoy Hashem's love, affection, and His complete and total embrace. Amen.

25. To Illuminate a Darkened Society
Chanukah

One of the greatest potential difficulties that man faces is living in a world of complete and total spiritual darkness. Throughout history, there were only a few generations who experienced this phenomenon. Among those who caused such darkness were the Nazis of 20th century Germany and prior to that were the barbarians who sacked and ravaged the grandeur of the Roman Empire. One of the first however, was Hellenistic Syria, which tried and almost succeeded at destroying the very fiber and substance of Judaism.

The Jewish people are commanded annually to kindle lights for eight nights beginning on the 25th day of Kislev. This commemorates the victory of the Maccabees over the Hellenistic Syrians. But what does the kindling of lights have to do with a military victory?

Many of our *Chachamim* maintain that the remarkable military success of the Maccabean forces was not the motivation for the institution of the Mitzvah to kindle lights. The reason rather, was to commemorate the miracle performed for the Jews when they entered the Beis HaMikdash in Yerushalayim, following the conclusion of the war.

After cleansing it of all the *tumah*, of all the spiritual impurities brought there during the Syrian occupation, the Jews attempted to light the Menorah. Much to their dismay, all of the oil for the Menorah had been defiled and contaminated by the Syrians. They finally found one flask of pure oil, but it was only enough to last for one day. Miraculously, the oil burned for eight complete days until fresh, pure, and unadulterated olive oil was transported to Yerushalayim. It is for this reason, say many of our *Chachamim*, that we kindle lights on each of the eight nights of Chanukkah.

However, if we carefully analyze all the available Rabbinic and historical sources, especially the various Midrashim and Gemaras, we would realize that there is yet another basis for this Mitzvah, namely, the almost complete elimination of the influence of Hellenism from Jewish life. Hellenism, especially as practiced by the ancient Syrians, emphasized depravity and decadence, rather than virtue and righteousness. It stressed physical prowess and aesthetic beauty over the intellectual pursuit of the mind.

For Jews whose lives are symbolized by light, who are taught to be moral and ethical and who are trained to learn and study, such a world represented complete and utter darkness. Unfortunately, Hellenism, along with its many perverse customs, attracted many thousands of Jews, including many religious and political leaders. When this danger, which almost completely engulfed and destroyed *Yahadus*, was over, the Jews celebrated and commemorated that event by annually kindling lights.

As a matter of fact, the concept of total spiritual darkness is completely remote and alien to Judaism. We are symbolized by the radiance of hope and optimism, rather than the twilight of despair and pessimism. At an earlier time in our history, during the last stages of our servitude in Egypt, during שעבוד מצרים, the Jewish characteristic of light vis-à-vis the darkness of its surrounding neighbors was most evident. In Sefer Shemos, Parshas Bo (10:21) we are told about the ninth *makah*, the next to last plague which *HaKadosh Baruch Hu* inflicted upon the Egyptians:

וַיֹּאמֶר ה' אֶל מֹשֶׁה נְטֵה יָדְךָ עַל הַשָּׁמַיִם וִיהִי חֹשֶׁךְ עַל אֶרֶץ מִצְרַיִם וְיָמֵשׁ חֹשֶׁךְ: וַיֵּט מֹשֶׁה אֶת יָדוֹ עַל הַשָּׁמָיִם וַיְהִי חֹשֶׁךְ אֲפֵלָה בְּכָל אֶרֶץ מִצְרַיִם שְׁלֹשֶׁת יָמִים:

And G-d spoke to Moshe, "Stretch out your hand to the heavens that there may be darkness over the land of Egypt, darkness which may be felt."

Harav Ovadia Seforno, the great 15th century, Italian commentator, is puzzled by the introduction of חשך, darkness, as a concept by itself. He says that darkness is nothing more than the absence of light. When there is no light, it is dark. This, however, can be rectified by simply kindling a light. The Sforno then expands on this and offers a new and novel interpretation. The darkness, he says, which engulfed Egypt, was a phenomenon in its own right. It was so real that it could be felt; it was so powerful that light could not penetrate and change it.

As the Torah continues its description of this *makah*, we are told (ibid. 10:23) that the Jews did not experience the same darkness which engulfed their Egyptian neighbors. The *posuk* states:

וּלְכָל בְּנֵי יִשְׂרָאֵל הָיָה אוֹר בְּמוֹשְׁבֹתָם:...

And all the children of Israel had light in their dwellings.

Much of our religious life centers around the symbol of light. The candles of Shabbos, the flame of the Motzei Shabbos Havdalah candle, the Yahrtzeit-Memorial lamp, and of course, the lights of the Chanukah Menorah are all basic to our faith. Light – the very symbol of hope.

From time immemorial, it has been the Jew who has helped illuminate the world. From the Rambam – first in Spain and later in Egypt – during medieval times, to Louis Brandeis in modern day America; from the Abarbanel during the 15th century Spanish expulsion of the Jews, to Professor Albert Einstein during the 20th century Nazi Holocaust of the Jews. In

Chanukah

every profession and in every aspect or walk of life, the Jew has shed light and has brought illumination to a darkened society.

Today, world Jewry looks towards the Jews of the United States of America as their beacon of light and their symbol of strength. It is we who are the most powerful of all the Jews, and it is we who have the resources to help our oppressed brethren. However, there is a very real distinction between having power and using it. It is one thing to have the ingredients for fire but quite another to actively ignite the flame. You can have two flintstones, but you must rub them together before you can actually start a fire. A room may have a light switch, but it will remain dark until the switch is turned on. We certainly have the ability to bring light to the world. The question is – have we been fulfilling our responsibility?

During the near total blackness of the Hitler era, American Jewry possessed the ingredients to help influence the powers that be to help minimize the effects of the Holocaust, the greatest destruction in the history of man. However, because of our own internal fears and due to our ongoing conflicts, our secular leaders did not produce the torch which could have and should have radiated throughout the world. Instead, we managed to ignite only a tiny spark, a mere momentary flame, which was barely visible to our government and not seen at all in the darkness of Europe.

For twelve long and most difficult years, between 1933 and 1945, we studied the events in Europe and composed and presented some of the most eloquent and brilliant resolutions and talking points. However, although we attempted to act on behalf of our condemned brethren, we were far more successful in our attempts at study and compositions of hollow documents. Had we but acted forcefully and with strength, courage, and determination, perhaps the Allies and especially our government would have responded positively. They may have attempted to mitigate Hitler's diabolical plan and perhaps, it would never have come to fruition.

We have thus seen that the Jewish mission of lighting the world will not be fulfilled by those Jews whose sole concern is themselves. It will be carried out only by those who are actively involved and totally committed to continually provide relief for their brethren the world over. We must not allow history to repeat itself. We must not disappoint another group of Jews who are living in darkness. We cannot forsake the Jews living behind the Iron Curtain of Russian Communism.

We are aware of the shadow of death – the גיא צלמות – which hovers over our Russian brethren. We are informed of the Soviets' denying them any form of religious freedom. We read of the occupational discriminations imposed on them, and we painfully observe the Jews being deprived of their right to emigrate to the land of their ancestors – the Land of Israel – or to any other country of their choice. We see their suffering, we hear their cries, we feel their anguish – but what do we do? The choices are very clear. We can either sit idly by and allow the third largest Jewish center in the world to be completely wiped out – first religiously and then, inevitably, physically – or we can at last ignite the flame which will bring light and freedom to the Jews of Darkness.

We must be brutally honest with ourselves. What good is lighting a match if it will be immediately blown out? Is the initial kindling of a fire enough to guarantee its continued existence? Fuel must constantly be added to any fire in order for it to grow and remain burning.

We should on this Chanukah, the Festival of Lights and dedication, rededicate ourselves to the concerns of all our fellow Jews and especially our Russian brethren. We must read and study all that we can about their plight and must constantly be prepared to aid and assist them physically, financially, and spiritually.

Most important, the Soviet authorities must be made aware that world Jewry and especially American Jewry will never remain silent while the Jews of Russia continue to be persecuted and their requests to emigrate to Israel are denied. They must be convinced that the Jewish people will "Never Again" allow any segment of its people to be physically destroyed or robbed of its religious freedom.

Only in this way can we hope and pray that all Jewry, including the Russian Jews of Darkness, will be able to celebrate future Chanukahs with freedom and joy, honor and gladness. We will make certain that the words of the Torah in Parshas Bo, will apply to all Jews including our imprisoned Russian brethren:

וּלְכָל בְּנֵי יִשְׂרָאֵל הָיָה אוֹר בְּמוֹשְׁבֹתָם:

And all the children of Israel had light in their dwellings.

Let us resolve on this Chanukah to individually kindle our lights of freedom. By placing our flickering flames together, we will turn our tiny individual candles into a great torch which will certainly illuminate our darkened society and bring hope and freedom to all our people and to all mankind. Amen.

Postscript:

This chapter was written in 1973. Eighteen years later, on December 28, 1991, the Soviet Union was dissolved. In its place came the newly independent Russian State. In fact, even prior to its formal demise, because of the great pressure placed upon it by the free and western world, the Soviet Union began allowing their Jewish residents to emigrate to the country of their choice. In addition, the new Russian entity now allowed its remaining Jews to learn and study their Jewish heritage, Jewish history, and all other areas of *Yahadus*.

American Jewry finally learned its lesson. It led the way in both public and private protests and influence. At the end of the day, American Jewry, sparked by a number of totally dedicated and committed Orthodox Jews, was able to shine forth in one area of a very darkened and bleak world. RHG

26. After Amalek, Why Pretend?
Parshas Zachor

This week we observe the second in a series of four special Shabbasos which precede the Yom Tov of Pesach. The first Shabbos, which was marked two weeks ago, was called Shabbos Parshas Shekalim. Today, the Shabbos just prior to Purim is designated as Shabbos Parshas Zachor - the Shabbos of remembrance. In addition to the regular weekly Sedra, which this year is Parshas Tetzaveh, we read a special section from the *Maftir* of Parshas Ki Seitzei found in Sefer Devarim.

The Torah there states (25:17-19):

זָכוֹר אֵת אֲשֶׁר עָשָׂה לְךָ עֲמָלֵק בַּדֶּרֶךְ בְּצֵאתְכֶם מִמִּצְרָיִם: אֲשֶׁר קָרְךָ בַּדֶּרֶךְ וַיְזַנֵּב בְּךָ כָּל הַנֶּחֱשָׁלִים אַחֲרֶיךָ וְאַתָּה עָיֵף וְיָגֵעַ וְלֹא יָרֵא אֱלֹקִים: וְהָיָה בְּהָנִיחַ ה' אֱלֹקֶיךָ לְךָ מִכָּל אֹיְבֶיךָ מִסָּבִיב בָּאָרֶץ אֲשֶׁר ה' אֱלֹקֶיךָ נֹתֵן לְךָ נַחֲלָה לְרִשְׁתָּהּ תִּמְחֶה אֶת זֵכֶר עֲמָלֵק מִתַּחַת הַשָּׁמָיִם לֹא תִּשְׁכָּח:

Remember what Amalek did unto you by the way when you went out of Egypt. How he met you by the way and smote the hindmost of you, even all that were feeble behind you, when you were faint and weary; and they did not fear G-d. Therefore, it shall be, when Hashem your G-d will give you rest from all your enemies in the land which G-d will give you for an inheritance, that you shall wipe away the remembrance of Amalek from under the heavens, you shall not forget.

As we read this section, we are confronted with two major questions. First - what was the significance of this battle that it warranted a special Shabbos to be set aside to recall and remember that event? Second - why do we read this portion about war and killings specifically today, on the Shabbos just before Purim, our most joyous and festive Yom Tov?

With even a superficial reading of this Parsha and the battle with Amalek, we may conclude that this specific encounter was indeed most significant. It marked the first time that the Bnei Yisrael were attacked after *Yetzias Mitzrayim*, the Exodus from Egypt. Their victory over the Amalek nation boosted the Jews' morale and gave them a feeling of pride in defeating a well-armed and well-trained enemy.

However, this certainly was not the most militarily significant battle in *Chumash* or *Nach*. The Torah does not record how many Jewish casualties there were nor how many Amalekites were killed. The Torah simply says that "Yehoshua weakened the Amalekites" (Shemos 17:13). The wars against Midian and the Emori, recounted at the end of the Book of Bamidbar, or Yehoshua's wars against the Canaanites in Sefer Yehoshua appeared to be much more decisive. Those wars resulted in captured territory and served as the foundation of the First Jewish Commonwealth.

However, if we study the *pesukim* quite carefully, we would see why this battle was so significant and vital and why *Klal Yisrael* is commanded to never forget this incident. The attack of the ancient Amalekites on our ancestors set a precedent which has been continuing for nearly four thousand years. Our forebears were attacked for no apparent reason or motive. A similar fate, unfortunately, awaited our relatives in each and every generation since.

Am Yisrael had recently been redeemed from their two hundred and ten years of slavery and persecution in Egypt. They were tired and weary, oppressed and downtrodden. They had not yet been given the Torah, nor were they set apart from the other nations. They were not yet designated as the *Am HaNivchar* or the *Am Kadosh*, the Chosen People or the Holy Nation. They were, in essence, no different than any other people in the world.

In fact, *Chazal* tell us that while enslaved in Egypt, the Jews had almost sunk to the lowest levels of immorality as did the Egyptians. They had reached the 49th degree, the next to the basest level of *tumah*, of impurity. Their actions and deeds while in Egypt were

Parshas Zachor

so corrupt and degrading that Moshe Rabbeinu himself wondered if they would ever merit to be redeemed (Rashi to Shemos 2:14). These were the individuals whom Amalek attacked.

The Jews were drawn into battle and were singled out and attacked simply because they were Jews. This has at all times been the modus operandi of the world, both then and ever since. The world community has always perceived us as different and distinct. Jews have always been subjected to attacks, persecutions, and killings simply because they were Jewish. It may have begun with the Amalek attack in the *Midbar*, but it has unfortunately been going on for thousands of years.

It is a sad reality that even today, many Jews believe that they are guaranteed safety if they imitate non-Jewish behavior and pretend that they are not Jewish. They assume that if they will assimilate and intermarry, the hatred of the antisemites will diminish and even disappear. History, however, has taught us otherwise. We learn this lesson from the Amalek attack on the nearly assimilated Jews from Egypt. We also learn it from the story of Purim.

We are all familiar with the historical events of Chag Purim. Due to Mordechai and Esther's rise to prominence in the Persian Empire, they were able to convince King Achashveirosh of the plot of his Prime

Parshas Zachor

Minister Haman to murder and to destroy all the Jews in his kingdom. What is not so well known is the lack of religious observance of the Jews at that time.

Chazal in various sources, specifically in Meseches Megillah and in the Midrash Rabbah to Megilas Esther, tell us that the Jews of that day were almost completely assimilated. They attempted every possible means of winning the respect and admiration of the Persians. They mimicked their religious practices, they ate the same foods, drank the same wines, and many actually participated in the same immoral acts. The Jews forgot the Torah's command of זכור את אשר עשה לך עמלק – "Remember what Amalek did to you." They forgot that assimilation and emulation do not work. Therefore, they were punished and subjected to the wrath of Haman, an ignominious and very emblematic descendant of Amalek.

My friends, we see a very strong connection between Parshas Zachor and the Yom Tov of Purim. Assimilation or attempting to conceal one's religion will not help you hide from the clutches of the antisemite. We have seen this down through the ages. We have observed this most tragically in our own times in Nazi Germany, during the Shoah, the Holocaust. The first Jews that Hitler persecuted, discriminated against, and murdered were not the traditional and religious Jews of Poland, Russia, or Hungary. They

Parshas Zachor

were the Jews of Germany and Austria, perhaps the most assimilated Jews in the world. Many of these Jews considered themselves 100% German and 0% Jewish. They were amazed and shocked when they were isolated from the rest of their fellow Germans, singled out and discriminated against merely because they were Jews.

We therefore read this Parsha about Amalek on the Shabbos just before Purim, since the major messages of Purim and Parshas Zachor are indeed very similar. The Jew is commanded to never forget that by giving up his religion and trying to win over the antisemite, he will only succeed in fooling himself.

The *Netziv*, Rav Naftali Tzvi Yehudah Berlin, in his *peirush* on Torah, *Ha'amek Davar*, said that the only way to end hatred of the Jews for all time is not to emulate the non-Jew. Rather, it is to walk in the path of the *Ribono Shel Olam*, to obey and observe all of the Mitzvos in the Torah.

By being proud, dedicated, and committed Jews, we will receive love, honor, and respect from *HaKadosh Baruch Hu*. By living an ethical, moral, and distinctive Jewish life, we will become an אור לגוים, a light and a beacon to the non-Jewish world. We will thereby set an example for our non-Jewish friends and neighbors. By our actions and deeds, all mankind will one day accept and practice the principles of an ethical and moral life found in the Torah. Instead of war and hatred, we will be blessed with peace and harmony, love and respect. Let us do what we can.

27. Fasting and Feasting

Purim

Of all the Yom Tovim in the Jewish calendar, the observance of the festival of Purim is most perplexing. Purim, as well as Chanukah, are not Biblically ordained festivals. Both were declared important Rabbinic Yom Tovim by *Chazal*. Thus, both holidays are considered minor when compared to the Yomim Noraim and the *Shalosh Regalim*: Pesach, Shavuos, and Sukkos. In addition, if, we would compare the observance of Purim to that of Chanukkah, we would find that Chanukah is much more widely observed throughout the Jewish community than Purim. Why is this so? This is especially difficult to understand when we read the differences between these two Yom Tovim as cited by the first Gerrer Rebbe, Rav Yitzchak Meir Alter (1799-1866), one of the foremost Chassidic teachers.

The Rebbe explains why a special *seudah,* a feast, was ordained for Purim but not for Chanukkah. On Purim, he says, we celebrate the annulment of a royal decree which was aimed at the physical destruction of all the Jews living at that time under Persian dominion. The Jewish people were saved from a potential Holocaust and a cataclysmic disaster. We therefore are commanded to partake of a festive meal in order to provide us with physical pleasure.

In fulfilling this Mitzvah, we recall not only our specific salvation at that time, but we also remember the ongoing and continuous miraculous nature of our survival as a people and as a nation. This joyous feast attests to Hashem's constant care and concern for us.

On Chanukah, however, our people were rescued from a decree which was aimed at destroying the spiritual and religious fiber of Judaism. The Syrian Greeks did not initially intend to kill and murder each and every Jew. Their desire was primarily to forbid our ancestors from observing the spiritual aspects of *Yahadus*. Therefore, to commemorate our salvation from that spiritual danger which we faced, we recite Hallel and offer additional *berachos*. We light the Chanukah Menorah so as to be spiritually gratified and religiously uplifted. Unlike Purim, we are not commanded to partake of any festive meal, any special *seudah*. This Yom Tov does not commemorate our escape from any potential physical annihilation. As such, it is quite surprising that the holiday of Purim, which appears to be of a more physical nature, should be less observed than Chanukah, which is aimed at the more esoteric and spiritual parts of *Yahadus*.

This problem of the non-observance of Purim is especially difficult to comprehend when we read about some of the other *Halachos* and *Minhagim* which it involves. For instance, Jewish children traditionally dress up and masquerade as either one of the heroes or villains of the Purim story. It is a Mitzvah to send *Mishloach Manos* to our friends and neighbors, and we are obligated to give Tzedakah, *Matanos l'Evyonim* to those who are in need. In fact, I would venture a guess and say that other than before Pesach, more Tzedakah is distributed on Purim than on any other time during the year.

Yet, if we would inquire as to the number of Jews from the non-Orthodox camp who give *Mishloach Manos* or *Matanos l'Evyonim,* or the number of individuals who partake in the *Purim Seudah*, we would be extremely disappointed. We would also find that even fewer people attend shul to hear the mandatory reading of Megillas Esther, either at night or during the day, than on a regular Shabbos morning. Why then, if Purim is really such an important Yom Tov, is it so widely ignored?

The answer can be found by analyzing a statement by the *Tikunei Zohar* and reiterated by the *Arizal*. The Kabbalists maintain that the holiday of Purim is perhaps more difficult to observe than even the holiest day of the year, Yom Kippur. On Yom Kippur, the Day of Atonement, the Jew is commanded to fast, to abstain from food and water for over 24 hours. He must do *Teshuvah*; he must repent for the sins and transgressions which he committed during the past year. He must additionally petition *HaKadosh Baruch Hu*, to forgive him for those sins.

Yom Kippur is considered a major Yom Tov and undoubtedly the most solemn day in our calendar. True, one must concentrate on spiritually perfecting himself. However, it is not too difficult for one to set aside a single day during the year and refrain from enjoying any physical pleasures. It is perhaps for this reason that Yom Kippur is the most widely observed of all our Yom Tovim even among our least observant brethren.

Purim, on the other hand, is a Yom Tov when we must approach Hashem on both a spiritual as well as a physical plane. We are told to eat, drink, and be merry, but we are also commanded to remember the poor, the needy, the oppressed, the widowed, and the orphaned. We are told to make noise during the reading of Megillas Esther when the name of our archenemy, Haman, is mentioned. By contrast, we must be perfectly quiet and listen to every word of the Megillah. We are not only allowed to eat on Purim, but are commanded to partake of a special Purim meal, the *Seudas Purim*. We are commanded to accompany this meal by sanctifying Hashem and acknowledging His most unique and continuous role in our history.

Purim, therefore, is indeed, a very arduous and challenging Yom Tov to observe to the fullest. And that is why many of our non-Orthodox fellow Jews tend to forget it or completely ignore it. It is my hope and prayer that Jews the world over, regardless of their religious affiliation, will once again begin to understand, appreciate, and internalize the true significance and importance of this very special, beautiful, and religiously inspiring Yom Tov. Perhaps one day the words written towards the end of Megillas Esther may be said about our generation: ליהודים היתה אורה ושמחה וששון ויקר -"The Jews had light and gladness, joy and honor." Let us hope that Hashem's great salvation from the days of Mordechai and Esther will be once again be experienced by all our people. Amen.

28. Matzah: The Everlasting Memorial
Pesach

The Yom Tov of Pesach is filled with many Mitzvos, *Minhagim* and traditions. The Seder, the Haggadah, the Marror, and the four cups of wine are all very important aspects of this festival. The most celebrated and widely observed Mitzvah however, is the eating of the poor man's bread - the food of affliction - Matzah.

There are two historical reasons for partaking of this food. First, this was the bread which our forefathers ate while enslaved in Mitzrayim. On this Yom Tov, when we recall our ancestors' afflictions and hardships, their many long and arduous years of slavery and back-breaking servitude, we eat the foods which they consumed, Matzah.

In addition, when leaving Mitzrayim, our ancestors did not have sufficient time to allow their dough to rise, as free men usually do. They had to bake their breads quickly for Hashem took them out of Mitzrayim in great haste. On Pesach, we therefore recall the miracle of *Yetzias Mitzrayim*, the exodus from Egypt, as well as our past servitude; we eat Matzah to commemorate both of these two historical facts.

What is it about the Mitzvah of eating Matzah that makes it the most observed custom of Pesach? There are very few Jews, even those who do not observe any other Pesach tradition, who do not eat Matzah on this Yom Tov. Why is this Mitzvah so widely observed?

Chazal inform us that in the non-Jewish community, when a person performs great and noble acts or deeds of distinction and his contemporaries wish to perpetuate his memory, they erect a statue of bronze or stone as a memorial and remembrance. However, after a few decades, the original people either move or pass away, and the succeeding generations completely forget this very significant and important person and the actual reason for erecting this statue. After a century or two, this beautiful and magnificent structure crumbles and falls apart. With it, the memory of this outstanding individual dies forever.

Hashem wished to keep alive the memory of *Yetzias Mitzrayim*, the Exodus from Egypt, as well as our ancestors' 210 years of hardship and servitude. He did not choose a lifeless, inanimate statue which would eventually disintegrate, disappear, and be forgotten. Rather, He commanded *Am Yisrael* to partake of Matzah. As we eat this piece of unleavened bread, we annually recall the miraculous Divine intervention and liberation of the Jewish people from Egypt almost 3,500 years ago.

In addition, the eating of Matzah proclaims not only that the *Ribono shel Olam* revealed Himself to our fathers in Egypt and personally wrought their emancipation. It also indicates that this revelation and intervention continues to occur even today for each of us individually and for all of *Am Yisrael* collectively, in every age and in every generation.

The *Zohar HaKadosh* expands upon this and adds another thought. The *Zohar* introduces the main ideas and differences between *Chametz*, leavened bread, and Matzah, unleavened bread. The basic ingredients of both are flour and water. *Chametz* is distinguished from Matzah only by the introduction of yeast. Yeast gives *Chametz* a better shape, taste, and appearance. *Chametz* is larger than Matzah and appears to be fuller. However, the actual substance of both is the same. Matzah contains the same nourishment as *Chametz*.

It therefore seems that *Chametz*, leavened bread, actually deceives man, since it appears to be something which it is not. Matzah, on the other hand, is straightforward and is unpretentious, unassuming and natural.

Leaven or *Chametz*, or that which it represents, when it is introduced into the human heart, allegorically acts in the same manner. It inputs into individuals the negative characteristics of greed, pomposity, and glory seeking. Matzah, on the other hand, does not possess these characteristics.

Matzah is plain, real, and unassuming. He who lives his life according to what Matzah represents is authentic, down to earth, and genuine. He cares and is concerned not only for himself and his own gratification. He worries about and works for the benefit and wellbeing of his fellow man. That is one of the reasons why we place so much emphasis on the eating of Matzah.

Chazal say that when the *Bnei Yisrael* ate Matzah during שעבוד מצרים, they truly represented its core components. They were not greedy or envious of one another, nor did they seek honor and glory at the expense of their fellow Jews.

Those Jews who completed their required daily quota of producing bricks before the others did not go home and spend time with their families. Instead, they helped their fellow Jews until they too fulfilled their quota. In addition, many of these individuals who were appointed by the Egyptians to oversee the back-breaking work done by their brethren actually suffered on their behalf. They subjected themselves to beatings and other forms of punishment and torture, rather than testify against and inform on their weaker and more

Pesach

vulnerable fellow Jews who could not complete their required workload.

Yahadus, in Mitzrayim and ever since, has always stressed the equality of man and the development of the intrinsic and innate characteristics of all people. Pesach, more than on any of our other Yom Tovim, truly reflects the concept of freedom and independence as well as equality, fairness, and evenhandedness. The young and old, the rich and poor, the scholar and the uneducated, all sit down together at the same Seder. We recite and study the same Haggadah and consume the same foods. Each of us, at the start of our Seder say: כל דכפין ייתי ויכול כל דצריך יתיב ויפסח. "Let anyone who is hungry come and eat; let anyone who is in need come and celebrate Pesach with us."

This Pesach, as we sit at our Seder and eat Matzah, let us recall the historical reasons for the partaking of Matzah, this poor man's bread. Most importantly, let us remember the very significant role that Matzah plays in both the Pesach celebration and in the ongoing, miraculous, and glorious story of our people. I wish each of you a חג כשר ושמח – a happy and healthy Pesach.

29. דם ואש ותימרות עשן

Haggadah shel Pesach

The crux of the Magid section of the Haggadah shel Pesach is the expounding of the *pesukim* at the beginning of Parshas Ki Savo. The final *posuk* cited in the Haggadah reads (דברים כו:ח):

וַיּוֹצִאֵנוּ ה' מִמִּצְרַיִם בְּיָד חֲזָקָה וּבִזְרֹעַ נְטוּיָה וּבְמֹרָא גָּדֹל וּבְאֹתוֹת **וּבְמֹפְתִים**:

And Hashem took us out of Mitzrayim with 1) a strong hand, 2) an outstretched arm, 3) with great awe, 4) with signs, and 5) with wonders.

The Haggadah takes two tracks in understanding the five components of this *posuk*. According to the first explanation, the final phrase, "ובמפתים"-"and with wonders" is interpreted as referring to blood. This is backed up by a *posuk* in Yoel (ג:ג) which states:

וְנָתַתִּי **מוֹפְתִים** בַּשָּׁמַיִם וּבָאָרֶץ דָּם וָאֵשׁ וְתִימֲרוֹת עָשָׁן:

And I will place wonders in the Heaven and Earth – blood, fire, and pillars of smoke.

The Haggadah then provides an alternative understanding, explaining how this *posuk* in Ki Savo is a reference to the 10 Makos, with each of the five phrases referring to two Makos respectively.

Pesach

At our Seder this past Pesach (5784), my grandson Moshe – Moshe Pesach Nissan ben Aryeh Chaim HaKohen Gross – raised a very thought-provoking question. He wondered why the *posuk* from Yoel was used to explain the word ובמפתים if that *posuk* has nothing to do with *Yetzias Mitzrayim* (it is, in fact, referring to the war of Gog and Magog). Moreover, this explanation appears to put a specific emphasis on blood, which was only one of the Ten Makos. Finally, why do we remove some drops of wine from our *becher* when we recite the three-part phrase of דם ואש ותימרות עשן?

After much research, I came up with a few variant explanations. The first was given by Rav Yosef Elias in his commentary to the Haggadah. He asserts that this phrase, speaking about our future redemption in the days of Moshiach, was deliberately chosen. We are declaring that at that time we will witness great and extraordinary miracles, heretofore not seen with these three elements.

The Ritva says that the דם in this *posuk* does, in fact, refer to the first *makah* of *dam,* blood. The *posuk* is telling us that the blood that had once been the Nile River boiled like fire and pillars of smoke during that plague.

Why do we remove wine from our *bechers* when we recite these words? Rav Elias says that by doing so here as well as when we recite the עשר מכות, we are indicating that the אצבע אלקים, the finger of G-d, was what actually redeemed Bnei Yisrael from Mitzrayim. We use our fingers to acknowledge and commemorate that historic fact.

The Abarbanel says that we remove a small amount of wine when we recite this phrase as well as when we list the עשר מכות to demonstrate our empathy with the suffering and killing of the Egyptians. Although they deserved these punishments as retribution for their tyranny and torturous acts, nevertheless, they were G-d's creations, and we still show our compassion and concern for them.

I would like to suggest an alternative understanding which is that the phrase ובמופתים and its attendant explanation of blood-fire-pillars of smoke have nothing to do with the 10 Plagues or the suffering of the Egyptians. Rather, this is a reference to *Klal Yisrael* itself. The *Arizal* tells us that the Bnei Yisrael were on such a low spiritual level in Mitzrayim to the point that they sunk to the 49th level of *tumah*. As such, they needed some *zechusim,* some merits, to be worthy of being redeemed. Without these *zechusim* they would have remained permanent and perpetual slaves. Thus, Hashem commanded them to perform *bris milah* as well as to slaughter the *Korban Pesach* and to consume it. These two acts – wherein *dam*-blood was an integral aspect – gave Bnei Yisrael the merit and the favorable quality to be worthy of redemption.

In addition, throughout their forty-year sojourn in the Sinai Desert, they were constantly led by Hashem's cloud, which during the day manifested itself as a pillar of smoke while at night appeared as a column of fire. Therefore, the phrase דם ואש ותימרות עשן can be understood as an expression of our great thanks and appreciation to the *Ribono shel Olam* for His care and concern which He exhibited for *Am Yisrael* both during the times of antiquity and for what He consistently does for us on a constant and ongoing basis.

If this be the case, why then do we pour out some small amount of wine at this juncture of the *Seder*? Rav Yitzchak Sender in *The Commentator's Haggadah* says that by our actions, we are indicating that whatever טובה we receive from Hashem is only a small representation, a minute sample of Hashem's kindness and benevolence which He does for us. If we are indeed זוכה, Hashem will do much more for us. And for this and for all else that He does for us, we must be forever grateful. We must, at all times, demonstrate our appreciation and thanks.

30. Death Need Not Be Final
Yom HaShoah

Today, the 27th day of Nissan, is *Yom HaShoah v"haGevurah*, Holocaust Remembrance and Memorial Day. In 1951, the Knesset, the Israeli Parliament, designated this day to be one of commemoration and observance. Even though we are still in the month of Nissan, where public mourning is frowned upon, even though we are less than one week past the end of Pesach – our celebration of emancipation and freedom, renewal and rebirth – today, we remember the greatest tragedy ever to befall our people, the Shoah, the Holocaust.

From 1948 to 1951, the Knesset debated and discussed which day should be designated as a memorial to the Six Million Jews. Some wanted it held earlier in Nissan to coincide with the start of the Warsaw Ghetto Uprising. Others, not wishing to mar the celebration and observance of the Yom Tov of Pesach, advocated to have this day set in Iyar. Eventually, a compromise was reached with the 27th of Nissan, the anniversary of the end of the Warsaw Ghetto Uprising. This day was deemed most appropriate because enough time would have lapsed after the celebration of Pesach. It was also one week prior to the observance of Yom HaAtzmaut, Israel's Independence Day. According to many scholars, Yom HaAtzmaut, the rebirth of the modern State of Israel, is the fundamental and essential response to the Holocaust.

The Jewish people reacted to the total assault of death and destruction of European Jewry by an outpouring of life. Many survivors who lost everything during World War II came to the shores of the United States, or to the new and fledgling State of Israel, and rebuilt their lives. They established new families and continued to build and add to our glorious *Mesorah*, the Jewish chain of destiny. After 12 catastrophic and debilitating years, Jewish life was made precious again. Nothing more could profoundly capture the relationship between the Holocaust and the State of Israel than the designation of this day as Yom HaShoah. The birth of Medinat Yisrael is not a reward or merely a product of the Holocaust. It is a response; it is a reaffirmation of life.

It is also most instructive that on Shabbos Chol Hamoed Pesach, just about 10 days ago, we read in the Haftorah about the prophet Yechezkel's awesome and extraordinary vision of the Valley of Dry Bones. While, on the surface, this Haftorah is apparently quite contrary to the mood of exhilaration and celebration of Pesach, it is, in fact, most fitting. It has, I believe, great significance and serves as a bridge, a *gesher*, between Pesach and Yom HaShoah.

We read in the Haftorah that Hashem said to Yechezkel (37:3-6):

וַיֹּאמֶר אֵלַי בֶּן אָדָם הֲתִחְיֶינָה הָעֲצָמוֹת הָאֵלֶּה וָאֹמַר ה' אלקים אַתָּה יָדָעְתָּ: וַיֹּאמֶר אֵלַי הִנָּבֵא עַל הָעֲצָמוֹת הָאֵלֶּה וְאָמַרְתָּ אֲלֵיהֶם הָעֲצָמוֹת הַיְבֵשׁוֹת שִׁמְעוּ דְּבַר ה': כֹּה אָמַר ה' אלקים לָעֲצָמוֹת הָאֵלֶּה הִנֵּה אֲנִי מֵבִיא בָכֶם רוּחַ וִחְיִיתֶם: וְנָתַתִּי עֲלֵיכֶם גִּדִים וְהַעֲלֵתִי עֲלֵיכֶם בָּשָׂר וְקָרַמְתִּי עֲלֵיכֶם עוֹר וְנָתַתִּי בָכֶם רוּחַ וִחְיִיתֶם וִידַעְתֶּם כִּי אֲנִי ה':

"Son of Man, can these bones live?"
And I said, "My L-rd, Hashem, You know."
And He said to me, "Prophesy over these bones and say to them, 'O dry bones, hear the word of Hashem. Thus. says Hashem to these bones: Behold, I am bringing breath unto you and you shall live. And I will put sinews upon you and bring flesh upon you and I will cover you with skin. And I will breathe into you and you shall live; and you shall know that I am the L-rd."

The *Navi* goes on to recount how the bones joined together and became covered with flesh and skin. Yechezkel prophesied again and the spirit entered their bodies, whereupon they stood upon their feet. The *Navi* continues: (37: 11-13):

וַיֹּאמֶר אֵלַי בֶּן אָדָם הָעֲצָמוֹת הָאֵלֶּה כָּל בֵּית יִשְׂרָאֵל הֵמָּה הִנֵּה אֹמְרִים יָבְשׁוּ עַצְמוֹתֵינוּ וְאָבְדָה תִקְוָתֵנוּ נִגְזַרְנוּ לָנוּ: לָכֵן הִנָּבֵא וְאָמַרְתָּ אֲלֵיהֶם כֹּה אָמַר ה' אלקים הִנֵּה אֲנִי פֹתֵחַ אֶת

Yom HaShoah

קִבְרוֹתֵיכֶם וְהַעֲלֵיתִי אֶתְכֶם מִקִּבְרוֹתֵיכֶם עַמִּי וְהֵבֵאתִי אֶתְכֶם אֶל אַדְמַת יִשְׂרָאֵל: וִידַעְתֶּם כִּי אֲנִי ה' בְּפִתְחִי אֶת קִבְרוֹתֵיכֶם וּבְהַעֲלוֹתִי אֶתְכֶם מִקִּבְרוֹתֵיכֶם עַמִּי:

And He said to me: "Son of Man, these bones, they are the whole family of Israel. Behold, they say, 'Our bones have cried, and our hope is lost. We are doomed.' Therefore, prophesize and say to them: 'Thus says Hashem: Behold! I am opening your graves and I will raise you up from your graves, O my people, and I will bring you to the land of Israel. Then you shall know that I am the L-rd....'"

This initially gloomy scene, which became quite glorious, was Yechezkel's prophecy about the eventual revival of *Am Yisrael* as a nation, as a people, and as a sovereign State. We recall this *nevuah* on Pesach because that is the main Yom Tov which celebrates Israel's original redemption from their Egyptian servitude and oppression. According to our *mesorah*, our final redemption and the ultimate revival of the dead, תחיית המתים, will also occur during the Yom Tov of Pesach.

Yechezkel's vision was offered to a nation that had lost its independence and had become enslaved. They were bereft of their national sovereignty and freedom following the destruction of the first Beis HaMikdash by the Babylonians in 586 BCE. This vision helped revitalize the exiled Judeans, and it gave

Yom HaShoah

them *chizuk*, the strength and encouragement, to continue living their lives as Jews. This *nevuah* also imparted an additional and most essential message of Jewish belief – the concept that death, the cessation of life, is not absolute or final. The placing of a body into an open grave does not necessarily terminate life from a Jewish perspective. The revival of the dry bones demonstrated in a very forceful manner that there is hope in death. From a traditional Jewish vantage, there is even life in death – life in the sense of תחיית המתים, individual spiritual rebirth as well as national physical resurrection.

The Holocaust stands alone as the most horrendous and devastating event which occurred to *Klal Yisrael* since the destruction of the Second Beis HaMikdash. All felt that the future of Judaism was in doubt. To our mortal minds, it remains the most perplexing tragedy in all of Jewish history. As such, it may appear sacrilegious and an act of hubris to devote a single day to its memory. However, by memorializing the victims of the Holocaust on Yom HaShoah, we are declaring with complete faith that in the great plan of Hashem, this was apparently a necessary component in the חבלי משיח, the birth pangs of Mashiach. It serves as the beginning of the Messianic era which will ultimately conclude, hopefully in the very near future, with תחיית המתים, the resurrection of the dead.

The Jewish ideal of standing up to our enemies, regardless of whether they outnumber us two to one or fifty to one or even one hundred to one in terms of men and weapons, was not an innovation of our modern Israeli brethren in the IDF, the Israeli Defense Forces. They have a *mesorah*, a tradition, a heritage and an inheritance. This was taught to them by the heroic Jewish men and women of Europe. In almost every ghetto and in a number of concentration camps such as Treblinka, Auschwitz-Birkenau, Sobibor, and others, Jews by the thousands rebelled and revolted against their mighty Nazi tormentors. They did not give any thought to the fact that were greatly outnumbered and under-armed. In addition, all too many of them were starving and were stricken with illness and disease.

And what about the millions of our fellow Jews who went to their deaths strong, erect, and brave? They did so without even begging or pleading to be spared. On the other hand, the millions of captured Russian soldiers begged for and groveled for clemency and mercy before many thousands of them were slaughtered.

These wonderful and exceptional people are our real heroes. They smiled and looked up to heaven and said שמע ישראל and sang the famous, heartrending

Yom HaShoah

declaration of אֲנִי מַאֲמִין. "I believe in G-d. I believe in the destiny of Israel. I believe in the very quick arrival of the Mashiach. If I must, I will go to my death willingly in order to sanctify and glorify the holy and revered name of Hashem." This, my friends, was true bravery. This was, indeed, death with dignity.

However, it was on Pesach, 1943, that the most remarkable event during the entire Holocaust occurred – the start of the Warsaw Ghetto Uprising. With homemade, crude, and quite primitive weapons, the few thousand remaining Jews of this most famous ghetto battled the Nazi beasts and held them at bay for almost a month. A new respect filled the world for these fighters who wished only to prove that the Jew can fight valiantly and bravely if only given the chance.

It was on Pesach, my friends, the holiday of freedom and independence, that these precious and pure people began the modern-day recreation of the Exodus. These heroes, who did nothing to deserve their tortuous experience except to be born Jewish, were the very ones who began putting sinews, flesh, and skin on these dry, old, and so very weak bones.

Hashem challenges Yechezkel (ibid. 37:3):
וַיֹּאמֶר אֵלַי בֶּן אָדָם הֲתִחְיֶינָה הָעֲצָמוֹת הָאֵלֶּה ...
"Will these bones live?"

Our קְדוֹשִׁים וּטְהוֹרִים, our holy and pure brothers and sisters responded with an unequivocal "Yes! We will, indeed, survive! For whether we live or die, our ideals, our aspirations, our religion, and our hope in the very future of *Yahadus* will live on, survive, and will never perish."

Unfortunately, the insurrection began when only a very small segment of the Jewish community remained alive in the Warsaw Ghetto. These Jews discovered that hundreds of thousands of their precious brethren who were taken from the ghetto were not, in fact, resettled to another area of Poland as the Nazis claimed. Instead, they were all systematically and ruthlessly murdered in Treblinka and in other death camps. The few thousand surviving Jews concluded that they must take action. They knew that doing nothing would certainly lead to their deaths. They hoped that by their uprising, they would inflict a great price on the Nazis. They were hopefully optimistic that by their revolt, the deportations would perhaps cease, or, at the very least, slow down in pace. In any event, they knew that by their actions they would at least send a message of encouragement to Jews in other ghettos and concentration camps to begin and start their own insurrections.

While their heroic actions did not prevent the liquidation of the Warsaw Ghetto, nor did it slow down the deportations, it did indeed inflict a significant military and psychological price on the purportedly

Yom HaShoah

invincible German war machine. It also made a very strong impression upon the remaining European Jews as well as Jews throughout the world. In that sense, their sacrifice could be viewed as an overwhelming and monumental success.

It is no accident, my friends, that just three years after the last concentration camps were liberated in 1945, the next step towards the final redemption, the אתחלתא דגאולה, occurred. The prophecy of Yechezkel (37:12) came true:

לָכֵן הִנָּבֵא וְאָמַרְתָּ אֲלֵיהֶם כֹּה אָמַר ה' אלקים הִנֵּה אֲנִי פֹתֵחַ אֶת קִבְרוֹתֵיכֶם וְהַעֲלֵיתִי אֶתְכֶם מִקִּבְרוֹתֵיכֶם עַמִּי וְהֵבֵאתִי אֶתְכֶם אֶל אַדְמַת יִשְׂרָאֵל:

"Behold, I am opening your graves and I will raise you up. I will bring you into the land of Israel."

In so short a span of time, this prophecy of the creation of the modern State of Israel came true. The spirit of these heroes of the Holocaust lived on and continues to live on in the lives of our brethren in Medinat Yisrael.

Last week, on אחרון של פסח, as we do on three other occasions during the year, we memorialized the souls of our departed relatives by the recitation of the Yizkor service. We said, as did the prophet Yechezkel, that we will put our spirit in them. We can by our positive actions and our fulfillment of the Mitzvos fuse life into their dry bones. We can cause them to live again through our lives. By dedicating our lives to Torah and Mitzvos, we assure them that they will never have completely died. They will live on through our deeds and actions, through our Mitzvos between man and Hashem as well as with our Mitzvos between man and his fellow man.

On this day of memorial and observance, on this very special day of Yom HaShoah, we can do the same for our Six Million brothers and sisters who were so barbarically and systematically murdered. If we can alter our lives just a bit, if we can become better Jews and better human beings, if we never forget our holy and precious martyrs, then they too can spiritually remain alive. We can make sure that their deaths were only in body but that their spirit will continue to invigorate us until the time of תחיית המתים. Through our deeds of צדקה and מעשים טובים, through our constant devotion and dedication to *HaKadosh Baruch Hu* and to Torah and Mitzvos, we will guarantee that *Am Yisrael,* Eretz Yisrael, and *Toras Yisrael* will continue to live, grow, and thrive. The Six Million will remain alive in our hearts and in our souls and we will never ever forget them. Amen.

31. Rebbe Akiva's Mesorah

Lag Ba'Omer, 1972

This week, two very important events on the Jewish calendar are being observed and commemorated. One event is an old, established, and very traditional semi-Yom Tov which has occupied a great deal of our *Mesorah* for thousands of years. The other is not a Yom Tov at all. Rather, it is a day which our current political Jewish leaders have designated as a specific time to remind Jews throughout the world of a great contemporary cause. With a mere superficial perusal, glancing at each of these events, we would think them to be very dissimilar and almost totally unrelated. However, close observation shows that they indeed have a great deal in common.

On Sunday, April 30, 1972, many Jews throughout the United States will gather in their individual communities, both large and small, to demonstrate their care and concern for the plight of their Russian brethren. That day has been designated as "Soviet Jewry Solidarity Day." The purpose of these planned rallies and demonstrations is to send two very special messages to President Nixon before his

departure in May for the Moscow Summit Conference. They are:
1. American Jews are very much concerned about their fellow Jews in the Soviet Union. We pray for them and are prepared to do whatever we can to help alleviate their plight.
2. We urge the president to help intercede on their behalf. We implore him to speak to the Soviet leaders to provide their Jewish citizens with the right to practice their religion as well as to emigrate to any country in which they choose to reside.

In addition, this coming Tuesday, May 2, we celebrate Lag Ba'Omer, the thirty-third day of the counting of the *Omer*. The *Shulchan Aruch* states (תצג:א):

נוהגים שלא לישא אשה בין פסח לעצרת עד ל"ג לעומר, מפני שבאותו זמן מתו תלמידי רבי עקיבא.

The forty-nine-day period between Pesach and Shavuos is observed as a period of *aveilus*, mourning. The reason which the *Shulchan Aruch* gives is that during the second century C.E., thousands of the finest students of the great sage, Rebbe Akiva, perished because of a mysterious plague. *Chazal* tell us that their affliction came about because they fell short in their adherence to one of the most important Mitzvos.

Their own Rebbe famously declared: ואהבת לרעך כמוך זה כלל גדול בתורה – *"Love your neighbor like yourself—this is a great principle of the Torah."* Although these students were great *Talmidei Chachamim*, they showed no real respect or concern for one another.

However, for one day, on the thirty-third day of the Omer, Lag Ba'Omer, they stopped dying. During the *Omer* period – the exact duration is subject to various customs – we do not take haircuts or participate in weddings. On Lag Ba'Omer, however, the *aveilus* period is suspended and a sense of joy pervades the Jewish people.

On the surface, it may appear that Lag Ba'Omer and Soviet Jewry Solidarity Day have almost nothing in common. If, however, we were to look a little closer, if we examine and study these two observances very carefully, we would find a common denominator, as there is a clear and definite link between these two events.

The central figure of the entire *Omer* observance is Rebbe Akiva. He was, in fact, the greatest Rav and scholar of his time. He exerted more influence on the development and growth of תורה שבעל פה, the oral tradition, the continuity of our *Mesorah*, than any other individual. He was also the religious leader and the most significant force behind the Jews' second insurrection against Rome in 133 C.E., the Bar Kochba Revolt.

Following the Roman destruction of the Second Commonwealth of Israel in 70 C.E. and, concurrently, the *Churban Bais HaMikdash* in Yerushalayim, our ancestors immersed themselves completely in the study of Torah. From the great new center of learning in Yavneh to smaller outlying areas throughout Eretz Yisrael, *Am Yisrael* spent their time fulfilling the Torah's command of ללמוד וללמד לשמור ולעשות: "to study, to teach, to adhere, and to observe all the *halachos* of the Torah. By their actions and deeds, they were able to preserve and maintain Yiddishkeit in the only possible way.

Unfortunately, after a number of years, the Romans changed their attitude. Soon after his accession to the throne, Emperor Hadrian instituted a number of decrees which forbade the Jews from observing much of Jewish law. Mostly, he demanded that they refrain from any further study of Torah on penalty of death. Yet, despite these hardships and threats, Rebbe Akiva and his colleagues continued to study and teach the Torah and encouraged their students to do the same. The Gemara in Meseches Berachos (61b) explains how Rabbi Akiva responded when he was asked why he was risking his life by studying the Torah.

Lag Ba'Omer

The Gemara says:

תנו רבנן: פעם אחת גזרה מלכות הרשעה שלא יעסקו ישראל בתורה, בא פפוס בן יהודה ומצאו לרבי עקיבא שהיה מקהיל קהלות ברבים ועוסק בתורה. אמר ליה: עקיבא, אי אתה מתירא מפני מלכות? אמר לו: אמשול לך משל, למה הדבר דומה - לשועל שהיה מהלך על גב הנהר, וראה דגים שהיו מתקבצים ממקום למקום, אמר להם: מפני מה אתם בורחים? אמרו לו: מפני רשתות שמביאין עלינו בני אדם. אמר להם: רצונכם שתעלו ליבשה, ונדור אני ואתם כשם שדרו אבותי עם אבותיכם? אמרו לו: אתה הוא שאומרים עליך פקח שבחיות? לא פקח אתה, אלא טפש אתה! ומה במקום חיותנו אנו מתיראין, במקום מיתתנו על אחת כמה וכמה! אף אנחנו, עכשיו שאנו יושבים ועוסקים בתורה, שכתוב בה כי הוא חייך וארך ימיך - כך, אם אנו הולכים ומבטלים ממנה - על אחת כמה וכמה.

Once, the wicked Roman regime decreed that the Jewish people may not engage in the study of Torah. Papus ben Yehudah came and found Rebbe Akiva publicly teaching Torah. Papus said to him, "Akiva: are you not afraid of the Roman regime? Why do you continue teaching Torah publicly?"

Rebbe Akiva responded to him: "I will give you a parable which will explain my actions. To what is this comparable? It is compared to a fox who was walking along the banks of a river. He noticed a group of fish who were jumping from one section of the river to another. The fox asked the fish, 'From what are you running away?' They responded that they were attempting to escape from the nets that the fishermen were bringing in order to catch them. The fox then said, 'Perhaps, you should come on dry land where you can escape from their nets and we will live together just as our ancestors dwelled together?'

"*The fish responded, 'Are you the one whom they describe as the cleverest of all the animals? It seems that you are not very clever at all. Indeed, you are a fool. If we fear for our lives in the habitat that sustains our life (the water), should we not be afraid even more of the habitat that will surely induce death to us?'*"

Rebbe Akiva concluded: "If now, as we sit and study Torah, about which it is written: 'For it is your life and the length of your days," we are nonetheless threatened by such dangers, then if we would proceed to absent ourselves from the study of Torah, we would be endangered all the more so."

In essence, Rebbe Akiva compared the lives of all of *Am Yisrael* to the fish in the sea. Fish require water in order to survive, and without it they would certainly die. The same is true for the Jewish people. In order for them to spiritually stay alive and be vibrant, they must be totally immersed in the study of Torah, for if not, they would die. Rebbe Akiva was so committed to this idea that he eventually gave his life and was mercilessly tortured by the Romans so that the study of Torah could be continued.

Lag Ba'Omer

The recent political reassertion of the Soviet Jews was also due primarily to religious principles. For fifty years they were forbidden from practicing their religion. They were not allowed to study Torah and they were not permitted to publicly daven. They were forbidden from preforming any Mitzvos such as making a Bris Milah, baking Matzos, or even placing a Mezuzah on their doorposts. They certainly were not allowed to immigrate to the State of Israel or even to any other country of their choice.

However, immediately following Israel's dramatic and overwhelming victory in the 1967 Six Day War, the Russian Jews were suddenly infused with tremendous courage and fortitude. They began to demand their religious rights. They wanted to be given all the privileges accorded other minority groups as well as the right to immigrate to Israel where they could faithfully observe and practice their religion. It was thus the desire to study the Torah and to practice Jewish law which, more than anything else, gave these Jews (like Rebbe Akiva and his followers centuries before) the courage and determination to fight for their rights.

My dear friends, whether it be remembering our brothers and sisters in Russia in our *Tefillos* or by contributing to organizations which help them emigrate from Russia, we must always have them in our minds. First and foremost, however, should be to make this cause a very special and important part of our lives. We must internalize and keep the plight of our Russian brethren embedded in our hearts. We should then spread the message and try to influence our non-Jewish friends and neighbors about their troubles and their very perilous predicament.

If we can, even in some small way, help bring world opinion to the side of our persecuted brothers and sisters, if the world community would ardently apply pressure on the Soviet leadership to "Let Our People Go," then we will then have fulfilled our task. We will have played a significant role in helping our brethren to be able to observe their Judaism, to study the Torah, and eventually, to be able to immigrate to Eretz Yisrael where they will be able to properly observe all the Mitzvos of the Torah. Let us do what we can to help fuse the observance of Lag Ba'Omer with this very important present-day cause.

32. Celebrating a New Beginning: Lag Ba'Omer- A New Perspective

The Torah in Sefer Vayikra, Parshas Emor (23:9-10) says:

וַיְדַבֵּר ה' אֶל מֹשֶׁה לֵּאמֹר: דַּבֵּר אֶל בְּנֵי יִשְׂרָאֵל וְאָמַרְתָּ אֲלֵהֶם כִּי תָבֹאוּ אֶל הָאָרֶץ אֲשֶׁר אֲנִי נֹתֵן לָכֶם וּקְצַרְתֶּם אֶת קְצִירָהּ וַהֲבֵאתֶם אֶת עֹמֶר רֵאשִׁית קְצִירְכֶם אֶל הַכֹּהֵן:

And Hashem said to Moshe saying: speak to the Bnei Yisrael and say to them: When you come to the land that I will give you and you reap its harvest, you shall bring an Omer of the first of your harvest to the Kohen.

A few *pesukim* later (23:15-16), the Torah continues:

וּסְפַרְתֶּם לָכֶם מִמָּחֳרַת הַשַּׁבָּת מִיּוֹם הֲבִיאֲכֶם אֶת עֹמֶר הַתְּנוּפָה שֶׁבַע שַׁבָּתוֹת תְּמִימֹת תִּהְיֶינָה: עַד מִמָּחֳרַת הַשַּׁבָּת הַשְּׁבִיעִת תִּסְפְּרוּ חֲמִשִּׁים יוֹם וְהִקְרַבְתֶּם מִנְחָה חֲדָשָׁה לַה':

You shall count for yourselves from the day after the Day of Rest (Pesach), from the day on which you will bring the Omer wave offering – seven complete weeks they shall be until the day after the seventh week; you shall count fifty days. And you shall bring a new meal offering to Hashem.

Chazal tell is that *Yetzias Mitzrayim*, the redemption, the Exodus of *Am Yisrael* from their 210 years of slavery and oppression, was not an end in itself. It was merely the initial, first step in the transfiguration of the descendants of the sons of Yaakov. They were transformed from twelve diverse and separate tribes into one homogeneous, like-minded and similar nation totally dedicated and committed to the *Ribono shel Olam*. They became a people willing and able to accept the Torah at Har Sinai. This momentous and once-in-a-lifetime event occurred on Shavous, just a mere seven weeks after their Exodus from Egypt.

Each generation of Jews, for the past 3,300 years, has reenacted this event. Beginning on the second night of Pesach, we begin to count the Omer. This is known as *Sefiras HaOmer*. We continue this process for 49 days until we reach the beautiful and wonderful Yom Tov of Shavous. We then annually recall and reenact *Ma'amad Har Sinai* by learning and studying Torah.

However, around 2,000 years ago, a monumental and historical event occurred. During the second century C.E., during the period that the Roman Emperor Hadrian ruled over Eretz Yisrael, an unprecedented tragedy occurred. One year, in approximately 135 C.E, for a period of thirty-three days, beginning on Pesach, all 24,000 *talmidim* of the great and incomparable Rebbe Akiva died. Some of our scholars[2] maintain that since Rebbe Akiva was the spiritual and religious leader and guide to the Bar Kochba revolt, naturally, his students would follow his lead. They joined the army and went to war. Unfortunately, they were all killed in battle by the Roman Legion. Other *meforshim*, especially those based on the Gemara (Yevamos 62b), feel that these great *Talmidei Chachamim*, they who held the key to the very future of our *Mesorah*, all died a mysterious death. The Gemara says that they perished because they did not give proper respect, *kavod,* to one another. The Midrash (cited by the great Provencal *Rishon*, Rabbeinu Avraham min HaHar) says that their deaths continued on a daily basis until the 33rd day of the Omer. On that day, they ceased dying.

The *Gaonim* determined that all of Bnei Yisrael should be in a state of mourning during this period between Pesach and Shavuos. They mandated that no weddings should take place. In addition, haircutting and shaving is forbidden. In essence, a pale of sorrow and mournfulness surrounds *Am Yisrael* during this time frame. The *Avudraham* states that this period of mourning should last only until the 33rd day of the Omer, in accordance with the Midrash. However, on the thirty-third day of the Omer, which has become

---

[2] See, for example, *Kisvei Rav Yosef Eliyahu Henkin vol. II Siman 107.*

known as Lag Ba'Omer, which corresponds to the 18th day of the month of Iyar, all areas of mourning cease. The *Rema* (493:2) says that on this day, מרבים בו קצת שמחה, "Some form of joy is practiced." This is because we celebrate the fact that the death of these great *Tzadikim* ceased on this day.[3]

This has been the accepted and normative explanation of Lag Ba'Omer for centuries. However, I have recently come across another idea, an additional thought, which places our observance of this semi-Yom Tov in a new and fascinating light. I saw a beautiful *d'var Torah* written by Rabbi Shmuel Silber of Baltimore, Maryland.

As mentioned, Rebbe Akiva's many *talmidim* died during the *Sefirah* period, and on Lag Ba'Omer they stopped dying. Therefore, we have a semi-Yom Tov. The question is asked: why do we celebrate the cessation of their dying? The dying stopped because there were no other students left to die. If this be the case, why do we celebrate? Shouldn't Lag Ba'Omer be instead a day of introspection, soul searching, and contemplation. Rabbi Silber sources the *Pri Chadash*, a 17th century *peirush* on the Shulchan Aruch. He explains the meaning and significance of Lag Ba'Omer with a new and completely different perspective.

---

[3] This is based on the *Meiri* to Yevamos 62b.

The *Pri Chadash* says that we celebrate Lag Ba'Omer because, specifically on this day, there was a new beginning, a new initiative. It was on Lag Ba'Omer, on the very day that the last of his *talmidim* died, that Rebbe Akiva decided to travel and find new talmidim. Even after losing all that he worked and toiled for so many years, Rebbe Akiva did not give up. He did not throw in the towel. He was not מְיָאֵשׁ. He felt that there was no time to cry and mourn. Rather, he looked to the future. He wanted to save and preserve the *Mesorah*.

He therefore travelled to the south of Eretz Yisrael and chose five great and brilliant individuals who now would be the future of Yiddishkeit. He chose Rebbe Meir, Rebbe Yehuda, Rebbe Yosi, Rebbe Elazar ben Shamua and Rebbe Shimon bar Yochai who eventually became his Talmid *muvhak*, his prized and special student. These five *talmidim* were to take the place of the 24,000 students who died. They would eventually produce the spark which would ignite the world of Torah. Inspired by their great Rebbe, Rebbe Akiva, they would continue teaching and imparting Torah and spreading our holy *Mesorah* to future generations.

Therefore, Lag Ba'Omer is a day of "קְצָת שִׂמְחָה" a day of a small amount of joy. Although we continue mourning for the great *Tzadikim* who perished during this period, along with the hundreds of thousands who lost their lives during the Bar Kochba revolt, Lag Ba'Omer is, nevertheless, a time to rejoice and be happy. For it was on this day that the future of Yiddishkeit and our holy *Mesorah* was preserved. A new beginning, a new opportunity, was established. Rebbe Akiva's transmittal of the Torah to his new students guaranteed that the *Mesorah* would be passed down from *Rebbe* to *Talmid*, from father to son. This has remained the case for nearly two thousand years. Therefore, Lag Ba'Omer is our celebration of a new and a great day, a new beginning.

I would like to end by quoting a small part of Rabbi Shmuel Silber's *dvar Torah*:

> Lag Ba'Omer is the day on which we confront our challenges and recognize that for many of us, life is filled with much adversity and difficulty. Yet, it is on this sacred day that we pledge to be like our ancestor, Rabbi Akiva, and find a way to regroup and rebuild. This is the little bit of *simcha* of Lag Ba'Omer. Lag Ba'Omer is a reminder that we can always start again.

33. G-d's Gifts and Israel's Responsibility
Yom Yerushalayim

This week, on the 28th day of Iyar, we will be observing Yom Yerushalayim, the day which commemorates the capture of the old city of Jerusalem by the Israeli Defense Forces in the Six Day War of 1967. With acts of heroism and dedication, the עיר דוד, the City of David, was reunited and placed in Jewish hands and control for the first time in almost 2,000 years. That event, I believe, more than anything else since the establishment of the State of Israel, provided our people with the optimism, determination, and the wherewithal to withstand all our enemies and face the future squarely and bravely. For Jerusalem, my friends, is not just another piece of land. It is not merely another chunk of territory which is here today and gone tomorrow. It is not an area which either we control or our enemies have dominion over. Rather, it is the cornerstone, the focal point of Jewish life.

Yerushalayim represents all that is sacred and precious to us. It was and remains one of the basic factors which has kept us alive as a nation and as a people. Twice a year, on Yom Kippur and Pesach, the

Yom Yerushalayim

holidays which represent, respectively, the spiritual and physical redemption of the Jewish people, we boldly and proudly recite the words:

"לשנה הבאה בירושלים"

"Next year in Jerusalem!"

After every meal, we mourn along with the Judean captives, who chanted the immortal words along the banks of Babylon:

שָׁם יָשַׁבְנוּ גַּם בָּכִינוּ בְּזָכְרֵנוּ אֶת צִיּוֹן.

"There we sat and cried as we remembered Zion."

We recite along with Dovid HaMelech in *Tehillim*:

אִם אֶשְׁכָּחֵךְ יְרוּשָׁלָם תִּשְׁכַּח יְמִינִי:

"If I forget thee, O Jerusalem, may my right hand forget it's cunning."

Wherever we were, whatever continent or country of oppression we found ourselves in, we cried along with Rav Yehudah Halevi:

לִבִּי בַּמִּזְרָח וַאֲנִי בְּסוֹף מַעֲרָב.

"I may be in the West, but my soul is in the East."

And finally, we continually remember that *Am Yisrael, Toras Yisrael,* and *Eretz Yisrael* are one. The future of the Jewish people is linked to these great spiritual ideals. For without Torah, we are a nation of heathens. Without the sanctity of the land of Israel, we are not a people. Thus, we recite at least four times a week:

כִּי מִצִּיּוֹן תֵּצֵא תוֹרָה וּדְבַר ה' מִירוּשָׁלָם:

"For out of Zion shall go forth the Torah and the word of G-d from Jerusalem."

I ask you, my friends: can a non-Jew truly understand what Eretz Yisrael, and especially the sacred city of Yerushalayim, means to a Jew? Can he conceptualize that for almost 2,000 years, the Jew has constantly longed to return to the land which G-d promised to his forefathers? No substitute was ever good enough. Argentina was unacceptable. Uganda was rejected. Russia was never even considered. Every nation and every people must be in the land of their own in order to remain alive, vibrant, and strong. If this be the case with all other people whose ties with their country are purely nationalistic, this is certainly true with our people. Jerusalem was never meant to be solely the seat of the government of Israel. Rather, it is the home of Hashem, the spiritual center of our people.

Would Catholics survive without the city of Rome? Could the Moslems exist without Mecca? Would anyone ever think of denying them their religious centers? Of course not. Only the Jews are denied control of and access to their spiritual capital. This concept of the *Kedusha*, the spiritual and moral uplifting of Yerushalayim for the Jewish nation, is an idea which the average non-Jew cannot even conceive of. Thus, he is not convinced of Israel's need to control her capital.

Can a non-Jew understand the Gemara in *Meseches Taanis* (5a) in which Hashem declared that He will not enter the heavenly Jerusalem, the ירושלים של מעלה, until He has entered the Jerusalem on earth, the ירושלים של מטה? Unless G-d is welcomed into Jerusalem on earth by the world political powers as well as by our actions, He will not enter the heavenly Yerushalayim. G-d's refusal to enter the Yerushalayim of above is a painful indication of the absence of His presence and influence over world affairs.

This idea cannot be truly understood by one who is not Jewish. It cannot be internalized by one who has not immersed himself in the richness of Jewish tradition and Jewish values. However, it can be understood by Jews. At the present time, my concern is not so much with the non-Jewish world and their hypocrisy and warped sense of morality; rather, it is with our fellow Jews and their lack of gratitude to Hashem.

For 2,000 years, we wept and cried bitterly until our tear ducts were dried up. We beseeched G-d to grant us our ancient homeland. We prayed to Hashem to bring us back to the land of our fathers. On every

Yom Yerushalayim

Yom Tov Mussaf, we repeatedly bemoan to G-d that as observant, faithful, and committed as we have been, we were only able to partially fulfill the duties of our faith. If only we could see Zion, if only we could possess Yerushalayim, how much more faithfully and completely would we be able to abide by all the laws of the Torah that are applicable only in the Land of Israel.

Hashem has now wrought miracles for us. He has delivered our people from the clutches of the enemy. He has provided us with our ancient homeland and given us complete control and jurisdiction over our most holy and sacred city. We now must ask ourselves one basic and elementary question. Have we lived up to our part of the agreement?

In the Hallel which we recite on all the Yom Tovim and which many say on Yom Yerushalayim, we read (Tehillim 116):

מָה אָשִׁיב לַה' כָּל תַּגְמוּלוֹהִי עָלָי:
"What can I tender to G-d for all His kind acts towards me?"

כּוֹס יְשׁוּעוֹת אֶשָּׂא וּבְשֵׁם ה' אֶקְרָא:
"A cup of salvations shall I raise, and I will call upon the name of the L-rd."

נְדָרַי לַה' אֲשַׁלֵּם נֶגְדָה נָּא לְכָל עַמּוֹ:
"My vows to G-d will I now pay before His entire nation."

After observing the great miracles wrought for our people by *HaKadosh Baruch Hu* in 1967, we of course celebrated. We rejoiced and we paraded. We lifted up our cup of deliverance for the entire world to see. There never was as much *simcha,* real and genuine joy and happiness in the Jewish community as there was during those first weeks and months following the reunification of Jerusalem. We sang and danced and pointed with pride to our great military victory.

We also called upon the name of the *Ribono shel Olam* by offering our thanks and appreciation. We went to our respective shuls and davened. We praised G-d for being with us and for providing us with this miraculous gift. Hundreds of thousands of Jews from all walks of life throughout the world made their way to the Kotel, the Western Wall, the last remnant of the second Beis HaMikdash, our holiest possession. During the first weeks after the war, there was a great upsurge of religious fervor. People who had been brought up on atheistic Kibbutzim wished to put on Tefillin and daven at the Kotel.

There was a feeling that we were about to witness the coming of Moshiach. There was love between Jews. Religious observance, it seemed, was about to be practiced by all segments of *Klal Yisrael*. Israel, the people and the state, was strong and

Yom Yerushalayim

powerful. However, that moment of exuberance and jubilation did not last for too long.

Somehow, after only a little less than a year after Israel's glorious victory, the zeal, the fervor, and the complete allegiance to Hashem waned. Instead of chanting ישראל בטח בה', *"Israel trusts and believes in Hashem,"* the new mantra became, ישראל בטח בצה"ל, *"The people of Israel put their complete faith and trust in the Israeli Defense Forces."*

My dear friends, when faith and religious belief in God's providence is replaced by man's belief in his own power and strength, כחי ועוצם ידי, then all progress and growth is completely lost. When that occurs, the happiness and joy which accompanied the aftereffects of the מלחמת ששת הימים is transformed into the cries, bitterness, and sadness of the מלחמת יום הכיפורים.

Indeed, the question is much deeper and even more profound. Has the religious commitment and spiritual deeds of our Israeli brethren who had not previously been observant increased because of our receiving the gift of Jerusalem? Are they still forever making excuses as to why they cannot be Shomer Shabbos and why real, genuine, and authentic Judaism is archaic and outdated? The answer, my friends, is quite obvious. Instead of increasing their religiosity and commitment, it has slowly dwindled to almost where it was previously. Some even dare question the omnipotence of G-d, exclaiming, "Where is G-d when we need him?" "Why did G-d let us down?" The non-Jew may not understand the Aggadah in the Gemara in Taanis, but we should. The fact is that because of the immoral, unethical, and spiritual deterioration of our society, G-d is unwelcome in the earthly Jerusalem. Because Jerusalem has not really become Yerushalayim, because the kind of Jewish behavior that Jerusalem merits is not there, G-d will not enter the heavenly Yerushalayim. And His not entering into the Yerushalayim of above is clearly indicated by the absence of His overt presence and influence over the affairs of the world.

The Torah in Devarim (31) says:

וְאָנֹכִי הַסְתֵּר אַסְתִּיר פָּנַי בַּיּוֹם הַהוּא...

"On that day, I will surely hide My face."

Thus, our fate, and even the actions of Hashem, if you wish, are determined by man's actions. This idea is described in very powerful terms in the Torah in Sefer Vayikra, Parshas Bechukosai. The Torah there describes the rewards that Israel will receive for observing the Mitzvos. In a rather lengthy chapter, it then details the horrors and catastrophes which will occur if Israel disregards G-d's laws. The *Sedra* begins:

אִם בְּחֻקֹּתַי תֵּלֵכוּ וְאֶת מִצְוֹתַי תִּשְׁמְרוּ וַעֲשִׂיתֶם אֹתָם:

Yom Yerushalayim

"If you will walk in My ordinances and keep My commandments, and do them."

The *Sedra* continues with a promise that by fulfilling the Mitzvos, the Jewish people will be greatly rewarded – economically, physically, and politically. There will be sufficient wealth for all. *Am Yisrael* will achieve great military success, and we will live in peace externally as well as internally.

Rashi, commenting on the words "אם בחוקתי תלכו" quotes the Sifri: שתהיו עמלים בתורה. This is an admonition that we should study Torah with great zeal and intensity.

The key and most important element in serving Hashem is through the study of Torah and all the Mitzvos contained therein. It is only at that time when we all faithfully follow the word of Hashem in all areas of life, that *HaKadosh Baruch Hu* will be happy and content with us. This hopefully will help bring about our salvation and our complete redemption.

The *Mincha Belulah,* a late 16th century Torah commentary, explains the opening word of the Sedra, "אם". He points out that each redemption of *Klal Yisrael* was led by two individuals whose names began with the letters 'א and 'מ. *Geulas Mitzrayim*, the Exodus from Egypt, was led by Moshe (מַשה) and Aharon (אַהרן). The redemption from the Golus of Paras and Madai, the Persian exile, was led by Esther

(אֶסְתֵּר) and Mordechai (מָרְדְּכַי). In the future, the ultimate redemption will come about through Eliyahu (אֵלִיָּהוּ) and Moshiach (מָשִׁיחַ). Thus, the word "אם" is included in the sentence to inform us that real, true, and authentic redemption and salvation will occur only if Israel will observe the Torah and its numerous *Mitzvos, Mishpatim,* and *Chukim.*

Thus, we clearly see that in order for Hashem to complete His promise of providing us with an era of peace and prosperity, brotherhood and tranquility, we must first complete our end of the agreement. We must pay our debt by observing all that we have pledged to Him. It is our responsibility to double our efforts and make a greater attempt at observing the precepts of our faith.

My friends, the future of *Yahadus*, the ushering in of the messianic era of brotherhood and unity in Israel, and, of course, peace and prosperity, will only come about when we begin to fulfill our responsibility and pay our debt to G-d. When we make Yerushalayim, the עיר שלם, the city that is whole and complete not only geographically speaking, but also in deed and observance.

Only then will we succeed. Only then, when this thought will spread far and wide throughout the Jewish world, will we be able to prove to the non-Jewish community that Israel, Jerusalem, and the Jewish people are indeed one. It is not only important to us strategically and nostalgically, but also religiously and spiritually. Only then will we have no difficulty in retaining Jerusalem and the other territories which are religiously important to us. For at that time, we will have witnessed the coming of the Moshiach. Hashem will then have entered into ירושלים של מעלה, the heavenly Jerusalem. We will bear witness to Bnei Yisrael's complete and total observance of the Torah and the Mitzvos as well as the building of the third and permanent Beis HaMikdash. במהרה בימינו אמן.

34. Who is a Jew?

Shavuos

During the past number of years, one of the major religious ideological questions to appear on the Jewish scene was not a new and novel one. It was merely a repeat, a re-run of a question long-since asked and answered. Nevertheless, it crops up time and again. The question was asked 3,500 years ago by the pharaohs of Egypt. It was asked by Torquemada, the vengeful and sadistic head of the Spanish Inquisition. It was asked 90 years ago by Hitler ימח שמו, and it was also asked by every despot and dictator whose goal was to eliminate and exterminate the Jewish people. The question is: "Who is a Jew?"

On the surface, this query is rather simple and elementary. Its response need not be profound nor exhaustive. Who is a Jew? A Jew is one who is either born to a Jewish mother or one who converts to Judaism according to all Halachic requirements.

Since the 19th century, the Conservative and Reform movements have tried to change this definition and make it easier for all individuals wishing to enter the Jewish fold. In fact, the Conservative movement, around 10 years ago, made a most radical change.

They have decided to join with the Reform movement and accept as members of their congregations the non-Jewish spouses of intermarried couples.

However, I believe it is unnecessary to comment on these anti-Halachic approaches. Rather, I contend that this question of "Who is a Jew?" can be understood to mean, "What is a Jew?" "What does it mean to be Jewish?" The question is not, "What is required of one who wishes to become a Jew?" That has already been made clear by our *Chachamim*, by our great sages down through the ages, from the Rambam to Rabbi Yosef Caro, the author of the *Shulchan Aruch*, to Rav Moshe Feinstein and to Rav Joseph Soloveitchik. What it means is, "What obligations and commitments must I make to demonstrate my Jewishness and my allegiance to Hashem and to my people?" This question, I believe, is quite relevant now as we are about to celebrate and commemorate the great event of the Theophany, Hashem's revelation of the Torah to the Jewish people at Har Sinai, the observance of the Yom Tov of Shavuos.

There are two questions that I wish to pose. With an exhaustive and comprehensive analysis of both, I believe that we will come to an even clearer understanding of what it means to be a Jew. First, the Torah was given to the Jewish people in the most unlikely surroundings, a desert, a barren and unfertile area. Why was this so? Second, one of the most beautiful customs of the Yom Tov of Shavuos is the reading of Megillas Rus. What is the significance of studying the Book of Rus on the Festival of Shavuos?

At first glance, it would appear that the Torah was given in an altogether strange environment. Perhaps it would have been more dramatic if Hashem would have brought all the Jews to Yerushalayim, gather them on *Har Habayis*, the Temple Mount, and present them with the Torah. Wouldn't that have been much more powerful and moving than a parched, sun-bleached, and empty desert? However, the fact of the matter is that this was not the case.

The Torah was given in the desert for a very specific reason. It was to teach *Am Yisrael* that in order to follow and observe the precepts of the Torah, in order to be an authentic and good Jew, one need not live in Yerushalayim, nor in pre-war Poland or Lithuania. To be a good Jew is something which is not dependent upon geographic location. You can be as good a Jew in Anchorage, Alaska, as you can be in Tel Aviv. You can be as good a Jew in Boca Raton, Florida, as you can in B'nai Brak.

There was a time when Jews did not nor could not believe that this was true. Years ago, it was said that only in specific Jewish havens such as the great Jewish centers of Europe could one authentically

Shavuos

remain true to his faith and heritage. The common refrain was, "America is a *goyishe Medinah* where even the stones in the streets are *treif*. To be a complete and total Jew in America is impossible." Forty and fifty years ago, eulogies were being written about Orthodox Jewry in this country. We were being consigned to obsolescence.

Today, my friends, this is not the case. Instead of being relics of the past, traditional, legitimate and authentic Orthodox Judaism is the wave of the future. There is no longer a question of whether Judaism in America will survive. The only question is what kind of Judaism will survive. We believe that only those Jews who are prepared to make a commitment to the totality of Jewish life can thrive in the climate of this society. Only those Jews who are prepared to stand up and be counted will be the ones who will survive. It will only be those Jews who are prepared to make sacrifices; those individuals who are prepared to endure suffering and afflictions; those who are ready to accept the yoke of Hashem like a Rus. They will be the wave of the future.

The end of *Megilas Rus* contains the lineage of Dovid HaMelech who was Rus' great-grandson. The *Shaarei Teshuvah (Orach Chaim #494)* tells us that it is for this reason that *Megillas Rus* is read on Shavuos for Dovid Hamelech was born and also died on that day.

The Vilna Gaon says that from the time of her birth, Rus was worthy of accepting the yoke of Mitzvos. In fact, the very letters of her name bear witness to this fact. The letters of רות add up to 606, which, taken together with the *Sheva Mitzvos Bnei Noach*, the seven Noahide laws, add up to תרי"ג, the 613 Commandments.

We are told in the Midrash (*Yalkut Shimoni* on Rus) that by reading this *Megillah* on Shavuos, we are taught that the Torah was often given through suffering and affliction. Rus' entry into the Jewish fold did not come easily. This Moabite princess, the daughter of the King of Moav, at all times expressed her deep, personal, and empathetic feelings for the Jews. She was loyal and helpful not only in good times but also when the situation of the Jews appeared most bleak and the future was in doubt.

During a famine, when she experienced the loss of her husband, her brother-in-law, and her father-in-law, her unswerving support never diminished. Rus expressed her friendship and love for *Klal Yisrael*. At a time of national catastrophe, when the future of the Jewish people looked bleak and was in grave jeopardy, she became a *Ger Tzedek*, the epitome and ideal of the righteous and authentic convert to Judaism.

There is no doubt that whether one is becoming Jewish or one is being reawakened to *Yahadus*, the traits of authenticity, genuineness, and commitment are absolutely necessary. Being Jewish is certainly not easy. The old saying, *"Is ez shver tzu zein a Yid,"* "It is difficult to be a Jew," should really be amended to read, *"Is ez shverer tzu zein an erlicher Yid,"* "It is even harder to be and remain a practicing, dedicated, loyal, and observant Jew."

While traditional and observant Judaism may, on the surface, appear hard and difficult, there is certainly a light at the end of the tunnel. Even though Rus lived through traumatic and difficult times, even though she could have turned her back on Judaism, she persevered and remained completely true to our faith. She was subsequently rewarded with seeing her great-grandson Dovid and his son Shlomo achieve the highest of honors. They were chosen as the מלכים, the kings and leaders of *Klal Yisrael*. They thus began the Davidic dynasty which will eventually bring the *Moshiach* במהרה בימינו.

Let us my friends, go back to our first question. Who is a Jew? A Jew is one whose heart cries out when he observes his fellow Jews throughout the world being subjected to anti-Semitic attacks. A Jew is one who will help, assist, and support Jewish causes and try to defeat the enemies of our people. A Jew is one who davens for and is concerned about the welfare of the citizens of Eretz Yisrael. A Jew is one who gives aid, comfort, and sage-advice to the widows, the orphans, and those stricken with illness. A Jew is thus one who was not merely born a Jew, but one who knows, understands, and observes the *Halachos*, Jewish laws and its many principles.

I wish to conclude with the beautiful words of the *Ohr HaChaim HaKadosh*. He said that the name of שָׁבוּעוֹת should be pronounced שְׁבוּעוֹת. The reason is that in addition to its translation as weeks, the term שְׁבוּעוֹת also comprises the idea of oaths, vows, and commitments. One שְׁבוּעָה was taken by Hashem, Who promised that He would never abandon or exchange us for another people. The second oath we took unto Hashem was that we would never exchange Him for another. *HaKadosh Baruch Hu*, my friends, has at all times fulfilled His oath. The task is for us to fulfill our part of the agreement.

Let us, on the Yom Tov of Shavuos, vow to become completely dedicated and committed Jews. In that way, in a very short time, the question of "Who is a Jew," no matter what the interpretation, will no longer be germane or relevant. At that time, the entire world will know that each of us is a shining example of what a true and genuine Jew is. We will then help bring about the coming of the *Moshiach*. We will then cause the universal glorification of G-d's name amongst all mankind, thereby creating the ultimate *Kiddush Hashem*. May this day come very soon, Amen.

35. A Day to Mourn, a Time to Hope
Tisha b'Av

Tisha b'Av, the ninth day of Av, is undoubtedly the blackest, saddest, and most mournful day on the Jewish calendar. This day commemorates numerous unfortunate catastrophes which have befallen our people. Both *Batei Mikdash* in Yerushalayim were destroyed - the first by the Babylonians in 586 BCE, the second by the Romans in 70 C.E. The Bar Kochba revolt against Rome was crushed on this day in 135 C.E. With that defeat, almost a million Jews perished at the hands of the Romans. One year later, the Romans plowed over the Temple Mount, Har HaMoriah, destroying much of the grandeur of that holiest of sites.

In 1290, the Jewish community of England—a *kehillah* which included many of the Ba'alei Tosafos—was expelled. The long and glorious history of Spanish Jewry ended on this day in 1492. Hundreds of thousands of Jews were forced to emigrate from the country which they had called home for almost 500 years. The First World War began on the 9th of Av in 1914. In addition, our people have experienced

Tisha b'Av

countless other unfortunate and catastrophic tragedies during the ages specifically on Tisha b'Av.

The origin of all these tragedies began when Bnei Yisrael were travelling in the *Midbar* on their way to Eretz Yisrael. The *Meraglim*, spies who scouted Eretz Yisrael, returned with a very distorted and negative report. They then convinced the Jewish people that, contrary to Hashem's promise of a swift and easy victory over its inhabitants, conquering the Promised Land was an impossibility.

The Torah in Parshas Shelach (14:1) says:

וַיִּבְכּוּ הָעָם בַּלַּיְלָה הַהוּא.

And the people wept that night.

The *Midrash Rabbah* says that Hashem responded by saying, "Tonight you cry for no reason; I will, in the future, give you many reasons to cry on this night." That night, say *Chazal,* was the ninth of Av, Tisha b'Av.

For almost 2000 years, Jews the world over have observed this day of mourning by fasting, gathering together for public prayer, the reading of Megillas Eicha, and by asking Hashem to restore Israel to its former majestic glory. However, for the last 200 years this day has become, especially for non-Orthodox Jews, perhaps the most neglected and most misunderstood of our major observances. The special significance of Tisha b'Av has been particularly confounded by the establishment and development of the State of Israel.

On Tisha b'Av, 2008, I attended an outstanding and very informative *shiur* given by the distinguished and very erudite Rabbi Dovid Gottleib, who then served as the Rav of Congregation Shomrei Emunah in Baltimore, Maryland. In his hour-long discourse, he detailed the thoughts and proposals of many well respected Rabbanim, especially in Eretz Yisrael, in regards to our continual, contemporary, and traditional observance of Tisha b'Av. He said that a number of Rabbanim ask: why is it necessary to continue remembering and mourning a catastrophe which occurred 2,000 years ago? This is especially so, they maintain, since Israel has been re-established as a Jewish National Homeland. The country has been built up and even Yerushalayim no longer lies in ruins. While we still do not have the Beis HaMikdash, some of the *tefillos* which we recite on Tisha b'Av concerning the ruins, the devastation, and the wreckage of Yerushalayim may seem to be no longer applicable through the method and manner in which we observed Tisha b'Av for two thousand years. Instead of prolonging our mourning, let us today alter some of the tefillos to be relevant and let this day's past catastrophes and tragedies become part of our historical record.

The second problem related to Tisha b'Av is that on this day, as opposed to other תעניתם, other fast days, *Tachanun* and *Selichos*, the penitential and supplication *tefillos* are omitted. *Chazal* explain that in spite of its sadness and its sense of gloom and foreboding, Tisha b'Av is considered a Yom Tov, a *Moed*, and it is described as such in the Shulchan Aruch. In Hilchos Tisha b'Av (תקנט:ד), the *Mechabeir* (Rav Yosef Karo) says:

אין אומרים תחנון (ולא סליחות – הגהות מהרי"ל) בתשעה באב, ואין נופלים על פניהם משום דמקרי מועד.

We do not say Tachanun nor do we say Selichos on Tisha b'Av because that day is called a Yom Tov"

The lesser fast days, such as Asarah b'Teves, Shivah Asar b'Tammuz, and Tzom Gedaliah, all of which also commemorate the events leading up to the *Churban Beis HaMikdash*, and which are, in essence, observed in a less rigorous and strict manner, are not considered as Yom Tovim. Why do we recite Tachanun and Selichos on these days and not on *Tisha b'Av*?

Rabbi Gottleib quoted the Rav, HaRav Yosef Soloveitchik *zt"l*, my Rosh Yeshiva, who completely disagreed with these other Rabbanim and brought a number of proofs as to why our traditional observance of Tisha b'Av must be maintained and continued as it has always been.

The Rav offered three rationales. He first said that the Jewish approach is that the events of Tisha b'Av, as well as so many other incidents in our history, must be considered as continuing to occur even until today. They are not just occurrences which took place thousands of years ago. As we say at the Pesach Seder:

בכל דור ודור חייב אדם לראות את עצמו כאילו הוא יצא ממצרים.

"In each and every generation, one is obligated to view himself as though he had personally gone out of Egypt."

In a similar manner, the Rav says that on Tisha b'Av, we sit on the ground, cry, and mourn as if the Beis HaMikdash is "presently burning and Yerushalayim is currently lying in ruins."

The second point he made concerns the status of Tisha b'Av during *Bayis Sheini*, the second Jewish Commonwealth. Did the inhabitants of Eretz Yisrael observe and mourn on Tisha b'Av at that time for the destruction of the first Beis HaMikdash which was destroyed by the Babylonians in 586 BCE? Rav Soloveitchik says that their observance was not actual mourning. Rather, it was the *Tefillah*, the hope and prayer that what happened with the first Beis HaMikdash should never, G-d forbid, happen again.

The Rav said, "The ghost of the *Churban* of the first Beis HaMikdash stalked the land." Similarly, today we observe and commemorate Tisha b'Av of the past and we pray that it should not *chas v'shalom* ever occur a third time.

Rav Soloveitchik also gave a third and most profound answer. He said that Tisha b'Av is not only dedicated to our mourning over the destruction of the *Batei Mikdash*; it is also dedicated to our historic recollection of all the tragedies and suffering which have afflicted *Am Yisrael* for the past two thousand years. Thus, even though Eretz Yisrael has once again become our homeland and Yerushalayim no longer lies in ruins, all of our traditional *tefillos* must continue to be recited.

The Rav said that when we read *Megilas Eicha*, it is not just the words of Yirmiyahu HaNavi that we recite. It is also the question of all of Jewish history. איכה—*Why* have we, both in the past and now also in the present, continue to suffer and despair? He says that during the time of the Moshiach, may he speedily arrive, we will then truly understand all the why's and how's of Jewish history. However, until that time, as long as איכה is followed by a question mark, *Am Yisrael* must continue to observe Tisha b'Av with all its mourning and sadness, with all its grief and lamentations.

An event in the life of the third of our *Avos*, Yaakov Avinu, may provide some insight into the second query as to why on Tisha b'Av we omit *Tachanun* and *Selichos*. Parshas Vayeishev, in Sefer Bereishis, discusses the jealousy and hatred which developed between Yaakov's ten oldest sons and Yosef - his most beloved son. We read how, in a moment of rage, the brothers seized Yosef, threw him into a pit, and then sold him as a common slave. They then dipped his coat in animal blood, leading their father to believe that he was devoured by a wild animal.

Yaakov was heart-broken and bereft by the news. He tore his garments and mourned for many days. For over two decades he refused to be consoled or comforted. Why did Yaakov not accept the inevitable? Why didn't he recognize and come to terms with the will of Hashem in Whom he had profound faith? Why did he not end his period of mourning? In fact, Halacha sets a definite period of time for one to mourn, after which he must begin to reconstruct his life.

Rashi, quoting the Midrash in Bereishis Rabbah, provides an answer. A person does not accept consolation for those who are thought to be dead but are actually living. Upon the dead it is decreed that their loved ones will eventually be able to be consoled. The living, however, will always be remembered, thus no comfort or solace can suffice. Everyone in Yaakov's household - including his sons - intuitively believed that Yosef was, indeed, dead. And after a certain period, they ended their own mourning. Yaakov however, intrinsically felt that Yosef was still alive. As long as there was even the slightest chance that he might one day see his son, Yaakov refused to be consoled, and thus, he never forgot him.

This, in essence, is the message of Tisha b'Av and all of Jewish History. When the first Beis HaMikdash was destroyed and Jewish sovereignty ended, those who were exiled passed the ruins of Judea as they were being led to Babylon. Their response to this tragic site was not one of despair and hopelessness, but one of hope and optimism for the future. They sang the words which Dovid Hamelech wrote in Sefer Tehillim 137:

אִם אֶשְׁכָּחֵךְ יְרוּשָׁלָם תִּשְׁכַּח יְמִינִי:

If I forget thee O Jerusalem, let my right hand forget its cunning.

To these individuals, Yerushalayim and Yehudah may have been physically destroyed, Jewish sovereignty may have temporarily ceased, but their hope and prayers for the future was very much alive. Eretz Yisrael will undoubtedly be rebuilt. Our capital, Yerushalayim will be restored to its former majestic glory. And Jewish self-rule and our self-government

Tisha b'Av

will one day be re-established. As long as this hope prevailed, they would never be consoled. Thus, on each Tisha b'Av, we mourn for the loss which is in our hearts.

The *Tefillos* of *Tachanun* and *Selichos*, the penitential and supplication prayers are omitted on Tisha b'Av to indicate the optimism and the forward thinking of the Jewish people. We believe, with our full heart and soul that this day of *aveilus*, mourning, will eventually become a Yom Tov, a day of rejoicing and celebration. We believe that on this, the saddest day in the Jewish year, the Moshiach was born. One day, hopefully very soon, from out of the depths of despair, the Jewish people will rise once again, phoenix-like, with renewed faith and determined purpose.

The hope of *Am Yisrael* is to have our lives fulfilled, as did Yaakov Avinu. For as he lived to see his beloved son Yosef alive again, so shall we see our dear homeland completely rebuilt amidst peace and tranquility, with love and unity from all its citizens, and with respect from its neighbors. One day soon we will see the Beis HaMikdash restored to all its glory, splendor, and honor.

Tisha b'Av, my friends, is not only a day of sorrow and mourning; it is also a day in which we gain determination and begin to hope for the future. It is a day when we are spiritually strengthened by the prophetic message (Yeshayahu 25:8):

בִּלַּע הַמָּוֶת לָנֶצַח וּמָחָה ה' אלקים דִּמְעָה מֵעַל כָּל פָּנִים...

Hashem will destroy death forever. He will wipe away the tears from our faces.

At that time, the entire world will be united in peace. They will all acknowledge *HaKadosh Baruch Hu* as the one true G-d and Master of all mankind. Amen.

Postscript:

This essay was originally written in 1972. It was revised and updated for this current edition. Beginning in 1971, Tisha b'Av has taken on an added dimension, one of deep personal sorrow and mourning. For on that day, my beloved uncle, teacher, and mentor, Rabbi Hyman Tuchman *z"l,* passed away very prematurely at the age of forty-nine.

My Uncle Hymie *z"l* was much more than a very dear and special uncle to me. He unfortunately never married and considered my sister Eamie and myself as his surrogate children. He spent most Yom Tovim and Shabbosim with my family. He learned Gemara, Chumash, and Jewish philosophy with me. He also helped me write, develop, and construct my early *drashos*. During my high school years, he spent many hours studying math and science with me. He was enormously helpful in assisting me prepare for the New

York State Regents exams on these subjects. It was in large part because of him that I received good grades on those exams. In addition, he, more than anyone else, was my inspiration and the greatest influence on my entering and serving in the Rabbinate.

My uncle was a genuine and bona-fide *Talmid Chacham* as well as a first-rate scholar and intellectual. He served briefly as a pulpit rabbi. He then spent the remainder of his brief but illustrious career in the field of *Chinuch*, Jewish education. Many of his progressive and forward-thinking innovations were implemented and remain even today, more than fifty years after his demise, the standard in many Yeshivos and Day Schools throughout the United States.

I want to also offer my sincerest *hakaras haTov* to my late dear cousin, Rav Mechie Schiffenbauer *z"l*, for his great help and assistance. On the day of my Uncle Hymie's *petirah*, which occurred on Shabbos, R' Mechie walked over four miles from his home to the hospital where he served all day as my uncle's *Shomer HaMais*. (As a Kohen, I was unable to do that Mitzvah myself.) My family and I will never forget that tremendous act of *Chesed shel Emes*.

May Uncle Hymie *z"l* continue to be a *meilitz yosher* for our family, and may he ascend higher and higher in *Gan Eden*. May his memory always be for a *beracha*. RHG

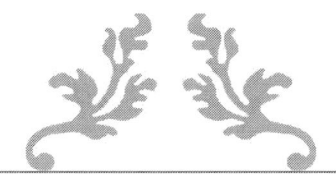

SPECIAL OCCASIONS

36. Singularly Important

Bar Mitzvah of my Dear Grandson - Yehuda Gross
(Parshas Eikev and Naso)

For the past seven years, since he was around six years old, Yehudah has very enthusiastically joined together with his dear father, Aryeh, and his older brothers, Simcha and Moshe, in performing *Birchas Kohanim - duchening*. Whenever Rivkie and I have been with Aryeh and Goldie for Yom Tov, I have had the great *zechus* to *duchen* together with them. Having three generations of Kohanim duchening together has been and remains for me an incredible merit, one which I never take for granted. It is therefore no coincidence that in Yehudah's Bar Mitzvah Parshah, Parshas Eikev, we find the original source for *Birchas Kohanim*.

One of the central themes of Parshas Eikev is Moshe Rabbeinu's review of the *Chet HaAigel*—the terrible sin of the Golden Calf. Jews across the spectrum of *Klal Yisrael* succumbed to this treacherous act. Only one Shevet, however, remained loyal to *HaKadosh Baruch Hu*.

In פרק י׳ פסוק ח׳ the Torah says:

בָּעֵת הַהִוא הִבְדִּיל ה' אֶת שֵׁבֶט הַלֵּוִי לָשֵׂאת אֶת אֲרוֹן בְּרִית ה' לַעֲמֹד לִפְנֵי ה' לְשָׁרְתוֹ וּלְבָרֵךְ בִּשְׁמוֹ עַד הַיּוֹם הַזֶּה:

At that time, Hashem separated the tribe of Levi to carry the Aron of Hashem's covenant, to stand before Hashem to serve Hin and to bless in His name until this day."

Hashem chose Shevet Levi over all the other *Shevatim*. He substituted them over the *bechorim* because my ancestors were steadfast in their determination and in their adherence to the *Ribono shel Olam*. Unlike the firstborn sons, who had originally been chosen to serve as Hashem's agents, Shevet Levi refused to be involved in the worshipping and the abominations surrounding the *Eigel HaZahav*. For this they were rewarded and chosen to represent Klal Yisrael in their service to Hashem.

However, Rashi tells us that in addition to this accolade granted to Shevet Levi, a very specific compensation was given to the Kohanim for standing up for Hashem's honor. The *posuk* we quoted concludes ולברך בשמו עד היום הזה—they will merit to bless in His name until this day. What is this referring to? Rashi says that ולברך בשמו refers to נשיאת כפים, otherwise known as *Birchas Kohanim* or *duchening*. We see that this special Mitzvah, which I and my family are privileged to perform, was a direct reward for the loyalty of the Kohanim in the aftermath of the *Eigel*.

In this light, I felt that it would be most appropriate today on Yehudah's Bar Mitzvah to share a thought on Birchas Kohanim.

The Torah in Sefer Bamidbar, Parshas Naso (6:22-27) says:

וַיְדַבֵּר ה' אֶל מֹשֶׁה לֵּאמֹר: דַּבֵּר אֶל אַהֲרֹן וְאֶל בָּנָיו לֵאמֹר כֹּה תְבָרֲכוּ אֶת בְּנֵי יִשְׂרָאֵל אָמוֹר לָהֶם: יְבָרֶכְךָ ה' וְיִשְׁמְרֶךָ: יָאֵר ה' פָּנָיו אֵלֶיךָ וִיחֻנֶּךָּ: יִשָּׂא ה' פָּנָיו אֵלֶיךָ וְיָשֵׂם לְךָ שָׁלוֹם: וְשָׂמוּ אֶת שְׁמִי עַל בְּנֵי יִשְׂרָאֵל וַאֲנִי אֲבָרֲכֵם:

And Hashem said to Moshe saying. Speak to Aharon and his sons saying, "This is how you shall bless the Jewish people: May Hashem Bless you and keep you. May Hashem cause His countenance to shine upon you. May Hashem lift up His face to you and provide you with peace. They shall bestow My Name upon the Bnei Yisrael and I will bless them."

Each of these *berachos* is written in *lashon yachid,* in the singular. There are two reasons given for this. One *pshat* is given by Reb Shlomo Leib of Lenchna. He contends that the main essence of these *berachos* is that they should unify and unite all of *Am Yisrael*. At Har Sinai, *Bnei Yisrael* were linked together and connected with one another for the first time. *Birchas Kohanim* serves the same purpose, as its aim and purpose is to cause *achdus*, to bring about the unification and consolidation of *Klal Yisrael*.

A second explanation is offered by the *Pnei Gedalya* who says that each *beracha* is, in essence, tailor made for every member of *Klal Yisrael*. Therefore, it is written in the singular.

This idea is certainly relevant for the first two *berachos*. However, when we arrive at the last beracha, that of "וישם לך שלום", that of making peace, this theory becomes problematic. The *beracha* of *Shalom* is undoubtedly the most important of this entire group. One can be blessed with everything in life. He can have health, wealth, as well as a great family. He can even enjoy a sterling reputation. However, without *Shalom*, without genuine and complete peace, a person, in essence, really has nothing.

However, the fact that even this *beracha* is in the singular is troublesome. For *shalom*, peace, is a concept that is realized only through the interaction of two individuals. It can be demonstrated fully only by the actions of at least two parties, such as two friends, two states, or two countries. If this be so, why is the *bracha* of *shalom* written in *lashon yachid*, in the singular?

An answer is provided by Rav Menachem Ben Zion Sachs *zt"l*. He was a son-in-law of HaRav HaGaon Rav Tzvi Pesach Frank *zt"l*, the former רב

הראשי of Yerushalayim. Rav Sachs, in his *Sefer Menachem Tzion* asserts that it indeed true that to have real, genuine, and authentic peace you need at least two individuals. Nevertheless, by necessity, *shalom* must be written in the singular, because prior to establishing peaceful relations with others, one must be at peace with himself.

Unfortunately, we find so many people who are cursed with inner conflict, personal strife, and total confusion. They are *farbissin*, bitter and angry. Each person must attempt to develop a life based on peace and tranquility. Once they develop this particular trait, they can then have an equilibrium in their own lives. They then can establish a sense of harmony and concordance with others.

This message is applicable to each of us in our observance of Torah and Mitzvos. It is indeed most relevant and germane to a Bar Mitzvah boy who is starting out in his role as a בר חיובא, an adult member of *Klal Yisrael*.

The message that I wish to share is that before we spread out our hands, before we attempt to help and assist others in their moments of need, we should try our best to personally have internal *shalom*. We should be at peace with ourselves. We should attempt to be content and satisfied with whom we are, with our personal station in life. We have to be comfortable and satisfied with our G-d given talents.

Our dear and very special Yehudah: in addition to the message of *Chazal* which I feel is most appropriate, I want to share a personal thought with you; from a loving grandfather to a wonderful and special grandson.

Yehudah, ever since you were born, Bubby and I have had a very special *kesher* with you. At your *bris*, I had the *zechus* to name you. We have had this bond, this connection with you for all these years since then. As the first Yehudah in the Torah said in Parshas Vayigash concerning his brother Binyamin's relationship with their father, Yaakov: "ונפשו קשורה בנפשו" – "His soul, his essence, is intertwined, it is connected with that of his father." So too, Bubby and I say to you: ונפשינו קשורות בנפשך. Our souls are interconnected and interrelated with you.

Yehudah, your kindness, your gentleness, and your sweetness, combined with your high intelligence is absolutely incredible. Each time that Bubby and I have come to your home, you are always ready and able to carry all our belongings inside. You and your siblings never even allow us to lift one thing. In addition, how often have you pleaded with your father to allow you to push me in the wheelchair to and from shul? And how many times have we sat next to each other and davened together, at which time I have seen your tremendous growth and maturity?

During each of our visits, you have always spent quality time with us. You have filled us in on your school schedule and your general activities. You have also enlightened us on some areas of thought which you enjoy and have read quite extensively. I also have had the great privilege in the past few years of learning both Chumash and Mishnah with you and have personally witnessed your prodigious progress and development in these areas.

You and your wonderful siblings, Simcha, Moshe, and Rena all have had זכות אבות. You have had the *mesorah* of Torah and Mitzvos, love of *Am Yisrael* and Eretz Yisrael. You have received these values from your great-grandparents, your grandparents, and especially from your incredible and extraordinary parents, our beloved children, Aryeh and Goldie.

I don't have to tell you about all that your parents do for almost every Jewish organization in Baltimore. They are always willing, ready, and able to help and assist anyone and everyone at all times and in all circumstances. However, I do want to emphasize what kind of example they set for you in the area of כבוד אב ואם as children to Bubby and myself. They have certainly set the gold standard in this area. Their love and concern for us knows no bounds. For this and for so much more we love them, we respect them, and we thank them.

Our *Beracha* to you, dear Yehudah, is that you continue on your path to becoming a *Masmid*, a future *Talmid Chacham*, as well as an expert in all your intellectual pursuits. May you grow and develop your truly wonderful *midos*. May you, together with your siblings, continue to give us tremendous *nachas* and happiness for many years to come. And finally, may you constantly bring pride and joy to our entire family, to *Am Yisrael,* and especially to *HaKadosh Baruch Hu.* We love you so very much. Mazel Tov.

Addendum

Aryeh and Goldie recently showed me an article which Yehuda wrote about me for a school. project. I was very moved and humbled by his beautiful and kind words; I thought that it would make a fitting epilogue to my drasha.

My Loving Grandfather
By Yehuda Gross

He was a Rabbi of a shul. He was a successful businessman. He was a chaplain in the army. He wrote many *seforim* and books. He is a cancer survivor. He always manages to have time for his children and grandchildren. He bought my tefillin for my Bar Mitzvah. I'm sure you're all wondering who "He" is. "He" is none other than my paternal grandfather. My grandfather, Rabbi Ronald H. Gross, is someone who I admire tremendously and look up to with utmost respect. He is a role model par excellence for my siblings and me and teaches us many valuable life lessons. I love him dearly.

My grandfather was born in Brooklyn in the 1940s. He immediately became well-liked and respected by his peers and everyone around him. Besides having great *middos,* my grandfather was also a great leader; he became the student president of his college. After college, he got *semicha* and became a chaplain in the army and later became a *rav* of a shul. Now my grandfather writes *seforim* and books and shows tremendous love for his children, grandchildren, and even great-grandchildren.

Throughout his life, my grandfather was always a leader and a role-model for everyone around him. These traits helped him accomplish many great things. One example was during my grandfather's time as student president of his college. Israel was threatened with a terrible trucidation when what is now known as the Six-Day War broke out. My grandfather still remembers being woken up at 3:00 a.m. to hear the horrifying news. Immediately, my grandfather decided to wake his friends to say *Tehillim* together for all those suffering from the war.

Another example of my grandfather's leadership was after he received *semicha*. He took on the daunting task of being one of the very few Jewish chaplains to help the plethora of Jewish people in the army. During his service as a chaplain, he helped many people, Jews and non-Jews, with various things they needed in regards to religion and other areas. While in the army, he gave a *shiur* every week on the *Parsha* and later compiled all of them into a *sefer* which was distributed to the Jewish world in the army. After his time in the army, my grandfather continued his career in the Rabbinate and became the *rav* of Sinai Congregation in Hillside, New Jersey. In Hillside, he was a respected *rav* and brought many people closer to Hashem. Knowing all the things he accomplished, I feel that my grandfather is the perfect role-model for me to emulate. He serves as an inspiration for everything in my life.

My grandfather has made a tremendous impact on my life and on my *avodas Hashem.* Since my grandfather bought my *tefillin,* I think about him every time I put them on, which is daily. He is a man with tremendous *Yiras Shamayim* and he fulfills the *mitzvos* in the best way he can. Therefore, when I think of him, it helps me have better *kavana* in my *davening,* and it helps me start my day on the right foot by reminding me to fulfill the *mitzvos* the way he would.

Another way my grandfather influences my life is in regards to our *mitzvah* of *Birchas Kohanim.* I was born into a family with the special gift of *Kehunah.* My grandfather views this as a unique privilege and tries very hard to be able to spend *Yom Tov* with my family so he, my father, my siblings, and I can all *duchen* together. When I am standing under my *tallis* saying the *bracha* together with my grandfather, my father, and my brothers, I feel the power of *kedusha* right there with me. This makes me feel special and elevated, knowing that we are bentching *Klal Yisrael*. I look forward to this experience all year.

Perhaps the most powerful message that my grandfather has imparted to me that I try to remember all the time is having *emunah* and *bitachon* in Hashem. My grandfather's illness has left him with an incredible boost in his faith in G-d. He truly believes that whatever Hashem does is for the good. No matter what disappointments and hardships life throws at us, they are special for us and they are meant to enable us to become greater people. I always think of this when I face all types of challenges in my life whether it's in school, at home, or in camp.

I love and respect my grandfather so much. I love when we get to spend time together, and I cherish every moment.

37. Gratitude and Laughter
Address at the Bris of Daniel Kohn
Fort Benning Jewish Center
February 13, 1972

It is my distinct honor and pleasure to welcome all the family, friends, and guests of Dr. Murray and Mrs. Susan Kohn, who have travelled from near and far to celebrate the *bris* of their son together with them. Your presence this morning has certainly enhanced this beautiful Simcha.

I want to make special mention of two couples who have travelled from the New York area to join us this morning. I first want to welcome Mr. and Mrs. Kohn, Murray's parents, who have come from Washington Heights, New York. I understand that they are very prominent members of the famous Breuer's Kehillah. They are intimately involved in the development and growth of that outstanding community.

I also want to welcome Mr. and Mrs. Simon Want, Susan's parents. They come from the Bedford Bay section of Brooklyn, New York. I have been told that for many years they have been prominent members of the Young Israel of Bedford Bay. That synagogue is led by Rabbi Samuel Fink, one of the most

Bris of Daniel Kohn

distinguished Rabbis in the United States. In fact, for the past few years, Mr. Want has served as the Shul President.

My dear friends, the birth and the *bris* of a baby boy is a monumental event in the lives of Jewish parents. It is a transformative and life altering experience. It imposes on Jewish parents a tremendous responsibility and obligation in transmitting our glorious and remarkable heritage and tradition to the next generation. I would like to begin my remarks this morning with a discussion of the Torah's description of the birth and *bris* of the first Jewish child, Yitzchak Avinu, the son of our first Patriarch and Matriarch, Avraham and Sarah.

The events surrounding this historic occurrence are recorded in the Torah in Sefer Bereishis in Parshas Vayeira which is read publicly twice a year. The first occurs on the Shabbos when we read this Parsha during the annual cycle of the Torah reading. The second is on the first day of Rosh Hashanah.

The Torah in Parshas Vayeira (21:1-3) describes the birth of the only child born to Avraham and Sarah, Yitzchok. The Torah says:

וַה' פָּקַד אֶת שָׂרָה כַּאֲשֶׁר אָמָר וַיַּעַשׂ ה' לְשָׂרָה כַּאֲשֶׁר דִּבֵּר: וַתַּהַר וַתֵּלֶד שָׂרָה לְאַבְרָהָם בֵּן לִזְקֻנָיו לַמּוֹעֵד אֲשֶׁר דִּבֶּר אֹתוֹ אֱלֹקִים: וַיִּקְרָא אַבְרָהָם אֶת שֶׁם בְּנוֹ הַנּוֹלַד לוֹ אֲשֶׁר יָלְדָה לּוֹ שָׂרָה יִצְחָק:

And Hashem remembered Sarah as He had said. And Hashem did for Sarah as He had spoken. She conceived and she gave birth to a son for Avraham in his old age at the designated time that Hashem had declared to him. Avraham named his son that was born to him, whom Sarah had given birth to for him, 'Yitzchok.'

Sarah and Avraham had anxiously awaited this blessed event for many decades. They were overjoyed by this gift that Hashem presented to them in their old age. Their progeny would now carry on their ideals, traditions, and faith. The religion which they had developed and the *hashkafah* which they had nurtured would now not die with them. Their faith and *bitachon* in *HaKadosh Baruch Hu* as the Creator and Master of the Universe would now live on and develop with their son whom they named Yitzchak.

Yitzchak is, indeed, a most interesting and rather unusual name. It is the future tense of the root צחק, to laugh. Thus, the son of Judaism's first Patriarch and Matriarch, persons who stood on the עבר אחת, on one side of the world against the rest of mankind in their complete belief in monotheism and in their total devotion to *HaKadosh Baruch Hu*, is named, "He will laugh." How strange; how odd. This name is even more difficult to understand when we read a little further in the same Parsha, which details the *Akeidas*

Yitzchak, Avraham's obedience to G-d's request that he offer Yitzchak as a *Korban* to Hashem.

In addition, throughout the תורה שבעל פה, our oral tradition, Avraham is represented by the attribute of *chesed*, performing deeds of loving-kindness to his contemporaries. Yitzchak, on the other hand, is represented by *Avodah* and *Gevurah*, sacrifice, courage, and strength – certainly not attributes that imply laughter, glee, and joy. It is therefore quite ironic that he was given such a name. Finally, we must also question: who shall he laugh at and why?

Chazal teach that the laugh of Yitzchak expresses not only his personal and individual laugh but the laugh and joy of his descendants as well. The vision of his parents was that he would, in essence, laugh and find happiness and contentment in the ideals and the G-dly life that he would inherit from them. His laughter indicates that he would become the carrier of the banner, the very symbol of a new faith proclaimed, demonstrated, and led by Avraham and Sarah.

Other *Chachamim* offer a different and a variant explanation. They say that the fact that the name Yitzchak is written in לשון עתיד, in the future tense, indicates the dominant role that laughter and joy will play in the future history of the Jewish people. In fact, our chronicle is made up of both the past as well as the future. It consists of history as well as prophecy.

Normally, Yitzchak and his descendants should have, at one point or another, given up. Human logic would have dictated that at any time in our traumatic and most difficult history, we should have put an end to our agony and suffering. We should have, in essence, renounced and repudiated our faith. We should have abandoned what appeared to be a sinking ship; we should have parachuted to safety away from the burning wreckage of the plane called Judaism.

Fortunately, with the help and assistance of the *Ribono shel Olam*, this has never occurred. A violent and treacherous world has repeatedly called out to us, saying, "Your G-d has abandoned and forsaken you. He does not care about you or your future. Come, join with us, desert your foolhardy, senseless, and ridiculous religion. You will then know no more suffering or discrimination." My friends, how did we respond? How did we answer these charges? We looked to the outside world and refused to be taken in by their hypocrisy and duplicity. In addition, we laughed.

No matter what the sacrifice, regardless of the difficulties and the price we had to pay, our faith, our *Emunah* and *Bitachon* in Hashem never weakened or wavered. And like our father Yitzchak, we laughed. We did so not because we were mocking or deriding our non-Jewish antagonists. Rather, we rejoiced and celebrated with the heritage and faith that was passed down from generation to generation, from father to son, from mother to daughter. We laughed because of our belief and conviction in the *Borei Olam* which is uniquely ours, no matter how many sacrifices go with it. Thus, Parshas Vayeira, which describes the birth of Yitzchak, is, in the final analysis, a message of hope and optimism, positivity and exhilaration.

My dear friends,

Today's *bris* is indeed a very special and unique *simcha* in our Shul. It marks the first time since I became your rabbi that we are celebrating a *bris* of one of our congregants. The parents of the new baby, Murray and Susan Kohn, have become my very close and special friends. They have been intimately involved in all aspects of our Shul and have supported and attended all of our programs and projects. They have given me tremendous *chizuk* and support for all of my efforts and initiatives.

Murray was extremely helpful in assisting me set up our beautiful and meaningful davening for the past *Yomim Noraim*. He was very instrumental in lining up our fantastic *Ba'alei Shacharis* and *Ba'alei Musaf*. Susan served as the chairman of our highly successful Chanukah celebration and observance. This event attracted many members of our congregation. All who attended had a very meaningful and enjoyable experience.

Since I began my duties at Ft. Benning in the fall of 1971, both Susan and Murray have volunteered as the chairmen of the adult educational committee. They have served in that capacity with great distinction, helping to bring a number of speakers and special programs to our Shul.

I also wish to recognize and thank Murray for his suggestion of instituting the "Thought of the Week" series which I have developed and currently send out each week to all members of the Ft. Benning Jewish Center.[4]

In addition, Murray and I both share a common great, great, great Grandfather. We are both descendants of the first *Kohen Gadol* of *Klal Yisrael*, Aharon HaKohen, the older brother of Moshe Rabbeinu. Both Murray and Susan are leading their lives by following in Aharon HaKohen's greatest attribute, that of being an אוהב שלום, and a רודף שלום. They are both the quintessential proponents of loving peace. They are always promoting and advocating harmony and brotherhood between all people at all times and in all circumstances.

---

[4] These thoughts served as the basis for this volume.

There has never been any time, since the day that I met the two of them, that I ever witnessed either of them being upset or angry by the words or actions of any other member of our Shul. Their entire modus operandi has been to promote and pursue *shalom* between all. That truly is a great and wonderful attribute which they can pass down to their children, their daughter Dena and their new son, Daniel.

As I look out at our newest addition to our congregation, Daniel Kohn, I am very optimistic about his future. With the *zechus Avos*, with the great and magnificent merits that he will inherit from both sets of grandparents and the many wonderful attributes that his parents will impart to him, I am quite certain that Daniel ben Moshe HaKohen will become a significant and important member of our people. May he grow to be a source of pride and *nachas* to his parents, to his entire family, and to all of Klal Yisrael. Mazel Tov.

Postscript:

In early 1973, Murray was discharged from the army. He had completed his tour of duty. He and Susan decided to move to the Bedford Bay area of Brooklyn, NY. They would be joining Susan's parents, Esther and Simon Want, who had lived in that area for many years and were among the main lay leaders of the

Young Israel, the largest Orthodox shul in that community.

Two and a half weeks prior to their move, they shipped their furniture and their household belongings up north. I invited them to move into my apartment where they remained with me until their army stay was completed. The time that we spent together truly enhanced and expanded our friendship. It elevated it to an even greater degree than what it had previously been.

After their move to New York, we maintained and continued our friendship. We spoke often and we corresponded on a regular basis. However, my relationship with both Murray and Susan would in the next few years reach new and even greater heights.

In June, 1974, less than one year after I returned to the New York area following my discharge from the Army, I received a very special call from Murray and Susan. They enthusiastically recommended a young lady from their shul to me, Rivkie Fink, the daughter of the Rabbi and the Rebbetzin of the Young Israel of Bedford Bay, Rabbi and Mrs. Samuel Fink.

I remembered Rabbi Fink, who was a Rebbe in BTA when I was a student. While I personally never had him as a Rebbe, some of my good friends were in his *shiur*. They spoke glowingly about his *mentschlichkeit* and his care and concern for each of his

Talmidim. He was known to be the most sincere and caring Rebbe in the entire yeshiva.

In addition, Linda Lauer, the wife of my closest friend, Teddy Lauer, was a classmate and a friend of Rivkie. She spoke glowingly of her. I then decided to call her and we scheduled a date. We went out a number of times and realized that we were a perfect match. January 7, 1975, our wedding day, was the happiest and most meaningful day of my life.

Baruch Hashem, now over 49 years later, with three fantastic and marvelous married children, 18 amazing grandchildren and three adorable great-grandchildren, I still can never thank Murray and Susan enough for their life-altering recommendation which they made to both of us.

Daniel has grown to be a distinguished member of his Bergenfield, New Jersey, Orthodox community. He and his wife and children have given his parents an abundance of *Yiddish nachas*.

Unfortunately, Murray passed away a few years ago. However, we still keep in touch with Susan. We wish her our continued and everlasting thanks and appreciation, אריכת ימים and ברכה, and happiness from her children and her grandchildren.

RHG

38. A Man of Kindness, Courage, and Principle

Hesped of אבי מורי, *my dear and beloved father, Moses (Moe) Gross, Reb Moshe Pesach Nisan ben Tzvi Hirsch HaKohen z"l*
February 28, 1990

In *Pirkei d'Rebbe Eliezer* (Chapter 33), we read:

שלשה אהובים יש לו לאדם בחייו, ואלו הן, בניו ובני ביתו וממונו ומעשים טובים,

"A man has three companions, his children and his household, his wealth, and his good deeds."

ובשעת פטירתו מן העולם קורא לבניו ובני ביתו ואומר להם בבקשה מכם הוציאוני מדין המות הרע הזה, והם אומרים לו הלא שמעת ואין שלטון ביום המות, ולא כך כתיב אח לא פדה יפדה איש,

"When a person is about to depart from this world, he appeals to his children and to his household. He cries out: 'Save me!' They reply, 'There is no power on the day of death; no man can redeem his brother.'"

ואפילו ממונו שהוא אוהב אותו אינו יכול לפדותו...וכשהוא רואה כן מכניס את ממונו ואומ' לו הרבה טרחתי עליך לילה ויום במישור ובהרים בבקשה ממך פדני

Hesped for Mr. Moe Gross z"l

מן המות הזה והצילני מן המיתה והוא משיבו והלא שמעת לא יועיל הון ביום עברה,

"His money replies: 'Wealth does not help on the day of death.'"

אחרי כן הוא מכניס מעשיו הטובים ואומר' להם בואו והצילוני מן המות הזה ותחזקו עמי ואל תניחוני לצאת מן העולם שעדיין יש לכם תוחלת עלי אם אנצל, וכן משיבים לו מעשיו הטובים לך לשלום עד שלא תלך לשם אנו מקדימין אותך, שנ' והלך לפניך צדקך,

"One's good deeds, however, reply, 'Before you come for judgement, we shall be there ahead of you. We will accompany you on your final journey and stand together with you during your final judgement before the כסא הכבוד.'"

My father, Moe Gross *a"h*, lived his life on three distinct and different levels. He was first and foremost a family man. He loved and was totally involved with and devoted to his בנים ובני בנים – his wife - my mother, his children, and his grandchildren. From his earliest years, he was committed to the care and wellbeing of his widowed mother, who in 1930 became a very young widow and had to single-handedly raise her three young children. In his later years, he was totally devoted to his Aunt Fanny, who never married and loved my father as a son.

In fact, when she became elderly and needed assistance, both my father and our very dear cousin,

Fruma (Potok) Schiffenbauer, who over the years has become like a close sister to me, became her guardians. They took care of all her physical and financial needs.

My father raised my sister and me with love and affection and provided us with all our needs, both physical and, especially, spiritual. He taught us the Torah way of life through his extraordinary example. He devoted himself heart and soul to my mother. He did everything possible to guarantee that she would enjoy life to the fullest.

In his later years, he was a very doting, affectionate, and extremely loving grandfather to his seven grandchildren. This love was reciprocated by each of them. They were all very devoted to and adored him.

He was also a wonderful, loving, and very dedicated brother to his older sister and brother-in-law, Jean and Ben Genauer, my dear aunt and uncle. He lived with them during his college years in Seattle, Washington, while attending the University of Washington. For that, he always had tremendous *hakaras haTov* towards them. They were his role models, and he constantly looked to them for advice and counsel. For all his life, he loved them both very much.

I also see my father on a second level, perhaps as no one else here could see him, on the level of ממון,

his business. For I stand here today not only as a son who is overcome with overwhelming grief and intense mourning over the sudden and tragic death of my father. I also stand here as one who had the great privilege, the great *zechus,* to have worked together with him in business for the past twelve years.

Many with whom he had business transactions loved and respected him. They admired him for his moral and ethical dealings and for his genuine honesty, integrity, and decency, his total and complete *mentschlichkeit*.

I learned so much from him about the business world and life in general. Most significantly, he instilled in me the importance of always being completely honest and above board. He taught me that at all times and in all circumstances, one must never compromise when confronted with truly moral and ethical matters. I loved him as a business partner; I especially loved him as a father. He was my dearest and closest friend. He was there for me at all times and in every aspect of life.

Thirdly, my father *a"h*, has many מעשים טובים. His years of devotion, involvement, and service on behalf of Congregation B'nai Yehuda, Shulamith School for Girls, the Young Israel of Boro Park, and especially Yeshiva Toras Emes-Kamenetz are his true מעשים טובים. They will certainly accompany him on his final journey and serve him well in his *din v'Cheshbon* in *Shamayim*.

However, my friends, what truly defined my father were his countless acts of *chesed*. His kindness, his benevolence, and his many deeds of altruism towards his friends and neighbors were quite remarkable.

His friends from each era of his life all admired, respected, and truly loved him. He remained close with some friends from his elementary school, Yeshiva Eitz Chaim and with his Rebbe and *chavrusos* from Mesivta Torah Vada'as. In his later years, his wonderful friends, with whom he spent so much time in shul and in social settings, were always together to the very end.

Despite his very busy business and volunteer schedule, he made sure to take care of his friends who were in need. He would always come to visit those who were ill and were either confined to their home or were hospitalized. He brought *chizuk* and good cheer to his friends, as well as comfort and support to the families.

He tried to attend every *shiva minyan* that was in his neighborhood. In addition, he was also very concerned about those who were recently widowed or divorced. He helped make sure that they had the means to support themselves and their family.

Hesped for Mr. Moe Gross z"l

When a dear friend of mine was going through some very difficult personal and financial problems, my father stepped up and arranged for interest free loans to be given to this individual, which he personally guaranteed. These private acts of *chesed* and kindness were done without any fanfare or publicity. They will forever remain an inspiration to me as well as to those whom he assisted.

There is one incident that I believe will help give a better understanding of who my father really was. Around twelve years ago, on a *Motzei Shabbos*, my parents were hosting *Sheva Berachos* in their home for my sister and brother-in-law, Eamie and Joel, who had just gotten married. When Rivkie and I arrived, we discovered that my father was not home. When I inquired as to his whereabouts, my mother informed us that he was in shul, where he had organized a *minyan* to say Tehillim for one of his oldest and dearest friends who was terminally ill.

When he returned home about an hour later, he explained his absence. "My dear friend is deathly ill, and he needs the help and *rachamim* of Hashem. The *Sheva Berachos* could wait; Hashem's intervention could not." That was my father. This was his *chesed*. These were his מעשים טובים, his deeds of genuine and sincere good and loving kindness. This, my friends, was my father's real legacy and his genuine heritage

Hesped for Mr. Moe Gross z"l

The Gemara in *Meseches Berachos* says: צדיקים במיתתם קרויין חיים. The righteous, even when they are dead, are considered alive." I hope and pray that my family and those who were close to my father will, in his memory and in his honor, always keep alive his ideals, his convictions and his principles. In this way, my dear and beloved father, Reb Moshe Pesach Nissan ben Tzvi Hirsch HaKohen *a"h*, will remain alive in each of our hearts, our minds, and our souls. He will never be forgotten.

To my mother, a true אשת חיל. She was my father's inspiration and strength. She anticipated his every need. She was his life partner for almost forty-five years. Mom, I pray that Hashem should give you the courage, the strength, and the wherewithal to carry on. May you be able to continue perpetuating Dad's wonderful deeds and his amazing legacy. I wish you only *gezunt*, good health, and many more years of demonstrating your love to your family and to all your very dear friends.

בלע המות לנצח ומחה ה' דמעה מעל כל פנים. "Hashem shall destroy death forever. He will wipe away the tears from our faces." יהי זכרו ברוך. May my father's memory always be for a *beracha*. Amen.

Postscript:

My father's very close chaver and confidant, Rabbi Shimon Segal a"h, the Executive Vice President of the Kaminetz Yeshiva, made all the arrangements for my father's funeral. He even organized the police escort which accompanied the large procession of cars that travelled from the Kaminetz Yeshiva to Beth David Cemetery in Queens.

The levaya itself was held in the main Beis Midrash of the Kamenetz Yeshiva. There were hundreds of individuals who came to pay their final respects to my father. Amongst them were Roshei Yeshivah, Rabbanim, lay leaders, and our immediate and extended family. Also present were my parents' friends from all eras of their lives. In addition, many of my friends as well as my sister's friends came from near and far. The entire Yeshivah High School and Beis Medrash of Kaminetz as well as the upper elementary grades were in attendance.

There were over ten hespeidim given that day. I had the zechus to deliver the final hesped. It was by far the most difficult speech I had ever delivered. I hope I made my father proud.

39. Finally At Peace

Hesped for אמי מורתי, my Dear Mother, Lilyan (Lil) Gross, Chayah Leah bas R' Alter Moshe a"h
August 14, 1992

Previous speakers have spoken about my mother's loyalty, devotion, and love for my father *a"h*. They detailed how she dedicated her life to be his helpmate and partner, how she was a wonderful and devoted mother, and how she was a very doting and extremely loving grandmother. I want to add a few words and speak about my mother as a person and especially as a parent.

The *Midrash Tanchuma* on Parshas Vayakheil (סימן א') quotes a *posuk* in *Sefer Koheles* (ז:א) which states that the day of one's death is inherently better than the day of his birth:

ויום המות מיום הולדו. אמר ר' לוי למה הדבר דומה לשתי ספינות שהיו בים מלאות סחורה, אחת באה ואחת הולכת, אחת שהיתה באה היו מקלסין אותה, עמדו להם תמהים, אמרו למה אתם מקלסים לזו, ואין אתם מקלסים לזו, אמרו להם לזו שבאתה אנו מקלסין, כי אנו יודעים שהלכה בשלום ובאה בשלום, אבל זו אין אנו יודעים מה היא עתידה לעשות, כך כשאדם נולד, אין בני אדם מכירין מעשיו...

Hesped for Mrs. Lil Gross a"h

The *Midrash* talks of two ships passing each other in the water. One ship – laden with merchandise and filled with people – is leaving on its maiden journey. A second ship – which has completed its journey – is returning back to port. The ship arriving back at the port is being met by throngs of people greeting her as she prepares to dock. The other ship, which is leaving on its initial trip, does not have huge crowds prepared to wish her a bon voyage. There are only a few family members and close friends who are standing by and wishing her a successful journey.

Chazal say that this a parable for life. The first ship represents each and every person. When one is born, he is, in essence, on his inaugural voyage in life. No one actually knows what the outcome of his journey will be. It is uncertain what kind of destiny, what fate or future this individual will have. Will she be a good, kind, and decent person, or will she lead a life that is unsatisfactory and unpleasant? Will this person be successful on his life's voyage or will he or she, unfortunately, be a failure?

The Midrash continues:

כשנפטר מן העולם הן יודעים מה היו מעשיו, הוי ויום המות מיום הולדו.

"However, at the time of one's death, we know very well what his life has brought."

Hesped for Mrs. Lil Gross a"h

A person's life's work is written in the heavenly ledger in black and white. Therefore, at that time, we praise and cheer for the ship that is returning back, the individual who is coming home from the port of life.

My dear friends, all who are gathered here this morning can certainly attest to the fact that my mother's ship has traversed the journey of life. She has passed her test with flying colors. She began her life's journey pure, authentic, and wholesome. She has now ended it with dignity, courage, strength, and conviction.

My mother came from a very distinguished and respected family. The main focus of the Tuchman family was on Torah learning, education, and intellectual pursuit. My mother and her siblings excelled in their scholarly endeavors both religiously as well as secularly.

My mother was a strong and courageous woman. She was steadfast in her beliefs. She was a fiercely loyal friend who went לפנים משורת הדין, well beyond the call of duty for those whom she admired and especially for those whom she loved.

Growing up, I remember with fondness how my mother would, on countless occasions, stay up late at night to help me write and type up my school assignments and term papers. She was always there to help mold and constantly impart life's lessons to me and my sister. She did it with love, affection, and total dedication.

What I remember most is that during my formative years, at certain times when things were not going well, when perhaps my spirits were a bit low, my mother was always at my side, encouraging me to think positively. She assured me that the "sun will truly come out tomorrow." The days ahead will certainly be brighter and shinier than they presently appear.

Of course, the love of my mother's life was my father. He was everything to her. When anyone ever mentioned Moe Gross, one automatically thought of Lil Gross. They were always a team. They did everything together. They walked together, they shopped together, and they travelled together. They truly lived and loved life together.

Then, tragically and suddenly, their lives ended almost simultaneously. Even though my father passed away two and half years before her, a good part of my mother died with him. She was never the same. Her vitality, her spark, her smile, and her happiness left her, unfortunately, never to return.

To the seven grandchildren who love her so much and whom she adored, I say to them, that while you may no longer have your physical grandmother, she will always remain an important and significant part of your lives. You will always carry the wonderful and beautiful memories of a strong, caring, and very loving grandmother.

On behalf of Rivkie, Eamie, and Joel, I want to offer a sincere and heartfelt thanks and a genuine הכרת הטוב to her group of wonderful and caring friends who stood by her at all times. They helped her, they heard her cries, and constantly invited her to their homes and took her out to dinner. They assisted her in so many ways, always trying to make her life meaningful and full.

Finally, I want to publicly thank and express our family's appreciation to my Aunt Rose. She single-handedly kept my mother alive for these two and a half years. She became her partner, her alter ego. She picked her up when she was down. She kept her going when she didn't want to go any longer. To you, Aunt Rose, we will forever be most grateful for at all times going לפנים משורת הדין, always going the extra mile.

To my mother, I say: Mom, our entire family, both our nuclear and our extended family, and all your dear friends hope that you are finally at peace. You are now together with Dad and your other loved ones. In the words of my darling daughter Frumie, your oldest grandchild, "The only thing that consoles me is that Grandma is now where she wanted to be, together with Grandpa."

We pray that you, together with Dad, should be a מליצה ישרה for each of us. In addition, one day, hopefully very soon, with the coming of the *Moshiach*, we will all once again be reunited. יהי זכרה ברוך.

40. Tribute to Rabbi Steven Dworken z"l
A Dear Friend and Beloved Colleague on the Occasion of his 20th Yahrtzeit, January, 2023
(Parshas Lech Lecha)

January, 2023 marked the 20th *Yahrzeit* of my very dear friend and colleague, Rabbi Steven Dworken, *z"l*. His family reached out to a number of his close friends and Rabbinic colleagues and requested that we each prepare a *D'var Torah* which reflected his life and accomplishments, as well as our personal recollections of him. They published these reminiscences in a commemorative book which they prepared for their family and for his closest friends. In addition to the *D'var Torah* which I wrote, I also composed a short missive, which I felt best reflected my personal relationship with him. The following were my remarks:

Steve and I initially became friends while attending the Semicha program at Yeshiva University. He was two years my senior. During my first year, in 1968-1969, I was a dorm counselor in the Yeshiva. Steve was then in his last year and served as the senior dorm counsellor. That year, we began a friendship

Tribute to Rabbi Steven Dworken z"l

which lasted until his very untimely death 35 years later.

In 1976, Steve became the rabbi of Congregation Anshe Chesed in Linden, New Jersey, a neighboring town to Hillside, where I was serving as the rabbi. We immediately picked up where we had left off years earlier.

Rivkie and I then began socializing with both Steve and his wife, Susan. Our relationship grew and developed exponentially over the next few years. We attended Rabbinic conferences together both in New Jersey and throughout the United States. We spoke very often, and we truly enjoyed each other's company.

Steve had a very special and holy *Neshama*. He was extremely bright, very dynamic, and charismatic. He also had a fantastic sense of humor. He was an exceptional and wonderful pulpit rabbi. Both his congregants as well as his colleagues respected, loved him, and truly enjoyed being around him. He had the most unique quality of making each of his friends feel that he was their best and closest friend. The fact of the matter is that he really was best friends with each and every one of us. That was what made him so very special and distinctive.

In addition, I would often marvel as to how he could accomplish so much each day. He was the rabbi of a growing shul, while at the same time he earned his

PhD. He later served as the Director of Placement at YU. Towards the end of his life, he was chosen to be the Executive Vice President of the Rabbinical Council of America, the largest Rabbinical organizations in the world. Yet, in spite of all of his many professional demands, he still took the time to almost daily call and speak with his many friends, both Rabbinic and laymen. He was never rushed; he always had the time for each and every person.

His very untimely and sudden death in early 2003 at the age of fifty-eight shocked and saddened all of us who knew and loved him. We each felt that we had lost our closest friend and mentor. As I wrote at the time of his *petirah*, "I doubt if there will ever be another person like him. He was unique and special. He was a leader of men and was respected by all. He was one of a kind. In many ways he was larger than life."

There is one incident that I wish to highlight which demonstrates his kindness, his closeness, and his genuine *mentschlichkeit*. This occurred just a few years before his *petirah*. In 2001, I had become quite ill and had to undergo many weeks of intensive chemotherapy treatments. I had by then, left the Rabbinate and had begun my own small business. In addition to his constant visits and around the clock calls, Steve did something extraordinary which I will never forget.

One evening, he came to our home and said, "I know that with the many doctor's visits and continuous rounds of treatment, you will probably have to temporarily close down your business. You will not have a continuous source of income." He then took out his checkbook and said, "Tell me how much money you will need for the next few months. You can pay it back whenever you get back on your feet, even if it takes years." *Baruch Hashem*, I did not have to close down my business or accept his very magnanimous and most generous offer. However, his incredible, compassionate, and beautiful act of pure and genuine friendship and love will forever be etched in my heart and my mind.

The following is the *D'var Torah* that I wrote for the commemorative book:

There is a *posuk* in Parshas Lech Lecha which I feel is most appropriate for this very special commemoration. The Torah says:

וְאֶעֶשְׂךָ לְגוֹי גָּדוֹל וַאֲבָרֶכְךָ וַאֲגַדְּלָה שְׁמֶךָ וֶהְיֵה בְּרָכָה: (בראשית יב:ב)

"I will make you a great nation, I will bless you, I will make your name great, and you will be for a blessing."

The Gemara in Meseches Pesachim (117b) says:

אמר רבי שמעון בן לקיש: ואעשך לגוי גדול - זהו שאומרים אלקי אברהם, ואברכך - זהו שאומרים אלקי יצחק, ואגדלה שמך - זהו שאומרים אלקי יעקב, יכול יהו חותמין בכולן - תלמוד לומר והיה ברכה - בך חותמין, ואין חותמין בכולן.

R' Shimon ben Lakish says: ואעשך לגוי גדול corresponds to the words in Shemoneh Esrei of Elokei Avraham. ואברכך is a reference to Elokei Yitzchak. ואגדלה שמך alludes to Elokei Yaakov.

The Gemara then concludes:

One would think that the ending of the beracha should include all three of the Avos. The posuk therefore says: והיה ברכה. Hashem says that the beracha concludes only with the name of Avraham and not the other Avos.

HaRav Shimon Schwab *zt"l* in his *Ma'ayan Beis HaShoeivah* says:

עבודת האדם מישראל תפרד לב' ראשים: א) מסורת אבותיו שבידו, ב) עבודת עצמו.

There are two ways in which a person develops a connection with Hashem. The first is that which is passed down from his ancestors. Each individual must realize and understand that his observance and adherence to the Mitzvos and traditions of *Yahadus* did not originate with him. It was established thousands of years ago by our great ancestors and has been passed down in each generation, from father to child, as a *mesorah*.

There is, however, says HaRav Schwab, another manner in which one can connect and attach himself to Hashem. He refers to this method as מגן אברהם, the "shield of Avraham." It is incumbent upon each Jew to create his own individual connection, his personal and exclusive interaction and synergy with the *Ribono shel Olam*.

Each Jew must, in the grand tradition of Avraham Avinu, make a genuine and sincere effort to find Hashem on his own. While both Yitzchak and Yaakov contributed mightily to the furtherance and continuity of Yiddishkeit, we look primarily to Avraham. He had to combat and fight against an entire world who denied his belief in monotheism. Avraham stood alone on עבר אחת, on one side. The rest of his society was on "עבר אחרת", the opposite and opposing bank.

Avraham was a trailblazer and a pioneer. He was the groundbreaker and the innovator. It is for this reason, says Rav Schwab, that we conclude the *beracha* of *birchas Avos* only with Avraham Avinu and not with the other *Avos*.

When I remember the life and legacy of my dear and wonderful friend, Rabbi Steven Dworken *z"l*, this idea and interpretation of HaRav Schwab comes to mind. He certainly understood and accepted his role of serving as the next link, the continuing tie in the great and magnificent *mesorah*. However, his *ahavas Hashem* and his love and devotion towards his fellow man was uniquely his own. That came through his continuous and ongoing personal searching, seeking, and constant growth and development in all areas of *Yahadus*.

His *Avodas Hashem*, his performance of the מצוות בין אדם למקום was only matched by his fulfillment of the מצוות בין אדם לחבירו. Steve Dworken loved all Jews. It did not matter to him whether they were observant or not yet religious. It was not important to him if one's religious philosophy was to the right or to the left of his *hashkafah*. He loved and respected each and every Jew. He was a true *eved Hashem* in every sense of the word. He most definitely fulfilled the charge and directive issued by HaRav Schwab.

יהי זכרו ברוך. May his memory always serve as a *beracha*.

Rivkie and I have, over these many years, remained very close to Susan. We tried to give her comfort and support in the years when she was alone. In addition, we have continued and maintained our friendship with her and her new husband, Freddy Koss. We see them often during the winter in Boca. Rivkie and Susan speak almost every Erev Shabbos. I also have become very close to Freddy. We are very proud to count them among our very close and dear friends.

41. A Woman for All Seasons

Dedicated to the blessed memory of my paternal grandmother, Yetta Gross, Yenta bas Harav Binyamin Halevi a"h in commemoration of her recent 54th Yahrtzeit, 21 Cheshvan. The following is an enhancement of the Hesped, the eulogy which I gave at her funeral in November 1969.

A few weeks ago, the *Sedra* which we *lained* in shul was Parshas Noach. There, we were told that Noach was perhaps the only individual in the Torah who had the distinction of being designated as both a *Tzadik* as well as a *Tamim*. He was righteous as well as wholesome. He walked together with Hashem. *Chazal* however, as quoted by Rashi, were undecided as to the degree of his virtue. Was he a genuine, full-time and bona-fide *Tzadik*, or perhaps he was a pious and upstanding individual only on a comparative basis? Was he considered distinctive and illustrious only compared to his wicked and evil generation? Perhaps, according to this view, had he been born in a different era or age, in which the population was not so evil and immoral, he may not have been considered anything out of the ordinary.

On this particular aspect, our *Chachamim* argue and debate. However, on another of his attributes, there is no dissension, there is no difference of opinion. On this, there is total unanimity and agreement. When the Torah says (Beraishis 6:9):

אֵלֶּה תּוֹלְדֹת נֹחַ נֹחַ אִישׁ צַדִּיק...

These are the generations of Noach; Noach was a righteous man.

What this means is that he was a good, decent, and upstanding person when he was an איש, when he was young and vibrant, when he still had the means and the ability to influence and change the life choices of others. On this feature, there is no disagreement.

Many of us, I am sure, have during our lifetimes encountered individuals who, for a number of years may have been off the דרך הישר, the right and proper path of *Yahadus*. However, years later, after they grew older and wiser or perhaps after they retired from their business career, they made the decision to return to the דרך ה', to become *ba'alei teshuvah*. These people became fully committed to a life which encompassed all of the Mitzvos of the Torah. These individuals certainly deserve our praise, our support, our appreciation, and our commendation for transforming and changing their lives. However, at the time that they made their personal change, it was unfortunately, too late for them to have any positive influence and impact

Hesped for Mrs. Yetta Gross a"h

on the next generation. Their children and, in many cases, even their grandchildren were already grown and had already established their own families and were set in their non-religious lifestyles.

I personally knew one such couple who had completely turned their religious lives around. They became fully Torah observant and remained so for the rest of their lives. However, they only embraced complete Yiddishkeit when they were in their high 60's. Unfortunately, their children and grandchildren were non-observant and their parents' religious lives did not have much of an impact or influence on their family.

The great Chassidic master, Rav Chaim of Sanz, in discussing the life of Noach, said that the true hallmark of a *Tzadik* is that he becomes and remains a righteous and pious person when he is an איש. One must be a *Tzadik* when he is still powerful and dynamic, when he is young and vibrant. It is insufficient to make his own personal life one of קדושה וטהרה. The true test of an איש is to use his ability, his strength, his determination and his wherewithal to alter the lives of his family.

Each of us has individuals whom we look up to with reverence and awe. Some of these people we may hope to emulate and pattern our lives after. Some look up to great ballplayers. Others look to great figures in history, perhaps an enlightened head of state or a major political leader who has positively contributed to society. Still others look to great military leaders. For Jews however, although we may very well admire some of the accomplishments of these individuals, they should never, at any time, serve as our real heroes or role models. We should never try to pattern our lives after them. We must have our own worthy and noble individuals after whom we can follow.

Avner Gold, the famous Jewish author, in his book, *The Long Road to Freedom,* describes the Jewish attitude and concept of heroism. He writes: "The world measures heroism by feats of valor on the battlefield and other acts of a similar nature. There is, however, nothing more heroic or valiant than the devotion of our people to the Almighty and to His Torah, despite all the persecutions that we have suffered."

Our heroes, the individuals whom *Am Yisrael* should look up to and admire are our great ancestors: the *Avos HaKedoshim*—Avraham, Yitzchak and Yaakov, Moshe Rabbeinu, Aharon HaKohen, Dovid Hamelech, and Eliyahu HaNavi, among others. We look to all the great and holy *Tzadikim,* our *Kedoshim* and *Tehorim,* who have formed and fashioned *Yahadus* throughout the ages, as well as to the millions of our brethren who have sacrificed their lives for its perpetuation.

Each of us individually has at least one or two people who have truly impacted our lives in a positive and meaningful manner. We look to them with pride, delight, and honor. We hope that we could, one day, follow in their footsteps. We admire the lives that they have lived, the sacrifices that they have made, and the examples which they have set.

For me personally, I have a few people who have had a profound impact and influence on my life: my father, Moe Gross *a"h*, my Uncle Hymie Tuchman *z"l*, my revered father-in-law HaRav Samuel Fink *zt"l*, and some of my *Rebbeim*. However, there is one person more than anyone else whom I look up to, one individual who has set the bar so very high. I hope and pray that one day I can leave a legacy and a heritage even half as great as hers. I am referring to my paternal grandmother, Mrs. Yetta Gross- Yenta bas Harav Binyamin HaLevi *a"h*.

My grandmother was diminutive in appearance. I don't think that she was even five feet tall. She was not very loud or boisterous; in fact, she was quite soft spoken and unassuming. It was only years after her passing that I discovered her true depth, her tremendous faith, and her incredible and remarkable courage. She, in essence, was the standard-bearer for me and for my entire extended family.

My grandmother was widowed in 1930 when she was only 40 years old. She had three children, two teenagers as well as my father who was then only eight years old. She needed to support her family after the sudden and unexpected death of my grandfather, Harry Gross *a"h*. She chose to open a houseware/hardware store on 13th avenue, in her neighborhood, the Boro Park section of Brooklyn, New York.

The Great Depression had just set in; as such, making a living was extremely difficult. Her relatives who had immigrated to the United States before her and were now "Americanized" attempted to convince her to keep her store open seven days a week. They felt that this was absolutely necessary for her to earn a living and to help support her young family. However, my grandmother grew up in a home of Torah and *Yiras Shamayim* and always remained *frum* and committed to all the Mitzvos. Her life in the United States was patterned after her formative years in Europe. She absolutely refused to listen to her relatives. She felt that Shabbos was a day that Hashem decreed for us to rest and observe its multitude of Mitzvos. There was no question that her store would remain closed on each and every Shabbos and Yom Tov. Whatever income Hashem would provide would be satisfactory for her. Therefore, in 1931, she opened the first *Shomer*

Hesped for Mrs. Yetta Gross a"h

Shabbos store on 13th Avenue and one of the only ones of its kind, at that time, in all of Boro Park.

My grandmother was a pioneer and a trailblazer. She was also a very clever, astute, and fair businesswomen. She was admired by her customers for her decency, generosity, and honesty. In fact, during the secular holiday season, her non-Jewish customers remained completely loyal to her, even though her store was closed on Shabbos. Many of them waited until the end of Shabbos and stood in front of her house which was around the corner of her store. At the conclusion of Shabbos, they would often ring her bell and say: "Mrs. Gross, there are three stars in the sky; your Sabbath is over. You can now open up your store for business."

In this vein, I am reminded of a story told by Rabbi Yissocher Frand, a Rosh Yeshiva in Yeshiva Ner Yisrael and a long-time family friend. Rabbi Frand related the time that Harav Mordechai Gifter *zt"l*, the late Rosh Yeshiva of the Telshe Yeshiva, came to visit Yeshiva Ner Yisrael.

Rav Gifter addressed the Yeshiva on Parshas Noach. He said that the Torah gave Noach three approbations: He was a צדיק, a תמים, and an איש. Before a person can become either a *Tzadik* or a *Tamim*, righteous or wholesome, said Rav Gifter, he must be an *Ish*, he must be a mensch. He must be as considerate and kind to his fellow man as he is to Hashem.

I truly feel that this *pshat* of Rav Gifter so aptly applies to my grandmother *a"h*. She, like Noach, was a *Tamim*. She was wholesome and pure. She was a *Tzadeikes*, she was truly righteous in all of her actions and in every facet of her life. However, first and foremost, she, like Noach, was an *Ish*, or in her case, she was an *Isha*; she was a real and genuine mensch.

Today, in the mid-21st century, it is not too difficult to own a business and keep it closed on Shabbos and Yom Tov. However, ninety-three years ago, it was a monumental and herculean feat. It took someone of superhuman spiritual and religious strength and conviction not to buckle in, not to give in to the mores and the irreligious conduct of that time. Many Jews, even those who came from very frum and even Yeshiva European backgrounds folded under the enormously intense pressure. They succumbed to the times and the behavior of the day.

My grandmother, my hero, was different. She saw the challenge and the *nisayon*, the test, and followed her heart. She stood by her convictions, by the Torah and Mitzvos that her parents and her forebears had implanted in her. She was bold and courageous, daring and fearless. She, like Noach before her, was a genuine and authentic *Tzadeikes*. By her tremendous deeds she set a beautiful example for her children, her grandchildren, and for many future generations to follow in her footsteps and to try to emulate her life.

I truly believe that it was because of her heroism and in the great merit of her sacrifice for *shmiras Shabbos*, that today, close to three hundred of her descendants are *Shomer Mitzvos* and are *Yirei Shamayim*. Many are learning Torah in yeshivas both in the United States and in Israel. Some have become Rabbis. A few have become spiritual leaders of congregations. Many are teachers and *Rebbeim* in various Yeshivos, Mesivtos and Seminaries. All however, are of the same mind. We all believe in the priority of Torah and Mitzvos and in transmitting these beautiful and most meaningful ideals and values to succeeding generations.

I became the person I am today in no small part because of my grandmother's sacrifice and total commitment to *Yahadus*. My children and grandchildren and, G-d willing, their children after them should be forever grateful to this *Isha Chashuva*. To me she will forever be my heroine. To me, she was a "Woman for All Seasons."

May the holy *Neshama* of *Ha'Isha Hachashuva* Yenta bas Harav Binyamin Halevi *a"h* go למעלה ולמעלה in *Olam HaBa*. May she continue to be a מליצה ישרה

for our entire family. May we continue to look to her and to her life of ideals and commitment as a springboard to our own growth in Torah and in *Avodas Hashem*. May our combined מעשים טובים help to speedily bring the Moshiach, במהרה בימינו אמן.

42. My Suggestions for the Enhancement of our Lives in America

Over the past few years, I have dedicated many hours to studying and developing certain ideas and programs which I feel can enhance and strengthen the future of the Orthodox American Jewish community. I have come up with two thoughts, which if implemented would, I believe, have a very positive impact on the future growth and development of our community.

While I enjoy my senior citizen status and all its perks and benefits, I wish that I still had the strength, the courage and the wherewithal to undertake and play a leadership role in these projects. Unfortunately, I no longer have the physical ability or the energy to promote and advance these ventures. I must leave them to others. Therefore, I will merely suggest and recommend a few ideas that are near and dear to my heart.

One proposal which I would recommend would be to attempt to convince every Orthodox shul in the United States, both small or large, from modern orthodox to Agudah, from Yeshivish to even Chassidic, to recite the *tefillah* for the United States government each Shabbos and Yom Tov morning. In addition, I would propose that they should also say the *tefillah* for the welfare of our brethren in Medinat Yisrael and especially for its very valiant IDF who continuously protects and defends Eretz Yisrael and all elements of *Am Yisrael*.

This plan, if implemented, would accomplish two very important objectives. It would firstly be a constant reminder to our country's governmental leaders that the American Jewish community is extremely loyal and patriotic. We would be indicating and demonstrating our gratitude and thankfulness for living in this great and welcoming country. We would show that we are dedicated, faithful, and loyal citizens who love and respect our nation. By our actions, we would demonstrate that we, who are the *Am Kadosh* and the *Am HaNivchar*, the holy and chosen people, believe in and integrate within us the democratic values which this nation has been built on, stands for, and has extended to all its citizens.

In addition, while we may not always agree with every policy or act which the State of Israel executes and carries out, it nevertheless behooves us to show and demonstrate our appreciation to the *Ribono shel Olam* for giving us this great gift, the miracle which is the modern State of Israel. At the same time, we would exhibit our *areivus*, our camaraderie and closeness with

Suggestions to Enhance our Lives in America

our beleaguered and isolated brothers and sisters in Medinat Yisrael.

I realize that this is, undoubtedly, a pipe dream. It will probably never even get off the ground. The reason is that a large majority of Orthodox shuls throughout the Diaspora will continue to refuse to ever recite either *tefillah*. However, I can still hope and pray that one day this dream of mine will come to fruition.

Secondly, with the cancerous spread of antisemitism, anti-Zionism, hatred, and bigotry recently afflicting and sweeping the entire world and even our country, the Jewish community must, I believe, attempt to do something to ameliorate it. Yes, there are numerous scholarly individuals throughout the United States who are currently implementing various educational programs. By their actions, they are hoping to change the minds and hearts of many of our antagonists and our enemies. They have begun sophisticated, educational, and social endeavors towards this end.

Nevertheless, however successful this might eventually be, I don't believe that these efforts will ever completely change the opinions and remove the hatred from, unfortunately, millions of Americans. These people have, over the past few decades, become either sympathetic with these Jew-haters or have become antisemites themselves. Their primary goal continues to be to hurt and cause harm to the American Jewish community.

In response to this malignancy, I believe that we must learn how to protect ourselves from our enemies. Our late and sacred European brothers and sisters were unprepared in the Shoah to fight their arch-enemy, the Nazis, ימח שמם וזכרם. Our generation must be ready, prepared, and on guard if this situation, G-d forbid, gets any worse,

We must teach our children, from the youngest grades up, some degree of self-defense. The Torah itself mandates us to do so. In Sefer Shemos, in Parshas Mishpatim, we are told that when someone attempts to harm or kill us, we have an obligation, a *chiyuv*, to prevent it from occurring. As our children get older, they should be taught to defend themselves in every possible way.

In addition, every Yeshiva and shul throughout this country needs an inordinate amount of funds to hire well trained and armed security guards who will hopefully protect our school children and the adults who attend shul. In that regard, I believe that we should attempt to institute a four-pronged approach to help these institutions.

1. Every shul and Yeshiva should request that each *mispaleil* and all parents provide at least a token contribution towards the security of their

institution. This must be over and beyond the regular membership fees and tuition. While this should be purely voluntary, it should be encouraged and inspired by the organizations themselves. In addition, the amount given by each participant would of course depend upon each family's financial situation. By participating and contributing we are at least doing our own *hishtadlus*. We each are doing our share.

2. I hope that a few brave and courageous individuals from our community would step forward. They should try to convince the ever-growing number of the super-rich committed and observant Jews in this country to donate the funds that are needed to protect our Jewish institutions.

3. For a number of years, there has been a grant funded by the United States Homeland Security Department. This endowment has provided millions of dollars to help protect religious institutions throughout the country. We must continue to apply for these grants. In addition, we must try to convince our legislative leaders to extend additional funding for these most important programs.

Suggestions to Enhance our Lives in America

4. Every shul in this country should have responsible members on their security team who are trained in self-defense. And, if possible, they should be licensed to carry a weapon which will help protect our *mispallelim* from a potentially cataclysmic event.

While I still believe wholeheartedly in the overall goodness and decency of our fellow Americans, we must continue to be vigilant and be on guard against those who wish to do us harm.

Finally, and indeed, most important, we must at all times have complete *Emunah* and *Bitachon* in the *Ribono shel Olam*. He is, and will always be, our שומר, our protector and defender. However, we must do our own *hishtadlus*. We cannot, nor dare not, ever be complacent or smug in this area. Only in this manner will we hopefully help guarantee our continued growth and development in our wonderful adopted country, the United States of America.

43. The Simchas Torah Massacre Israel in an Existential War of Survival

The following essay was written on October 30, 2023, a mere few weeks after Israel was brutally and barbarically attacked by Hamas savages and their fellow, so-called, "peaceful" Palestinian supporters.

Dear friends:

Just a mere eight days after the start of Chag HaSukkos, our festival of great joy and celebration, the Jewish world and especially the lives of our brothers and sisters in Medinat Yisrael were upended and changed forever. The brutal, barbaric, and inhumane pogrom and massacre of over 1,200 beautiful and holy Jewish lives on Shemini-Atzeres/Simchas Torah in the Southern area of Israel has left a permanent hole in the hearts of all of Klal Yisrael. When those חיות רעות, those sub-humans, the members of Hamas and their associates, smashed through the highly vaulted and supposedly impregnable security wall at the southern border of Israel and ruthlessly killed innocent civilians, our previously positive and optimistic faith in the future peace and prosperity for Eretz Yisrael was permanently shattered.

I realized that I must summon up all my broken courage and tear-filled feelings and try to share some of my thoughts with my family and dear friends. While many of the past wars and other historical events which the State of Israel has experienced were written about in hindsight –after many years and decades have passed – this cataclysmic, disastrous and tragic event is very different. I feel that it must be written about and discussed in real-time. We must have a discourse on this now.

I do not believe that today is the right time to sit and reflect upon how these tragedies were able to occur. Our Rabbanim, world class historians and outstanding Jewish and military scholars will in the next few months, years and decades, dissect and analyze the events leading up to the attack and the inevitable blame and repercussions that will certainly occur. However, I feel that this chapter which details the events of the current and ongoing war must be penned at this time.

Chag HaSukkos is sub-titled in Halacha as זמן שמחתינו, our primary Yom Tov which symbolizes joy, celebration, and happiness. *Chazal* are replete in their reasons for the Torah's designation and our reciting in our Tefillos of the classification of this Festival as one of exuberance, celebration and unbridled joy. This description of זמן שמחתינו is also carried over to the final days of the Yom Tov. Shemini Atzeres/Simchas Torah share the same nomenclature and appellation of זמן שמחתינו as well.

For my family, the Yom Tovim of Sukkos and Shemini Atzeres has for decades been a very personal time of joyousness and *simcha*. It first began on Chol Hamoed Sukkos of 1974 when Rivkie and I became engaged. Two years later, on the first day of Sukkos, 1976, our oldest child, our dear and beloved daughter, Frumie, was born. A week later, on Shemini Atzeres, I named her for my late mother-in-law, Rebbetzin Fruma Fink *a"h*.

Twenty-four years later, on Shemini Atzeres, 2000, my third grandchild, Moishe, was born. I had the *zechus* to be his *Sandek* and he was named for my late and beloved father, Moshe Pesach Nissan *a"h*. Thus, besides the national observance of this Festival as a time of joy and happiness, for our family it has always been a personal time of exceptional ebullience and high spirits.

This year, it was only later in the day, on the eve of Simchas Torah in Chutz l'aretz, that we began hearing of the devastating and horrific news coming out of Israel. I only heard some sketchy reports on Yom Tov. Upon the conclusion of Yom Tov, when we were all able to turn on our phones, computers, televisions, and radios, we began absorbing and internalizing the unfathomable and disastrous events of the past few days.

Unlike my children and especially my grandchildren for whom this was the first major Israeli war that they experienced, I have lived through all of Israel's past wars. I was a young child during the 1948 War of Independence. I was a 10-year-old elementary school student during the 1956 Sinai campaign. I was a junior in college during the 1967 glorious and spectacular Six Day War. And I was beginning my first Yom Kippur as the Rabbi at Congregation Sinai Torath Chaim in Hillside, New Jersey, during the start of the very difficult but eventually very successful and overwhelmingly victorious 1973 Yom Kippur War.

After watching all the news channels and absorbing and internalizing the events of Israel's current crisis, I was completely shocked and disappointed. After living through the Yom Kippur War, I always felt that each successive Israeli government and its Prime Minister would have learned their lessons from their country's past miscalculations. The calamitous nature of the inception of that war was due to its total lack of preparedness, its taking the enemy Arab countries for granted, and its dereliction in not placing enough personnel both at the Suez Canal and in the Golan Heights.

The Simchas Torah Massacre

Over the past five decades, all Israeli leaders stated that they would "never again" be unprepared for any armed conflict. Each Isru Chag, after the conclusion of every Yom Tov for the past fifty years, I was always quite grateful when I would turn on the news and find out that no hostilities or surprise attack occurred on Yom Tov. I was especially relieved after every Yom Kippur. This year, both after the conclusion of Yom Kippur as well as after the first days of Sukkos, I was confident that *Am Yisrael* and especially Medinat Yisrael were at peace. After speaking to some very dear and close friends and relatives who reside in Israel, I was convinced that this year would be one of Shalom and *beracha* for all of *Am Yisrael*. And then came Simchas Torah. That became a day unlike any other in the lives of all of us who were born after the conclusion of the Shoah, the Holocaust, the worst period, the nadir in all of Jewish history. It became Israel's "Day of Infamy." It became Israel's 9/11.

When I went to Shul on Simchas Torah, I felt that this year, Simchas Torah should not be the same day of celebration and frivolity as we usually observe each year. I spoke to the Rav of the Shul where I was davening and expressed my sentiments to him. I had a very warm relationship with the Rav. I asked that we have modified and abbreviated *hakafos*. I was told that a *shailah* was asked to a *poseik* in Lakewood who felt that the *hakafos* should be the same as in all other years. His reason was that our celebration of the Torah would be a *zechus* for the current very difficult *matzav* in Eretz Yisrael. Although I personally felt that due to the life altering experience which we suffered this year we should at the very least modify our joy and happiness, I abided by the *psak* issued by a well-respected Rav.

After the conclusion of Yom Tov, I spoke to a number of friends from other communities across the United States. Most informed me that they either had a very modified and abbreviated *hakafos*, or at the very least, no drinking of alcohol and certainly no inebriation was allowed in recognition of the very dire situation. I then felt justified that my feelings on this issue were shared by many other people.

I would like at this time to present three takeaways from the current crisis which our brethren in Eretz Yisrael face. Two are quite positive, while the third is extremely disturbing. I would like to begin first with the latter. I wrote in chapter 42 about the very dangerous and ongoing threat of antisemitism which is raising its ugly head both here in the United States and especially around the world and how we can possibly try to combat it. However, since the war began, we have become witness to even more widespread nefarious and villainous attacks both domestically and world-wide.

While I expected large and vocal protests against Israel and in support of Hamas and the Palestinian cause throughout the Arab and Muslim world, I did not ever expect to see all the hate, venom, and vitriol against Israel and the entire Jewish community coming from some of the major cities in the United States and Western Europe.

What was even more troubling was the malice and acrimony towards Israel and all Jews which emanated from some of the most prestigious, esteemed, and prominent colleges and universities throughout the country. Institutions of higher learning such as Harvard, Yale, Columbia, NYU, Stanford, Cooper Union, University of Pennsylvania, and countless others spewed much more than merely their backing of Hamas and their hatred of Israel. They made it very clear that their goal and purpose was the elimination and destruction of all Jews both in Israel and throughout the world. Even more troubling was the fact that these vociferous activities and the hate spewed was led and encouraged by many professors and heads of departments in these universities.

Equally troubling was that the leaders of these institutions, the deans, the provosts and even the presidents and chancellors gave these antisemites total and complete license to express their first amendment rights, even at the expense of the hurt and fear caused to their Jewish students. I never thought that I would see the day when so-called enlightened and liberal academia would rear its ugly and bigoted head and demonstrate its true colors of hatred and vociferousness toward any group, especially our brothers and sisters.

I have been a student of history for many decades. I took numerous courses on the Holocaust, I have read Holocaust literature extensively, and I have also published a number of times on different areas of the Holocaust. The Nazis ימ"ש in Germany did not suddenly and without any planning, wake up one morning and decide at the Wannsee conference in 1942 to systematically murder all of European Jewry. This was planned out and instituted in a step by step, gradual process of demonization of the Jews. This lasted for 9 years, beginning in 1933 until 1942. By the time the Nazis officially decided to murder all of European Jewry in 1942, the Jews had been persecuted and discriminated against and had been marginalized for many years.

In addition, the average German citizen was influenced by and categorically believed all the negative and hateful propaganda spewed against the Jews by the Nazi propaganda machine. They were then quite ready and willing to be silent bystanders and sometimes quite willing accomplices as their neighbors and former friends were herded into cattle cars and brought to their deaths in the concentration camps.

These were the thoughts that came to my mind these past few weeks as I watched the tens of thousands of Americans demonstrating for Hamas and against the State of Israel on multiple college campuses and in major cities throughout this country. Their venomous insults and their irrational hatred were not just limited to Israel and her war against the Hamas terrorists. It morphed into an all-out attack against the Jewish community, both in this country and throughout the world. It reached such a low point that in certain areas, signs were being carried and voices were raised which called for the "murder and incineration of all Jews." Thus began the demonization, the gradual and continuous lowering of the Jewish community in the eyes of our fellow countrymen.

On October 28, there was a fascinating interview in the Wall Street Journal with Natan Sharansky, the former Soviet Prisoner of Conscience and past Israeli politician and statesman. He discussed Israel's current war against Hamas and the world's very negative reaction towards Israel's plight. He said, "Israel is subjected to the three D's: demonization, double standard, and delegitimization." The intellectual community and the leaders of colleges and universities "refuse to call the most primitive acts of antisemitism by its name." They instead dignify the Hamas murders as a form of anti-colonial struggle.

If this is the reality, how then do we combat it? What do we do to fight this insidious and potentially catastrophic toxicity? One thing we cannot do is to ignore it. We cannot, nor dare not remain silent when we are being attacked and maligned.

I believe that the first thing each of us must do is to resolve to strengthen our religious and spiritual commitment and practices. We each have to take on additional Mitzvos, recite more Tefillos and Tehillim, and increase our Torah learning. We must demonstrate to the *Ribono Shel Olam* that we have become different and better people. We must beg Him to change this *gezeirah* against us. We cannot feel that things will get better merely because we will it. We must show Hashem that we have personally taken the initiative and that we are different, better, and more spiritual Jews.

Second, we have to determine who are our real friends and allies. Be they in the United States Congress (House and Senate), be they in industry, in the business world, and in the various professions or arts, we must request and implore them to step forward and speak loudly and forcefully for our cause, for what is right and just.

Third, I believe that we have to reach out to the thirty to forty million Evangelical Christians, the born-again non-Jews who reside both in the United States and throughout the world. They are our largest and most loyal allies. They love Israel and greatly admire the Jewish people. We must request that they join with us in different cities throughout this country in rallies and in pro-Israel demonstrations. We should implore their leaders to appear on the various news shows and voice their support for our people and for Medinat Yisrael. When the press and the world community will see thousands of Jewish and non-Jewish supporters of Israel standing together, shoulder to shoulder, it can only have a very positive effect. Hopefully, it can counter some of the mass demonstrations taking place around the world in which anti-Israel and antisemitic rhetoric is being voiced.

In addition, since this war had begun. at least at this juncture, we have been witness to an incredible united front of almost the entire Jewish community coming together as never before. The past year had unfortunately seen terrible factionalism, in-fighting, and extremely bitter divisions in Israeli society and in world Jewry as never before. Secular, anti-religious, and extreme liberal Jews took to the streets and protested every week for months at a time. Their anger was generated against the right wing political and religious coalition led by Prime Minister Netanyahu and their attempt to reform the judicial process throughout Israeli society.

This attempt at judicial reform appeared to have taken over all aspects of the country, even to the point where the government seemed to pay scant attention to the larger and more existential threat, the fear of war from Iran and her proxies in the area, Hamas and Hezbollah. That factionalism within Eretz Yisrael and the potential for civil war was, by the start of this past Rosh Hashanah, so real and palpable that it was terribly frightening. The future for the internal affairs in Eretz Yisrael was very much in doubt. However, then came Simchas Torah, and everything changed.

When Eretz Yisrael had its guard down, when the government was completely absorbed in relatively insignificant areas, it was in essence unprepared to protect its citizens from the real enemy, the constant and ongoing external threat. Thus, when the חיות רעות from Gaza successfully attacked and sadistically and barbarically murdered and killed over 1,200 innocent Jews, the army was nowhere to be found. It was only following that unbelievable and unthinkable tragedy that everything changed.

Finally, all segments of Israeli and world Jewry awoke from its slumber. We began to understand, comprehend and realize that כל ישראל ערבים זה בזה – we are all one people. Whether we are to the right or to the left, whether we are *Chareidi* or *Tzioni*, whether we are *shomer Shabbos* or Shomer HaTzair, we are all one. An attack on one Jew is, for all practical purposes, an attack on all Jews.

This war has so far brought together almost all segments of *Klal Yisrael* in support of the people of Eretz Yisrael. There has never been a time in our history when so many of our fellow Jews throughout the world have donated to the countless charitable organizations which are helping support and give encouragement to our beleaguered brethren. Hundreds of people living in America and in Western Europe have already travelled to Israel to bring much needed supplies to the beleaguered civilian population and to show their support for the *chayalim* and for אחינו בני ישראל. Many *Chareidi* Jews, both in Israel and from abroad, have volunteered for the first time to join the Israeli Defense Forces or to help serve and assist in any possible manner. Thus, the degree of *achdus*, unity and camaraderie, is higher than at any other time in the history of the State of Israel.

In addition, thousands of men and women both in Israel and in the United States who study full time in

Yeshivos and Seminaries have dedicated many hours of their day to learning and davening for their brothers and sisters who are putting their lives on the line while defending Eretz Yisrael and Klal Yisrael. Almost every Shul throughout the world has regularly been reciting numerous chapters of Tehillim both during the week and on Shabbos, for the success of Tzahal and for all our brethren in Eretz Yisrael. As religious and believing Jews, we are fully aware that we desperately need both areas of defense, spiritual as well as physical.

One of the most optimistic results of the war has been the steady and almost complete support of the State of Israel and its right to defend itself by the different agencies of the United States government. The US Congress, with the rare exception of the antisemitic "squad" and a few of their allies, is almost unanimously in favor of Israel's position. The Biden administration has already sent millions of dollars of military aid to help bolster her defense. It has also pledged over an additional billion dollars in armaments and in additional equipment for the Iron Dome defense against incoming enemy rocket attacks.

In fact, just last week, President Biden, in a highly unprecedented move, flew to Israel and spent a number of hours meeting with and showing support to the leaders and the citizens of the State of Israel. This is a very important and significant step. I just hope and pray that it continues and that America will remain very steadfast in supporting Israel's defense against an ever-increasing hostile, belligerent and antagonistic world.

I would like to suggest, as I have told my immediate family, to be prepared for a three-pronged approach:
1. We must make certain that our passports and those of our children are up to date and can be utilized immediately, if needed. We should also have a certain amount of liquid funds to access and use if needed immediately.
2. I believe that each person, both young and old, should be trained in some degree of self-defense. If, G-d forbid, we are ever attacked by ruffians or by individual antisemites, we should not just run away or cower and hide. We must be capable of defending ourselves. It has been shown over and over again that the only thing a bully or a tyrant understands and respects is strength.
3. Each adult who is capable, both physically and psychologically, should immediately apply for a license to purchase a gun and be trained to defend himself and his family.

If these actions are implemented, I believe that we will have a very good chance of overcoming and

The Simchas Torah Massacre

dealing with these very significant challenges facing our people. With the constant help and assistance from the Ribono Shel Olam along with our own *hishtadlus*, we will not only survive this dangerous situation, but we will emerge from this עת צרה and be stronger and more secure as a people and as a nation.

דבר תורה

Morai v'Rabbosai: As religious, committed, and observing Jews, we believe *b'emunah shleimah* that nothing in life occurs haphazardly. All events are pre-determined and ordained by *HaKadosh Baruch Hu*. We do not know nor could we ever understand or comprehend the ways and actions of Hashem. It was apparently G-d's decree that so many of our brethren were sadistically and inhumanely slaughtered and butchered on Simchas Torah by the sub-human Hamas terrorists from Gaza.

Additionally, it was ordained that exactly two weeks after this horrendous event, the Sedra read on that Shabbos was Parshas Noach. The main theme of the Parsha was the cataclysmic deluge, the great *Mabul* with which Hashem destroyed the earth, saving only Noach and his family. At the very beginning of the Parsha, after describing the very positive characteristics of Noach, the Torah indicates the reason why Hashem destroyed the world. The Torah says (Bereishis 6:13):

וַיֹּאמֶר אֱלֹקִים לְנֹחַ קֵץ כָּל בָּשָׂר בָּא לְפָנַי כִּי מָלְאָה הָאָרֶץ **חָמָס** מִפְּנֵיהֶם וְהִנְנִי מַשְׁחִיתָם אֶת הָאָרֶץ:

And Hashem said to Noach: The end of all flesh has come before Me, for the earth was filled with robbery through them; behold I will destroy them from the earth.

I would like to share a few interpretations of the idea of *chamas* by our *Chachamim*. I hope it will help you understand and internalize the depth of its depravity, perversion and viciousness.

Rashi, quoting the Gemara in Sanhedrin (103a), says that although the generation of the *Mabul* violated all of Hashem's laws, the decree of punishment was exacted only because of חמס, robbery, which they committed.

The Ramban explains that *chamas,* which can also be interpreted as violence or savagery, is given as the main cause of the earth's destruction. This was so because it was in essence a transgression both against man as well as against G-d.

Finally, the *Nesivos Shalom*, Harav Shalom Noach Berezovsky, says that the cruelty and savagery of the *Dor HaMabul* became so pervasive and entrenched that it contaminated and polluted all of creation. This occurred to such an extent that Hashem had to decree and follow through with the earth's total annihilation and destruction.

The root of the evil and nefariousness of the *Dor HaMabul*, says the *Nesivos Shalom*, was comparable to the deeds of the nation of Amalek. The Torah is very explicit in regards to Amalek. Each Jew has a *chiyuv*, we are at all times required to destroy and obliterate every vestige, every member of the Amalek nation. In a similar fashion, we have a charge to obliterate from our midst the reincarnation of the modern-day version of Amalek and its predecessor, the *Dor HaMabul*: Hamas. We should all be *mispaleil* that Hashem bestow strength, courage, and the wherewithal to Tzahal and wisdom and *chachmah* to the leaders of Medinat Yisrael to be able to carry out and complete this very important and significant Mitzvah, the total and complete annihilation and destruction of Hamas and all of our other enemies, Amen.

44. The Last Pesach

I am writing these words on the 28th day of Nisan, 5784, Yom HaShoah u'Gevurah. While it is only a mere six days after the conclusion of our most joyous and festive Yom Tov, Pesach, we nevertheless pause and reflect. Today we remember the lives and the deaths of our six million European brothers and sisters who were barbarically, systematically, and brutally murdered by the Nazi sub-human beasts during the Shoah, the Holocaust.

Today is also a most appropriate time to recall the latest group of Jews who were also killed by the modern-day Nazis. Just a mere seven months ago, our precious brethren were slaughtered in the most inhumane manner by the Hamas barbarians in southern Israel on October 7, 2023.

In addition, I wish to comment on the events of the past two hundred days. Israel's existential war is still going on. They have not yet achieved their two objectives, namely, 1) Getting back all the hostages taken on that fatal day, and 2) Completely destroying Hamas' military capacity.

This has become Israel's longest war since the War of Independence in 1948-1949. The reason, I believe, is that Tzahal, the IDF, is basically fighting

The Last Pesach

with one hand tied behind its back. There has been so much external political pressure placed on Prime Minister Netanyahu that his hands are practically tied. This is due to a number of factors:

- The ever-growing protests in Israel by the hostage families who are demanding a truce with Hamas at any cost
- The hundreds of thousands of anti-Israel and antisemitic protests on college campuses throughout the world and especially in the United States
- The complete back stabbing and duplicitous actions of President Biden and his entire administration

Israel stands at a real and genuine crossroad. They do not want to antagonize the entire world community and become a pariah, despised, hated, and alienated from the world community. On the other hand, they do not want to abandon their two major goals of the war.

Their intelligence (which is the best in the world) informed them that the remaining Hamas fighters have taken refuge in Rafah, the southernmost city in the Gaza strip. Most of the living hostages have been taken there as well. It is there that they must stage an all-out offensive attack to complete their war goals and to finally destroy Hamas once and for all.

The Last Pesach

After countless negotiations with Hamas for the release of the hostages continuously failed, the Israeli government, has no choice. They must go into Rafah and inflict tremendous punishment on Hamas despite the warnings from President Biden and other world leaders.

On this issue, Prime Minister Netanyahu has a *mesorah*. He has a tradition passed down to him from one of Israel's greatest Prime Ministers. In 1982, Prime Minister Menachem Begin *a"h* came to Washington. Begin had a meeting with then Senator Joe Biden, the head of an important Senate Committee. During the meeting, Biden threatened to withhold arms from Israel if the Israeli government did not accede to his demands regarding the so called "illegal" territories. The great Prime Minister Begin responded and said:

"אני יהודי גאה, לא תפחד אותי באיומים!"

[*I am a proud Jew; you do not scare me with your threats.*] Don't threaten us with cutting off aid to give up our principles. I am not a Jew with trembling knees. I am a proud Jew with 3,700 years of civilized history. Nobody came to our aid when we were dying in the gas chambers and in the ovens. Nobody came to our aid when we were striving to create our country. We paid for it. We fought for it. We died for it. We will stand by our principles. We will defend them. And when necessary, we will die for them again, with or without your aid.

Although the world appears bleak and foreboding, and the future of Judaism is in a precarious state, we can never give up hope or our dreams for the future. I recently saw a most beautiful *vort* which will cause us all to become optimistic and be positive for the future of *Yiddishkeit*.

The *Iturai Torah* brings down a source named *Matamim*. He explains why only on Chag HaPesach is the last day called *Acharon shel Pesach*. We don't have this appellation given to the last day of any other Yom Tov, whether it be Shavuos, Rosh HaShanah, or even Sukkos. Why is this so? He explains that Yirmiyahu HaNavi states (Yirmiyahu 16:14-15) that in the very near future, the day will come that the Jewish nation will not even mention *Yetzias Mitzrayim*, the Exodus.

לָכֵן הִנֵּה יָמִים בָּאִים נְאֻם ה' וְלֹא יֵאָמֵר עוֹד חַי ה' אֲשֶׁר הֶעֱלָה אֶת בְּנֵי יִשְׂרָאֵל מֵאֶרֶץ מִצְרָיִם: כִּי אִם חַי ה' אֲשֶׁר הֶעֱלָה אֶת בְּנֵי יִשְׂרָאֵל מֵאֶרֶץ צָפוֹן וּמִכֹּל הָאֲרָצוֹת אֲשֶׁר הִדִּיחָם שָׁמָּה וַהֲשִׁבֹתִים עַל אַדְמָתָם אֲשֶׁר נָתַתִּי לַאֲבוֹתָם:

The reason given is that the miracles which Hashem will perform for us at the time of *Moshiach* will be so great and monumental that the wonders of the Exodus will pale by comparison. We thus refer to

The Last Pesach

the last day of Pesach as *Acharon shel Pesach*. We pray that this past Pesach will be the last Yom Tov before the coming of *Melech HaMoshiach*. At that time, all Jewish suffering throughout the world will end. This should be the modus operandi of Prime Minister Bibi Netanyahu. We pray that the *Ribono shel Olam* should give him the strength, fortitude, and conviction to totally and completely obliterate all our enemies and all who wish to cause us harm, Amen

I want to thank my dear friend, Lenny Sausen, for sending me the quote from the late, great Menachem Begin a"h. RHG

45. Awaiting Our Greatest Victory

The Birth and Bris of Our First Great-Grandson

28 Elul, 5784; October 1, 2024

(Parshas Ki Savo and Netzavim)

Am Yisrael has, over these many years, been witness to all too many acts of violence and destruction towards our fellow Jews. This is true here in the United States, but it is especially so in Eretz Yisroel. The most recent atrocity was, of course, the attack last Simchas Torah by the sub-human Hamas terrorists. These beasts savagely and barbarically murdered over 1,200 innocent and beautiful Jewish souls in southern Israel and also took 251 Israelis as hostages. This act of terror resulted in the Gaza war which is the longest war in Israel's history.

For the past 12 months we, as a collective community, have cried bitter tears and have remained in a state of morose and gloom. We have, over this time, had very little to transform our sorrow and pessimism into feelings of optimism and hope. However, in the past 3 weeks, thanks to the help and assistance of the *Ribono shel Olam*, we have been witness to some brilliant and extraordinary Israeli actions. The State of Israel used their superior degree of military intelligence to successfully target and kill hundreds of Hezbollah terrorists. These subversive and radical thugs had continuously rained terror on Israel's northern border for a number of years. These murderers have launched thousands of missiles and drones which targeted many of Israel's civilian centers. This situation deteriorated so badly in the past year that over 60,000 residents of Northern Israel were forced to flee from their homes and have remained virtual refugees.

B'Chasdei Hashem, in the past few weeks, the IDF has successfully destroyed the complete inner structure of Hezbollah. In fact, on Friday, September 27, immediately following Prime Minister Benjamin Netanyahu's address to the United Nations, a *neis gadol*, a great and momentous event occurred. Tzahal successfully bombed Hezbollah's headquarters, destroyed its entire leadership, and eliminated one of the world's worst antisemites and Israel-haters, Hassan Nasrallah *yemach shemo v'zichro*. For over three decades, he had preached hatred and murder of all Israelis and Jews throughout the world. Killing him, together with the other leaders of Hezbollah, was one of the most successful acts ever performed by the IDF. It literally cut off the head of the snake.

While this heroic act may not in itself bring immediate and permanent peace to our brethren, it is a very positive and auspicious beginning. The entire leadership of this implacable foe has been greatly degraded. While they still possess a tremendous arsenal of lethal missiles which could cause great damage to our people, this enemy is currently on the run. On the Shabbos following this great event, Jews throughout the world celebrated and rejoiced. We drank a L'chaim and began to hope and pray for the possibility that a permanent peace will soon occur, one which will also bring us long term prosperity and continued growth and development.

Just one year ago, on October 7, 2023, on Simchas Torah, 5784, we were attacked and were utterly incapable of protecting our citizens for almost 24 hours. However, now the reverse occurred, a נס גדול היה פה. We experienced a series of incredible and miraculous acts. I asked myself, how can we reconcile these two contradictory experiences? I contend that there are two concepts that have made all the difference. They are – the awareness of Hashem's role in our lives and the expression of genuine *Achdus*.

Last year, just prior to the Simchas Torah tragedy, the Jewish world was witnessing divisiveness and disunity among all segments of Israeli society. The situation was so severe that it was bordering on the breakout of a civil war which had never before occurred in Israel. In addition, there was an anti-religious wave which appeared to denigrate the role and authority that the *Ribono shel Olam* plays in our lives. This then led to Hashem's hiding His face from world events. We suffered from a state of *Hester Panim* which, as detailed in Parshas Ki Savo, brings the experience of *klalos*, the curses and maledictions, the *tzaros* and difficulties which will befall and negatively impact our people. The Torah says (Devarim 28:45) that all this will occur because:

כִּי לֹא שָׁמַעְתָּ בְּקוֹל ה' אֱלֹקֶיךָ לִשְׁמֹר מִצְוֹתָיו וְחֻקֹּתָיו אֲשֶׁר צִוָּךְ:

"You have not obeyed Hashem your G-d to guard His commandments and His statues that He commanded you.

I believe that all of this has changed. Hashem's omnipotence and omnipresence is now recognized and celebrated by most of Israeli society. In addition, there is an overwhelming majority of Israelis who are beginning to join together and realize that the most important issue facing the country is not their small and petty ideological stands. Rather, their external enemy, Iran and its many proxies, Hamas, Hezbollah, and the Houthis of Yemen are the real and existential threats. These *reshaim* have the single aim of להשמיד ולהרג ולאבד את כל היהודים: to murder and annihilate all Jews throughout the world. The latest polls show that most of the country agrees with the decisions now being undertaken by Prime Minister Netanyahu that now is the correct time to once and for all destroy all our enemies

This unity of purpose and comradery as a recipe for success was delineated very clearly in the opening words of Parshas Netzavim (Devarim 29:9). The *Sedra* begins:

אַתֶּם נִצָּבִים הַיּוֹם כֻּלְּכֶם לִפְנֵי ה' אֱלֹהֵיכֶם...

Today, you are all standing together before Hashem your G-d.

The *Midrash Tanchuma's peirush* (Netzavim #1) is very instructive and insightful. It says:

וכן את מוצא שאין ישראל נגאלין עד שיהיו כולן אגודה אחת.

The Jewish people will not be redeemed until they are united as a single group.

The Midrash continues:

כשהן אגודים מקבלין פני שכינה.

It will only be when *Am Yisrael* comes together, when they act as one, when they are a united and unifying force, only then will they merit to greet the very presence of Hashem.

The Lubavitcher Rebbe, Rav Menachem Mendel Shneerson *zt"l,* offers an additional interpretation to this *posuk*. In addition to the unity and togetherness of *Am Yisrael* as a whole, the opening two verses of Parshas Netzavim continue to specify each and every sub-group:

...רָאשֵׁיכֶם שִׁבְטֵיכֶם זִקְנֵיכֶם וְשֹׁטְרֵיכֶם כֹּל אִישׁ יִשְׂרָאֵל: טַפְּכֶם נְשֵׁיכֶם וְגֵרְךָ אֲשֶׁר בְּקֶרֶב מַחֲנֶיךָ מֵחֹטֵב עֵצֶיךָ עַד שֹׁאֵב מֵימֶיךָ:

The heads of your tribes, your elders, your officers, and all the men of Israel. Your children, your wives, and the convert who is in the midst of your camp, from the woodchopper to the water drawer.

The fact that the Torah delineates the individual members of the nation is most revealing. The Rebbe says that while standing together as a united force and working together is of paramount importance, we cannot nor dare not ever forget the *yachid*, the singular and individual Jew. Each of us on a personal level makes our distinctive contribution to the furtherance and future of Yiddishkeit.

These two ideas – the unity of *Am Yisrael* as a whole versus the emphasis on each and every Jew – might seem contradictory at first glance. In truth, they are very much compatible and crucial to the furtherance of *Yahadus*, for it is only when we can appreciate the unique role of every individual that we can truly come together as a unified whole. By combining these two concepts we will merit to truly bask in the glory of Hashem.

While the present situation in Medinat Yisrael has not yet resulted in ushering in a period of peace and prosperity, I feel that it may very well be the אתחלתא דגאולה, the beginning of a period which will hopefully lead to our greatest victory – shalom, peace, and the coming of Moshiach במהרה בימינו.

Just as *Am Yisrael* has had a trying year on a national level, on a very personal level, Rivkie and I have had a very difficult and challenging year as well. We have each dealt with a number of health issues which have defined the past twelve months. However, just as we have been shown the Hand of Hashem in dealing with our national foes, we have seen a light from Heaven in our personal lives as well. Just a week ago, we received some beautiful and wonderful news. Our oldest grandson, Dovid Drebin and his very special wife, Tzippy, the children of our very dear children Frumie and Hillel Drebin, became the proud parents of their second child, their first son.

Rivkie and I have previously been blessed with two marvelous and delightful great-granddaughters, Aliza, the daughter of our dear grandchildren Shanah and Meir Nitsun, and Gelley, Dovid and Tzippy's oldest child.

At the Bris, I was *zoche* to receive a double honor. First, I served as the *Sandek* for my first great-grandson. Second, the baby was named for my dear and beloved father-in-law, HaRav Yehoshua Fink *zt"l*. Both in Volume One of *From Sinai Came Torah* as well as in my autobiography, *A Blessed Life,* I have written at length about my late and great father-in-law. Suffice it to say that in addition to his being a first rate *Talmid Chacham*, a Rabbi's Rabbi, and an educator par excellence, he was also a very wise and special father-in-law. In the many years that I had the honor of being a member of his family, his actions towards me were always with love and respect. He treated me much more than even a dear son-in-law; he considered me as a loving son. For that and for so much more, I will forever be grateful to him.

Rivkie and I want to thank Dovid and Tzippy for this very special honor which they bestowed upon me. We also want to show our gratitude to them for perpetuating my father-in-law's name in yet another generation. We wish them and Frumie and Hillel a huge Mazel Tov. May they have only *nachas* and *gezunt* from this baby and from all their other children and grandchildren.

This wonderful event occurred just a few days before the end of 5784 and the start of our new year 5785. I pray that this new year will be one of peace and happiness for all of *Klal Yisrael,* and may it bring complete *refuos* and *yeshuos* for our family. I wish each of you a *kesivah v'chasimah tovah.*

46. Our Very Blessed and Cherished Time
Celebrating Our Golden Fiftieth Anniversary

January 3-4, 2025 – 3-4 Teves, 5785
(Parshas Vayigash and Vayechi)

Parshas Vayigash is the culmination, the climax, the completion of the past three *Sedras* which detailed the acrimony, the animosity, and the hatred which existed in the home of Yaakov Avinu between Yosef and his older brothers. Now, in our Parsha, Yosef HaTzadik, the Viceroy of Egypt, finally reveals himself to his brothers and forgives them for their past negative actions against him. Thus begins a period of reconciliation and the strengthening of family ties.

This Parsha is filled with many very interesting and intriguing topics. One can spend a great deal of time dwelling on and interpreting each of these themes. I, however, wish to focus on one segment of the Parsha which I feel presents us with a very significant and meaningful lesson.

The Torah (45:14) tells us of the reunion between Rachel's two children. This marked the first time in over two decades that Yosef and Binyamin spent time together. However, instead of detailing their moment of joy and ecstasy, the Torah records something altogether different. It tells us of a reuniting that was accompanied with tears and weeping. The Torah says:

וַיִּפֹּל עַל צַוְּארֵי בִנְיָמִן אָחִיו וַיֵּבְךְּ וּבִנְיָמִן בָּכָה עַל צַוָּארָיו:

And Yosef cried on the neck of Binyamin, and Binyamin cried on the neck of Yosef.

Rashi says:

ויפול על צוארי בנימין אחיו ויבך - על שני מקדשות שעתידין להיות בחלקו של בנימין וסופן ליחרב:
ובנימין בכה על צואריו - על משכן שילה שעתיד להיות בחלקו של יוסף וסופו ליחרב:

Yosef cried over the two Batei Mikdash which, in the future, were to be built in Binyamin's territory and would eventually be destroyed. Binyamin grieved over the Mishkan in Shiloh which was to be built in the land which would be given to Yosef's descendants and would also eventually be destroyed.

Our *meforshim* ask: why did these two brothers, who now saw each other for the first time in decades, weep at this particular time? Why were they not ecstatic, joyful, and especially grateful that they could now be reunited? In addition, if they felt an urge to shed tears for a future tragedy, why didn't they shed tears over their own calamity instead of their brother's misfortune?

An answer is provided by the 19th century Chassidic master, Rav Yechezkel Taub, the first Modzhitzer Rebbe. He offers a most beautiful *pshat*. He explains that when Yosef and Binyamin were finally reunited, they recalled the reason for their long and bitter separation. It was, the Rebbe says, caused by the great *aveirah* of *Sinas Chinam*, baseless, groundless, and unfounded deeds of hatred and antipathy of one person for another, namely, the brothers' animosity towards Yosef.

In addition, through their sense of *Ruach HaKodesh*, Divine prophecy, they were able to foresee the two great tragedies and catastrophes that would befall *Klal Yisrael* in the future. These calamities would also come about because of *Sinas Chinam*, unbridled and unsubstantial hatred of one Jew for another.

The Rebbe then says:

והואיל והתיקון לשנאת חינם הוא חיזוק האהבה.

"The antidote, the solution to *Sinas Chinam* is *Ahavas HaBriyos*, the strengthening of the bonds of love and respect, esteem and high regard, of one Jew for another."

שצער הזולת יכאב לך יותר מצערך שלך.

Our Very Blessed and Cherished Time

"The other person's pain and difficulty should become as hurtful and distressing to you as though it was your personal loss." Thus, the tears that they shed were for each other's loss, not their own.

Binyamin knew that both *Batei Mikdash* would in the future be built on land upon which his Shevet dwelled. However, they would only be built after the destruction of Mishkan Shiloh, which was on territory inhabited by Yosef's descendants. Binyamin felt that he would rather not have the *Batei Mikdash* built if it meant that his brother would suffer his loss. Yosef, on the other hand, cried over the future destruction of the two *Batei Mikdash* which were destined to be built on land inhabited by Shevet Binyamin. He wept over his brother's loss.

The Rebbe said:

באהבה שכזו עשוי להיות תיקון לשנאת חינם.

"Such a love is so great that it serves as a remedy, as an antidote, for causeless and baseless hatred."

This *pshat* is so dear and special to Bubby and myself. We look out at our family, our wonderful and special children: Frumie and Hillel, Aryeh and Goldie, Dena and Yaakov. Each and every one of you has, at the drop of a hat, run to be at our side and has been completely and totally attentive to all of our needs. This has been done during your working time, when

Our Very Blessed and Cherished Time

you were on vacation, during the week, and even on Shabbos and Yom Tovim.

We see your amazing children, our incredible and very loving and dedicated grandchildren: Dovid and Tzippy, Shana and Meir, Moishe, Baila, Mordechai, Nechemiah, Simcha, Frumie, Asher, Moshe, Hindy, Chaya Leah, Yehuda, Miriam, Hindy, Rena, Shua, and Yehoshua, and our very precious great-grandchildren: Aliza, Gelly, and JJ, who have learned these beautiful *midos* from their parents. We constantly see these same concepts of אהבה ואחוה שלום ורעות – love, brotherhood, peace, and friendship.

We have witnessed over the years how each of you would go *lifnim mishuras hadin*, over and beyond the call of duty, to help, assist and aid each of your siblings and your very close extended family. All your dealings with each other, and especially your actions towards us, are always done with love, concern, and with the utmost respect.

Frumie remarked to me last night at our *seudah,* "It is amazing; it seems that just yesterday, we had only the five of us (Bubby and myself, Frumie, Aryeh and Dena) at our Shabbos meal, and now, *bli ayin hara,* we have 30 family members all together." For this and for so much more, we are forever grateful and thankful to the *Ribono shel Olam.*

Fortunately, unlike Yosef and Binyamin, you have never been apart and distanced from each other. I am quite confident that if any of you would ever experience a difficulty or adversity, you will each undoubtedly be vigilant for and be helpful to each other's needs and concerns. The *Ahavas Chinam*, the love and camaraderie, which you have for each other is very evident and manifests itself in all your actions.

I wish to conclude with a *pshat* from next week's Parsha. The Torah in Parshas Vayechi says that Yaakov Avinu lived in Mitzrayim for the last 17 years of his life (Bereishis 47:28). The Midrash (*Pesikta Zutrasa* on this *posuk*) says that the *gematria,* the numerical equivalent of 17, is טוב. These years, say *Chazal,* were, in essence, the best and happiest years of Yaakov's life. Why, they ask, were these the best years of his life?

The Midrash explains that this was the first time that Yaakov was truly in peace. He was able to live life to the fullest without experiencing any external or internal difficulties. He did not experience any trials or tribulations. In addition, for the first time in many decades, he observed that his entire family was at peace. There was finally *shalom* and respect between each child and his brother.

I recently saw a beautiful *pshat* in the *Iturei Torah* who quotes Rebbe Bunim of Peshischa. I feel that this interpretation is truly on target. He said that

Our Very Blessed and Cherished Time

although Yaakov lived these last years outside of Eretz Yisrael, in *golus*, and while he realized that these years were the precursor to *shibud Mitzrayim* – the Egyptian enslavement and all the difficulties and hardships which would accompany it – he did not focus on the future problems and adversities. Instead, he concentrated on the *Tov*, the good that he was now experiencing. He maximized the time that Hashem gave him with all his children and grandchildren. And they were all good – they were טוב מאד.

In a similar vein, while Bubby and I are currently going through difficult medical issues, we too only see the *Tov*. We only see the good and the wonderful life which Hashem has bestowed upon us, and we thank Him for everything. For we too believe that we are blessed with a life which is truly טוב מאד.

We love and respect each and every one of you. We acknowledge and are so proud of all that you do to strengthen Torah values both in your homes and for the overall Jewish community. Each and every one of you is held in such high esteem by your friends and colleagues.

From the bottom of our hearts, we thank you for this truly amazing and magnificent Shabbos and weekend. It is one which we will never forget. I am *mispallel* that we all be together for many years and only enjoy each other and continue to celebrate beautiful and glorious *s'machos*. Thank you for everything. We love you so much. Mazel Tov.

INDEX

A

Abarbanel 152, 267
Acharon shel Pesach 405
Adam and Chava 22, 67, 173
Aharon HaKohen .. 137, 178, 183, 301, 342
Alpert, Rav Nissan 140
Amalek 115, 194, 221, 248
American First Committee 156
American Jewish Committee .. 72
American Jewish Congress 72, 155, 166
Ananei HaKavod 222, 231
Antisemitism .. 96, 156, 167, 196, 251, 309, 380, 389, 403, 408
Aschalta d'Geulah 277, 413
Avos
   Avraham Yitzchak and Yaakov ... 67, 114, 143, 152, 201, 217
Avraham Avinu 36, 41, 46, 54, 67, 201, 213, 337, 364

B

Baal Shem Tov 235
Begin, Menachem – Israeli Prime Minister 188, 404
Biden, Joe
   46th President of the United States 397, 404
Bilam
   non-Jewish prophet 116, 215
Birchas Kohanim 177, 324
Black Americans 78, 126
Bris Milah 79, 267, 285, 336, 407
Brown v Board of Education ... 78

C

Chasam Sofer 128, 193, 233
Chillul Hashem 141, 152
Chizkiyahu HaMelech 104
Churban Beis HaMikdash 317
Cohen, Arthur
   author 52
Congo Republic 126

D

Devorah the Prophetess 103
Dor Haflagah 30
Dor HaMabul 30, 400
Dworken, Rabbi Steven 360

E

Eban, Abba - Israeli Statesman and Diplomat 119, 188
Eigel HaZahav 127, 136, 325
Elias, Rabbi Yosef 266
Eliezer, servant of Avraham Avinu 48
Eruv Rav, the mixed multitude 136, 149
Eshkol, Levi - 3rd Prime Minister of the State of Israel 120, 188
Evangelical Friends 394
Eved Ivri, a Jewish slave 207

Index

F

Fink, Rabbi and Mrs. Samuel 336, 372, 386, 414
Frand, Rabbi Yissocher 374

G

Gemara
    Bava Metzia 59b 163
    Bava Metzia 71a 169
    Berachos 352
    Berachos 61b 282
    Kiddushin 23a 127
    Megillah 252
    Pesachim 117b 363
    Sanhedrin 103a 400
    Shabbos 153a 209
    Sukkah 11b 230
    Taanis 5a 296
Gerrer Rebbe, Rav Yehuda Aryeh Leib Alter - Sfas Emes 237
Gerrer Rebbe, Rav Yitzchak Meir Alter 205, 255
Gifter, HaRav Mordechai 374
Gold, Avner - author 371
Gross, Lilyan (Lil) (Tuchman) 3, 354
Gross, Moses (Moe) .3, 346, 357, 372
Gross, Moshe Pesach Nissan ben Aryeh Chaim 266
Gross, Rivka (Fink) 192, 324, 344, 351, 361, 386, 413
Gross, Yehudah 324
Gross, Yetta (Genauer) 368

H

Hadrian, Roman Emperor 223, 282
Haganah 74
Haggadah shel Pesach 265
Halevi, Rav Yehudah 294
Hallel 297
Har Sinai 83, 123, 132, 136, 195, 198, 222, 235, 288, 305, 326
Hellenistic Syria 83, 239
Heroes 274, 371
Hertzberg, Rabbi Arthur 166
Hillel and Shammai 176
Hirsch, Rav Samson Raphael. 23, 50
Holocaust (Shoah) 39, 63, 72, 74, 95, 108, 117, 155, 169, 189, 221, 224, 242, 243, 252, 269, 381, 388, 402

I

IDF
    Israeli Defense Forces, Tzahal 75, 274, 293, 299, 379, 396, 402, 408
Intermarriage 50, 52, 224
Irgun 74
Israel, State of. 28, 64, 74, 94, 97, 159, 164, 189, 190, 270, 285, 293, 314, 379, 384, 385, 408, 413
Israel-Hamas War .189, 384, 402, 407
Iturai Torah 405

J

Jewish defense 74

Index

Jewish Defense League 107
Jewish rallies and demonstrations 162, 279
Jewish unity - Achdus .. 194, 327, 396, 409
Johnson, Lyndon - 36th President of the United States 99, 118

K

Karo, Rav Yosef - author of Shulchan Aruch 315
Kayin and Hevel 22, 67
Kennedy, Senator Robert 87
Knesset, Israeli Parliament ... 269
Kohn, Daniel 336
Kohn, Murray and Susan 336
Korach and his rebellion 176
Kotler, Rav Aharon 111

L

Lag Ba'Omer 279, 287
Lamm, Rabbi Dr. Norman 176
Lavan HaArami 54
Lenchna, Rav Shlomo Leib ... 61, 326

M

Ma'amad Har Sinai 136, 174, 235, 305
Mabit, Harav Moshe ben Yosef D'Trani 232
Maccabees 83, 239
Machlokes l'sheim Shamayim 178
Machlokes shelo l'sheim Shamayim 179
Matzah and Chametz 260
Megillas Eicha 218, 313

Megillas Esther 83, 251, 257, 301
Megillas Rus 306
Meir, Golda - 4th Prime Minister of the State of Israel 159
Midrash Pesikta Zutrasa 421
Midrash Rabbah 42, 81, 115, 165, 252, 313
Midrash Tanchuma .55, 128, 151, 354, 411
Midrash Yalkut Shimoni 308
Mincha Belulah 301
Mishkan, the Tabernacle 132, 162, 180, 236
Modzhitzer Rebbe, Rav Yechezkel Taub 418
Moshe Rabbeinu 82, 89, 101, 114, 127, 136, 149, 178, 183, 198, 235, 251, 301, 324
Munich Olympic Massacre of Israeli Athletes (1972) 28

N

Nashim tzidkaniyos, righteous women 137
Nesivos Shalom, Rav Shalom Noach Berezowsky (Sloinimer Rebbe) 400
Netziv, Rav Naftali Tzvi Yehudah Berlin 91, 253
Noach 30, 41, 368, 399

O

Ohr HaChaim HaKadosh 310

P

Palestinian protests 390
Papus ben Yehudah 283
Parah Adumah, Red Heifer ... 136

Index

Parshas Parah 136
Parshas Shekalim 123
Parshas Zachor 248
Pesach, Shabbos Chol HaMoed 270
Peshischa, Rebbe Bunim of .. 228, 421
Pinter, Rabbi Mutel 4
Pirkei Avos 61, 93, 100, 176, 198, 204
Pirkei d'Rebbe Eliezer 33, 346
Protests on College Campuses 390, 403
Przemysl, Rebbe Meir of 60

R

Ramban 132, 152, 179, 400
Rashi ...31, 42, 84, 102, 123, 143, 184, 192, 231, 251, 301, 318, 368, 400
Rebbe - Rabbi Yehudah HaNasi 199
Rebbe Akiva.. 223, 230, 279, 288
Resistance against the Germans in World War II 277
Ritva 266
Roosevelt, Franklin D. President of the United States 72, 156
Rosh Hashanah 212, 237, 337

S

Sachs, Harav Menachem Ben Tzion 327
Sanz, Rav Chaim of 370
Sarah Imainu 47, 337
Schwab, Rav Shimon 364
Security for Jewish Institutions 381

Sefas Emes, Rav Yehudah Aryeh Leib Alter 237
Sefer Shoftim 103
Seforno, Rav Ovadia 241
Self-defense 381, 398
Sender, Harav Yitzchok 268
Shavuos 304
Shelah HaKadosh 101
Shemini Atzeres 386
Shibud Mitzrayim 88
Shmiras Shabbos 218, 376
Shoah ...... *See* Holocaust
Shul 378
Shulchan Aruch 280, 305
Shulchan Aruch - Rav Yosef Karo 125, 315
Shver tzu zein a Yid 309
Silber, Rav Shmuel 290
Sinas chinam 71, 188
Six Day War – June, 1967 ... 118, 188, 285, 293, 387
Soloveitchik, Rav Joseph B.. 196, 305, 315
Sorotzkin, Rav Zalman . 140, 195
Soviet Jewry . 107, 169, 245, 279, 285
Sukkos 230, 384

T

Tefillah for Medinat Yisrael.. 379
Tefillah for the U.S. government 378
Tefillah for Tzahal 379
Tehillim 206, 294, 319
Teller, Judd - author 155
Tiatron 165
Tisha b'Av 222, 313, 314

Index

To Be a Man 87
Truman, Harry - President of the United States 95
Tuchman, Rabbi Hyman ... 3, 171, 219, 321, 372
Tzahal .... *See* IDF

U

United Nations 99, 118, 408
United States Congress .. 126, 393

V

Valley of Dry Bones 270
Vilna Gaon 71, 235, 308

W

Want, Esther and Simon 336
Warsaw Ghetto Uprising – April, 1943 269
Weiss, Rav Asher 130
Who is a Jew? 304
Wise, Dr. Stephen 72
World War II 93, 156, 270

Y

Yechezkel HaNavi 270
Yerushalayim ... 54, 70, 103, 293, 306, 312, 314, 328
Yirmiyahu HaNavi . 75, 133, 218, 317, 405
Yisro 114
Yom HaShoah - Holocaust Memorial Day 269, 402
Yom Yerushalayim 293
Yosef and Binyamin 416
Yosef and his brothers 68, 80, 89, 318

Z

Zionism 380
Zohar 201, 257, 262

מ

מה יאמרו הגוים 147
מה יאמרו ישראל 160

נ

נצח ישראל לא ישקר 212, 229

ת

תורה שבכתב ותורה שבעל פה 136, 199, 203

Other Works by this Author

1. *Public Demonstrations Sponsored by and Participated in by The American Jewish Congress et al, 1933-1945* (Unpublished Masters Dissertation –1971)
2. *To Illuminate a Darkened Society: Essays on Jewish Thought and Contemporary Life* (First Edition – 1973)
3. *From Sinai Came Torah Volume 1: Essays on the Jewish Festivals* (2018)
4. *From Sinai Came Torah Volume 2: The Life Cycle of the Jew* (2019)
5. *The Kibel-Gross Legacy Haggadah*, written with Rabbi Nechemiah Kibel *zt"l* and Rabbi Yaakov Kibel (2020)
6. *From Sinai Came Torah Volume 3: An Elucidation and Explanation of the Weekly Parsha: Beraishis-Shemos* (2021)
7. *From Sinai Came Torah Volume 4: An Elucidation and Explanation of the Weekly Parsha: Vayikra-Bamidbar-Devarim* (2023)
8. *A Blessed Life: My Autobiography* (2023)

Made in the USA
Columbia, SC
24 January 2025

d6ff2ec3-a6e7-4c91-97ab-46f0a13d6b15R01